UP AND DOING

UP AND DOING

Canadian Women and Peace

Edited
by

JANICE WILLIAMSON
AND DEBORAH GORHAM

The
Women's
·Press·

Janice Williamson gratefully acknowledges financial support from the Canadian Centre for Arms Control and Disarmament.

CANADIAN CATALOGUING IN PUBLICATION DATA

Main entry under title:
Up and doing: Canadian women and peace

ISBN 0-88961-130-0

1. Women and peace. 2. Peace – Literary collections.
3. Canadian literature (English) – Women authors.*
4. Canadian literature (English) – 20th century.*
I. Williamson, Janice Rae, 1951-   . II. Gorham, Deborah.

JX1965.U7 1989   327.1'72'088042   C88-095373-X

Copyright © 1989 Janice Williamson and Deborah Gorham

Cover art: Jane Ash Poitras, *Cover design*: Stephanie Martin, *Editing*: Valerie Alia and Kate Forster, *Copy editing*: Kate Forster

Published by *The Women's Press*, 229 College Street No. 204, Toronto, Ontario M5T 1R4. This book was produced by the collective effort of The Women's Press. This book was a project of the Social Issues Group.

The Women's Press gratefully acknowledges financial support from The Canadian Studies Directorate of the Department of the Secretary of State of Canada, The Canada Council and the Ontario Arts Council.

Part of the royalties of this book are donated to a prize for the best essay or creative writing on peace and social issues. The prize will be administered through the Women's Studies Program, University of Alberta, Edmonton, Alberta, T6G 2E5. For further information please write.

Printed and bound in Canada
1   2   3   4   1993   1992   1991   1990   1989

The Women's Press gratefully acknowledges permission to reprint the following material.

Reprinted by permission of the author. "Still There Are Wars and Crimes of War" by Phyllis Webb. From *Wilson's Bowl* (Toronto: Coach House Press, 1980). Copyright Phyllis Webb. Reprinted by permission of the author. "My Final Hour" by Margaret Laurence is a speech given at Trent University in 1983. It was published in *The Toronto Star*, January 17, 1987. Reprinted with permission. "Is There a Just Cause?" by Joy Kogawa. First published in *Canadian Forum*, March 1984. Reprinted by permission of the author. "Direct Action: Ann Hansen's Statement to the Court." First published in *Hysteria* vol. 3, no 2. Reprinted by permission. "from the Women's Conference on how to end the war in viet nam" by Maxine Gadd. From *Lost Language* (Toronto: Coach House Press, 1982). Reprinted by permission of the author. "Spain" by Dorothy Livesay. From *The Self-Completing Tree* (Press Porcepic, 1987). Copyright Dorothy Livesay. Reprinted by permission of the author. "40 days" by Nadine McInniṣ. From *Shaking the Dreamland Tree* (Coteau Books, 1986). Reprinted by permission of the author. "Learning the Bomb" by Marilyn Bowering. From *The Sunday before Winter: The New and Selected Poetry of Marilyn Bowering* (Toronto: General Publishing, 1984). Reprinted by permission of Stoddart Publishing Co. Ltd. "Grenada 1983" by Himani Bannerji. From *Doing Time* (Toronto: Sister Vision Press, 1986). "Praxis" by Sharon Thesen. From *Holding the Pose* (Toronto: Coach House Press, 1983). Reprinted by permission of the author. "delphiniums blue & geraniums red" by Daphne Marlatt. From *How Hug a Stone* (Turnstone Press, 1983). Copyright Daphne Marlatt. Reprinted by permission of the author. "Machine. Gun. Nest." by Margaret Atwood. From *Selected Poems II* by Margaret Atwood. Copyright © Margaret Atwood 1986. Used by permission of Oxford University Press Canada. "Einstein" by Lola Lemire Tostevin. From *'sophie* (Toronto: Coach House Press, 1988). Reprinted by permission of the author. "Y 2-Q 2-B 2-CL" by Louky Bersianik, translated by R. McGee. First published in *Parallelogramme* 10.1 (Fall 1984). Reprinted by permission of the author. Untitled poem by Leslie Hamson. From *Women's Peace Write: A Writing Campaign to Members of Parliament*, June 1985-May 1986 by West Coast Women and Words Society. Reprinted by permission of the author. "Elemental Poem" by Roberta Buchanan. First published in *Atlantis: A Women's Studies Journal* 12:2 (Spring 1987). "Where the Sky is a Pitiful Tent" by Claire Harris. From *fables from the women's quarters* (Toronto: Williams-Wallace, 1984). Copyright Claire Harris. Reprinted by permission of the author. "An Argentinian Script" by Rosemary Sullivan. From *The Space a Name Makes* (Black Moss Press, 1985). Reprinted by permission of the author. Excerpt from *serpent (w)rite* by Betsy Warland (Toronto: Coach House Press, 1987) Reprinted by permission of the author. "Five Miles from Detonation" by Erin Mouré. From *Domestic Fuel* (Toronto: House of Anansi Press, 1985). Reprinted by permission of House of Anansi Press.

CONTENTS

Still there are Wars
and Crimes of War

war crimes war crimes war cries cries war
war cries war cries cries cry crimes cry
crimes cry cry cries cries cry war cries
war crimes crimes crimes crime cries war
cries war war war war warm cries warm cries
cries cries cries cries still there are war
war war war still still warm cries still warm
warm warm cries CRIES WAR CRIES there are there
are still still still still still

Phyllis Webb

Introduction

THIS BOOK BEGAN as I sat as a defendant in a courtroom contemplating the politics of women and peace. As part of the collective defence in a feminist civil disobedience trial, I yearned for a book which would explore the experience of Canadian women with the issue of peace. Since that time several fine volumes have been published (see Resources, p.22); this book is intended to complement the others and participate in the ongoing dialogue women create in "speaking our peace."

My own activity in the peace movement became focused as a result of a workshop organized by Women's Action for Peace, an event which eventually led to my participation in nonviolent civil disobedience at Litton Systems Canada, the manufacturer of the Cruise missile guidance system. Linking environmental issues, women's experience and peace, Women's Action for Peace was committed to nonviolent civil disobedience as one response to the dangerous environmental and military hazards which we face. Margaret Hancock, an original member of Women's Action for Peace and an early inspiration for this anthology, commented on the need to demystify nonviolent civil disobedience:

> In a way, women commit civil disobedience all our lives. In order to maintain our humanness within the confines of the world we're given, we have to keep saying, "I'm going to go to school. I'm not going to have children. I'm going to live openly as a lesbian. We're going to open an abortion clinic on our own terms. We're going to have our rape crisis centre and confront the men who are raping women." All of these are acts of civil disobedience ... needed just to keep our heads above water.

In 1980, at the coalition meeting which organized the Toronto International Women's Day March, a proposal by Voice of Women to foreground peace as a special rallying cry for the day was voted down; the vote was an ironic "no" to the theme, "survival." Some of the disagreements which arose during the discussion involved the relation between peace and social justice. At public forums organized by the International Women's Day Committee, these issues took on a global character when they were articulated by women who faced a multitude of oppressions. Women from South Africa, Eritrea, Guatemala, the Philippines, El Salvador and Nicaragua spoke out about the everyday character of violence in their lives. In frustration, these women displayed courage and commitment within their communities by taking up arms in response to the institutionalized torture of brutal regimes and civil wars. Unable to adopt the single-edged surety of absolute pacifism, many of the women involved in these forums spoke of the specificity of circumstances which moved them to defend themselves with force.

These contradictions and feminist ethical issues continue to inform discussions within the women's community. In a *Peace Magazine* article, Nomi Wall, feminist activist and a member of Canadian Action for Nicaragua, offers her personal perspective on this issue:

> I don't call the Nicaraguan people or blacks in South Africa violent. Their terms "violence" and "terrorist" are laid on to mystify us so that we define violence as the same for everybody. An organization like the ANC – the only legitimate representative of an entire nation of black people – must have an alternative to lying down and submitting to genocide. Something like the Nestle's boycott isn't going to bring down apartheid in South Africa. What choice do people have but armed struggle? Otherwise they're dead, they're history.

Historical and cultural contexts informed the continuing discussions of the relationship between feminism, peace and nonviolent action. The bombing of Litton Systems in 1982 opened up the question of violent social action within the Canadian context. Many peace activists were fearful that the bombing of Litton had destroyed the educational and strategic gains their years of nonviolent activities had developed. Nonviolent peace groups actively protesting industrial military production in Canada were concerned about the media's representation of antimilitarist activists as "terrorists." While eager to vilify the Litton bombers, the media refused to call Litton Systems to task for its participation in the government's violent militarist "defence" production. In response to this, the nonviolent group Cruise Missile Conversion Project distributed a pamphlet to Litton workers that ironically echoed the words of one of Litton's managers: "Bombing Is Madness."

In order to develop an editorial position adequate to the interdisciplinary nature of this anthology, social historian Deborah Gorham joined the project. This was particularly pleasing since we initially met in her classroom during my first Women's Studies course at Carleton University in 1972. The energizing euphoria and painful recognitions which develop in the context of Women's Studies often initiate or complement students' engagement in activist feminist politics. Over the years, as friends, Deborah Gorham and I have discussed our perspectives about feminist issues. Our points of agreement and our differences are symptomatic of the diversity of positions and strategies within contemporary feminist debates about militarism, peace and social justice. A brief survey of several contemporary women's political activities illustrates their range – research and advocacy work directed towards interrupting defence experts with a different discourse; coalition group work organized around community action; and native women's public speaking and civil disobedience as part of the Innu struggle against NATO test flights in the North.

THE VOICE OF WOMEN AND CITIZEN ACTION

The Voice of Women members monitor the developments in current peace research. In April 1989, Science for Peace, a Canadian peace group of scientists, organized a Toronto conference on "The Control of Chemical and Biological Weapons: Strengthening International Verification and Compliance." The Voice of Women National office had persuaded the conference organizers that the VOW perspective on citizen action would bridge the gap between the activities of experts and concerned citizens.

The two VOW speakers at the conference were Diana Chown of the Edmonton Voice of Women, who has been active in the last three years with others in documenting and naming Canadian chemical and biological warfare (CBW) research, particularly at Suffield, Alberta; and Ursula Franklin, a longtime peace activist and professor at the University of Toronto, who has been identifying Suffield's CBW research since the 1960s. Their talk preceded an address by the Head of Suffield's Chemical and Biological Defence Section.

Chown noted how Canada's support of the U.S. binary chemical rearmament program appeared to contradict Canada's developing role in nuclear verification technology and minimize Canada's "credibility with respect to taking verification initiatives independent of U.S. policy initiatives." The following is an edited version of Chown's presentation:

> While governments tend to be preoccupied with national security, citizens working for disarmament are more interested in the merits of internationalism.... Although governments often

overlook the importance of citizens working for disarmament, government initiatives are sometimes the result of public pressure activated by citizen action; political will *can* come from fear of defeat in the next election.

Canada's most significant contribution to the chemical and biological arms race takes place at the Defence Research Establishment at Suffield in southern Alberta. Suffield was established in 1941 after 125 farms were expropriated to make way for a Canadian-United Kingdom chemical warfare experimental station; the area, 1,000 square miles of grassland, was remote, flat and huge. After the war, the Technical Co-operation program between Canada, the U.S., the U.K. and later Australia provided for continued chemical and biological warfare (CBW) research information sharing; while there were other Canadian CBW research facilities, Suffield – with its huge testing ground – has always been the most significant. According to a secret 1980 Memorandum of Understanding set up "to *integrate*" the chemical and biological defence programs of the U.S., the U.K. and Canada, work at Suffield is in collaboration with CBW research in the U.S. Even though Canadian policy had not changed, this 1980 Memorandum marked a dramatic upsurge in Suffield which corresponded with U.S. chemical weapon rearmament.

Initiated in part by citizen group concerns about open-air testing of surprisingly large amounts of nerve gas at Suffield in recent years, the 1988 Barton Report, a review of Canadian CBW research, noted that a staff of 100 is employed at Suffield for research which includes far more than the design and testing of protective equipment which has been the standard government description of the Suffield research. Most ominously, the Barton Report reveals research into "the potential of biotechnology for use in [chemical and biological] defensive applications" and "antibodies and immune systems." This of course refers to biological warfare. In Canada, the U.S. Department of National Defence vehemently denies that binary chemical weapons are being tested at Suffield, and continues to claim that Canadian CBW research is defensive. If, however, the Canadian research is shared with the U.S. by agreement and contributes to the U.S. ability to use these weapons offensively, this Canadian participation has to be considered offensive research.

As citizens, we ask this question: When CBW agreements are being drawn up or re-signed, how many of our decision makers understand or acknowledge that, just as we've seen in Vietnam and Iraq, chemical weapons are weapons of mass destruction to be used mainly against civilians?

In her concluding commentary at the conference, Ursula Franklin outlined how citizens must overcome their "lack of confidence" in governments which "lie to their own citizens.... The civilian population, disadvantaged with respect to their government as all civilians are who are not members of the ruling class, will be the ones who are unprotected and at risk." Her strategizing as to how to work against chemical weapons is twofold. First Franklin suggests that "all letters to government officials protesting chemical weapons be copied and sent, let's say, to the International Red Cross, where a data base would be established. This would not be done behind the backs of the letter writers' governments but, without relying on the good will of the press or other agencies, would openly bring citizens' legitimate concerns to the attention of an international agency which has concern for the welfare of ordinary people in the face of disasters, be they natural or man-made – and I use the word 'man-made' very intentionally." Her second proposal rethinks chemical warfare as, in Arthur Forer's words, "public health in reverse." Franklin suggests that public health agencies rather than secret defence installations need to be informed of available antidotes. Her final commentary locates her recommendations in "the long and usually frustrating experience of people like us who care, deeply care, about the fate of the earth, about the honorability of their country, and the future that is either for all of us or for none."

COALITION POLITICS

The Canadian Peace Alliance was established in November of 1985 and has 400 member groups across Canada. As a result of women's participation in the coalition, feminism has played a role in structuring patterns of debate and decision making. During the first meetings, twice as many men spoke for twice as long as the women. But the "basis of unity" adopted in 1985 insisted on gender parity as well as regional parity. Thus representative sessions were "timed" to alert participants to their gendered speaking patterns. According to Wendy Wright, coordinator of the Toronto Disarmament Network, the most recent meetings revealed that more women were speaking for longer periods. In May 1989, Wright was interviewed about her participation in a changing peace movement.

When the government's June 1987 white paper, "Challenge and Commitment: A Defence Policy for Canada," was made public, submarines were central to the defence of the north. The government was accused by peace groups of "seeing red," but 59 percent of Canadians supported the purchase of nuclear-powered submarines. However, by last fall, an Angus Reid poll commissioned by the Canadian Peace Alliance showed that 71 percent of Canadians were against the submarines. In terms of our work in the peace movement, this shift in public opinion came at a time of crisis when even some peace activists were talking about the death of the peace movement. In spite of this ebbing spirit, we've been able to see changes. During the federal election, the peace movement made the issues visible and a matter for public debate. Peace activists shadowed the prime minister, disrupting his speeches, keeping the issue alive throughout the election even though Mulroney didn't want to debate it. But the 1987 Defence White Paper was only the first step of the right-wing agenda; it would be followed by Free Trade and the brutal 1989 federal budget.

From my personal perspective as an organizer in the peace movement and a feminist interested in a coalition perspective, I support autonomous women's groups. For example, the Voice of Women has built a strong continuing organization, which is fantastic. But, over the past eight years, peace has not remained the number one issue; surveys show that the environment and AIDS, in that order, are now more important to Canadians. This is a very positive development. Those who are interested in peace issues are expanding their concerns to link environmental issues to what is happening to humanity on a broader scale. After this federal election, I asked myself whether I still wanted to work on peace issues as a primary concern; I'm freaked out about my chromosomes. A few years ago, the fear of the future was around nuclear weapons, rather than strictly environmental issues. But peace remains central to a range of issues which political activists have been struggling to publicize for years. The fear of nuclear war is still present, but militarism sustains our popular culture and and our economy; these systems of oppression need to be exposed. This is where the idea of coalition politics becomes even more significant. The coalition within the peace movement which organized the different constituencies internal to the movement has now become a coalition which reaches out to other environmental and political groups. For example, our annual walk for peace in Toronto last year was co-sponsored by the Coalition Against Free Trade, the National Action Committee on the Status of Women, the Basic Poverty Action Group, the Metropolitan Toronto Labour Council and the Ontario Environmental Network. More than 4,000 people came out to vote to take Canada out of the arms race, to stop the Free Trade deal, to save the environment and to fund human needs. The links we made here we're not going to lose, and these links change our own peace issues. For instance, in terms of our analysis of economic issues, the Free Trade debate has helped the peace movement develop a much more sophisticated analysis of militarism.

This transformation of coalition politics which Wright outlines corresponds to the politics of difference in current feminist strategizing. As feminists, we value both the commonality and diversity of women; we work to link issues while acknowledging the autonomy of distinct women's groups.

CIVIL DISOBEDIENCE
Civil disobedience as a strategy for change is, according to Wendy Wright, most effective when the protest issue is being ignored by the media and the public and there are few people to demonstrate active support. Recently civil disobedience tactics have been used by obstructionist antifeminist anti-abortionists to harass women seeking abortions at free-standing abortion clinics. Within Canada their anti-abortion sentiments represent a minority opinion and are fuelled by the right-wing U.S. anti-abortion group "Operation Rescue." This right-wing appropriation of the civil disobedience tactics traditionally used by pacifists and political progressives echoes the anti-women REAL (Realistic, Equal, Active for Life) Women's attempt to make themselves over not only as the bogus advocates of equality for women but as the "dominant" Canadian women's movement. The Conservative government provides a climate ripe for such appropriation, as we have seen in the diminishing resources for feminist organizations and the increased federal government support

of REAL Women. Witness their recent Toronto conference on "equality" which was supported by federal government funding.

In Toronto on March 8, 1989, a group of women, many from the Alliance for Non-Violent Action's Women's Collective, blockaded the intersection of King and Bay Streets, an action intended to stop "business as usual in the profit-from-pain heartland." Many of these women also take part in antimilitarist demonstrations. Reflecting on the effectiveness of their action, Anita Block noted that "the press picked up the blockade and reported it in context with other struggles, both local and international.... In addition to media coverage, word-of-mouth communication about the action was prevalent – EVERYONE in this city knew that the Broads (nostalgic term) took Bay Street on March 8th." Block points out the "broads" derived from Bette Davis's pronouncement: "There are two sorts of women, the female and the broad. The female marries for security. The broad is more forthright." Maggie Helwig, one of the nineteen women arrested for the criminal offence of public mischief, noted that the action not only empowered the participants but also affected the bystanders who watched the women "genuinely disrupt the operation of the rich white male system." Many of these women also participated in the protest against Ottawa's ARMX, "Canada's International Arms Exhibition." The 1987 ARMX exhibition included delegations from many countries known to have violated human rights. The 1989 theme, "Training and Simulation," was apparently designed to highlight Canada's "superiority" in simulations systems. The Ad Hoc Coalition to Disarm ARMX points out that Canada's aircraft trainers have proved popular with governments in Chile, Honduras, Iran, Iraq, and El Salvador, among others. On May 23, 1989, 145 protesters were arrested in a nonviolent civil disobedience action which grew out of a series of educationals on the relation between militarism, poverty, women's oppression, and native and Third World solidarity. As a result of the public outcry, the Ottawa city council voted to ban future ARMX exhibitions from the city.

The Canadian government's militarism has become evident across Canada in the antisubmarine warfare on Nanoose Bay, the Cruise missile and B-52 tests, and the low-level tests over the Quebec-Labrador Innu land. Civil disobedience has become one of the effective means for members of the 10,000 Innu, as the Naskapi-Montagnais people call themselves, to protect their homeland on the Quebec-Labrador peninsula, Nitassinan. Their hunting and fishing grounds have been designated one of five Canadian government military flight corridors in the Canadian north, and, at the invitation of the Canadian government, NATO is considering building an $800,000,000 Tactical Fighter and Weapons Training Centre in Goose Bay, Labrador. If this installation were to be realized, the current 6,500 low-level flights would be increased to 40,000 per year. Estimates suggest that 27,500 flights at a full NATO base would be at less than 500 feet. As well as training flights, supersonic fighter bombers would rehearse high-speed, air-to-air combat and nuclear strike flights. Four bombing ranges would be constructed on Innu hunting territory.

For the first time in its history, the Canadian Peace Alliance formally worked with the Assembly of First Nations on this issue, which links native rights and environmental issues with militarism. As a result of this collaboration, peace activists are continually encouraged to participate in the Innu campaign.

In May of 1989, Innu women left their homes to speak out to other Canadians in Ottawa, Montreal and Toronto. As part of their presentation, they played a videotape produced by the Innu Project Working Group in which one of the Innu men identified the NATO flights as "an invasion of our homeland. It's colonialism we're talking about." In their Toronto address sponsored by the Alliance for Non-Violent Action Women's Collective, the Canadian Friends Service Committee and the NATO Out of Nitassinan Toronto Coalition, the Innu women spoke of their insights and experiences. Rose Gregoire read aloud the women's collective rationale for their protest connecting militarism with environmental concerns and native land claim issues. The women condemned the Canadian government's lack of respect for the Innu hunting lands and way of life, and hunting lands they have inhabited for at least 9,000 years. Gregoire traced the effects of their relocation into villages to the social alienation of alcoholism, prostitution, and family and community violence. "[The last Innu] were moved into houses in 1972. [Before this] sometimes we were hungry but we never felt homeless and we always knew that our homeland belonged to us.... We are a hunting people. To keep us in a village is to keep us from hunting, our livelihood. Our self-reliance has become dependence. Even our ways of expressing our anger and sadness, our resources were cut off from us.... We are fighting for our land and for our rights as hunters on the land.... Our fight is not just about land claims. That is being used against us. We do not want to give up our Innu identity. We have become slaves in our own lands."

According to research by the NATO Out of Nitassinan Campaign, effects of these flights are disastrous: subsonic jet noise can have psychological effects and contribute to stress-related disease (sonic booms can blow out windows or crack walls); and high-level radio-frequency (RF) radiation has been linked to genetic abnormalities, cataracts, changes in spinal fluid and heart disease. As well, there are the more obvious risks of air crashes and the resulting civilian deaths.

While the environmental effects on wildlife and the land will be disastrous, the social effects of such a military base will be devastating to Innu women and men, who have already begun to suffer the disintegration of their economy and community. Seventy percent of women across Labrador are unemployed, and almost 30 percent are on social assistance, but the boom-bust economy of a military base town means that women and nonwhites are the last hired and the first fired. In particular, the women will suffer from militarized prostitution and sexual harassment. "The sexual abuse of women by military men for their "rest and recreation" occurs worldwide.... The women generally come from poor families. Prostitution is an attempt to escape poverty, it is often the only alternative.... Women in Labrador expect an increase in unwanted pregnancies as more military come to Goose Bay.... In Sheshatshit, 15 children have been born to Innu women from liaisons with British, American and West German men. These women must bear the economic burden of raising these children. In June, 1988, an 18-year-old Innu woman was raped by a member of the Canadian armed forces and later attempted suicide."

As part of their protest, last September the Innu set up camp on the Minipi Lake bombing range near Goose Bay and succeeded in halting bombing practice for two months. Throughout the year, they "trespassed" onto the base and were led by their elders in prayer on the tarmac. Two hundred arrests were made. During the Toronto meeting, one of the four Innu activists acquitted in May for civil disobedience actions, Elizabeth Penashue, wept while her court statement was read in translation: "We have always cared for our plants and animals. We have always killed with great respect. There has been too much destruction on our land.... Even though we accept the government's money, this is only bread crumbs to what they have taken away from us." At the end of their presentation, all three Innu women laid their heads in their hands and wept. This expression of their profound grief silenced the seventy or so native and non-native spectators, who sat speechless until a woman called out,

"What can we do to help?" In response to this question, the room filled again with conversations as the women and men began to work together on strategies to educate and inspire the public to action.

This book's cover, "Burial Stand #2" by Edmonton artist Jane Ash Poitras, is intended to embody both the despair and the effective creativity of women's peace activism. The written notations – Cree syllabics, English newspaper scraps, and Buddhist chants – link our writing, thinking and acting about peace with rites of renewal and connectedness.

The title of our book originates in the determination and strength of Margaret Laurence, the late novelist and peace activist. Feminist and peace activism is split at the root in a doubled consciousness of oppression and a utopian possibility: feminists active in the peace movement have linked militarism with domestic, sexual, class, racial, ecological and rhetorical violence. While our collective will struggles to transform injustices and inequities, our utopian vision inspires us with a different future. Pessimism sparks our consciousness of injustice and danger; empowering energy and positive action fuel our optimism. It is our fierce commitment to imagining and working towards a different world which inspires the title of our anthology, a title rooted in Margaret Laurence's "basic message": "Do not despair. Act. Speak out. In the words of one of my heroines, Catharine Parr Traill, 'In cases of emergency, it is folly to fold one's hands and sit down to bewail in abject terror. It is better to be up and doing.'"

– Janice Williamson

Thanks to Wendy Wright and Diana Chown
for their help and inspiration.

I WAS DELIGHTED WHEN Janice Williamson asked me to help her edit this volume, both because the question of how we can achieve a more peaceful, less destructive world is of such importance, and because I welcomed the opportunity to work with a dear and valued friend.

My own involvement with peace activism began in the United States in the early 1960s, when I took part in demonstrations organized by the Committee on Non-Violent Action, in Cambridge, Massachusetts. CVNA's main endeavour in those years was to protest the building of Polaris submarines in New London, Connecticut. Protesters handed out leaflets to the workers as they emerged from the factory, and on several occasions a small number of CNVA volunteers attempted to board a partially constructed submarine which was floating in the river along which the factory was situated. On these occasions, supporters lined both sides of the river bank, cheering the swimmers on, as a police boat chased after them. As soon as the swimmers reached the submarine, the policemen would haul them out of the water.

This was my first encounter with the difficulties and contradictions that peace activism involves – contradictions that are recognized and discussed in different ways by many of the contributors to this volume. The New London workers were not persuaded by the leaflets condemning the Polaris submarine: instead, they were angry that we were attacking their source of livelihood, so angry that they sometimes knocked the leaflets out of our hands. While there is no question that the arms race continues in large part because arms manufacturers profit from it, so do many ordinary workers, in the short run at least. The nature of our economy makes it difficult for peace activists to speak convincingly to such workers – just as it is difficult for environmentalists to speak convincingly to the people in South Moresby, British Columbia, or in the Temagami region of Ontario, who make a living as loggers. In developed economies, there are few people indeed who are not co-opted to some degree by a productivity that on the one hand provides unprecedented material abundance, but that on the other hand threatens the beauty, and indeed the very existence, of the earth and all its inhabitants.

The Committee on Non-Violent Action was dominated by pacifists, by people opposed absolutely, on moral grounds, to the use of organized violence. Some of them were people of great courage, who had maintained their pacifism, and had been vilified and imprisoned for it, during World War II. Is the position of absolute pacifism one that can be maintained in the late twentieth century? Or is it an outdated and suspect product of liberal individualism and the Judeo-Christian ethical heritage, an unrealistic, sanctimonious, perhaps even disingenuous response in the context of the injustice, racism and oppression propagated by regimes that practice violence against their own citizens? What can a pacifist say in response to someone like the member of Canadian Action for Nicaragua whom Janice Williamson quotes in her section of this introduction? Nomi Wall is of course correct when she says that "something like the Nestle's boycott isn't going to bring down apartheid in South Africa." And who am I, a comfortable academic who has lived only in fortunate countries like Canada and the United States, to argue with her? But although it may be a lame response, my answer to her question "What choice do people have but armed struggle?" is that we *must* find an alternate choice. Too much of the history of this century has demonstrated that in employing violence, even in defence of a just cause, individuals and revolutionary protesters, like nations, inevitably take on the characteristics of the enemy against whom they struggle. The pacifist conviction that there are no just wars, that violence itself is immoral, still deserves a hearing.

– Deborah Gorham

RESOURCES
Printed Materials
Atlantis: A Women's Studies Journal 12.1 (Autumn 1986). Special issue on Women and Peace, ed. Barbara Roberts. This volume includes a French-language section edited by Micheline de Sève.

Berenice A. Carroll, "Feminism and Pacifism," *Women and Peace: Theoretical, Historical and Practical Perspectives*, eds. Ruth Roach Pierson with Somer Brodribb (London: Croom Helm, 1987).

Wilma Needham, ed. *Women and Peace Resource Book,* A Project by Voice of Women Halifax, 1987.

Dorothy Goldin Rosenberg, a peace, security and environmental researcher, is compiling "A Directory of Women in Canada Specializing in Global Issues / Répertoire des femmes spécialisées au Canada dans les questions internationales." It will provide a book-form and a computer data base directory of women in Canada who have expertise in policy areas relating to development, peace, the environment and associated economic and social justice issues. It is intended to counter the "there-are-no-women-researching-in-this-field-so let's-appoint / hire / vote for / listen to-a-man" syndrome. International surveys indicate that where substantial groups of women are in policy-making positions, environmental programs and progressive social policies tend to be more prevalent. In order to reflect women's different value systems, this directory will provide a resource for organizations requiring consultants, workshop leaders and speakers. For further information contact Dorothy Goldin Rosenberg, Canadian Council for International Cooperation, 1 Nicholas Street, Suite 300, Ottawa, Ontario, Canada K1N 7B7, (613) 236-4547.

Films

A number of Canadian women peace activists are interviewed in *Speaking Our Peace*, a National Film Board Studio D film about "women, peace and power," directed by Bonnie Sherr Klein and Terri Nash. This film and a number of short films expanding on the issue of women and peace are available from the National Film Board of Canada.

Groups

For further information about the **Alliance for Non-Violent Action's Women's Collective**, call Alliance for Non-Violent Action at (416) 533-9567 or Maggie Helwig at (416) 967-6507.

The **Canadian Federation of University Women** has a committee which writes policy on peace and security issues. Contact Elizabeth Cureton, Executive Director, Canadian Federation of University Women, 55 Parkdale, Ottawa, Ontario, Canada K1Y 1E5, (613) 722-8732.

For more information about women's peace activities in Canada, contact **Canadian Peace Alliance**, 555 Bloor Street West, Suite 5, Toronto, Ontario, Canada M5S 1Y6, (416) 925-5308. The group publishes *The Canadian Peace Directory*, which lists its member organizations across Canada.

The **Survival Committee** of the **National Action Committee on the Status of Women**, 40 St. Clair Avenue East, Suite 306, Toronto, Ontario, Canada M4T 1M9, (416) 922-3246.

Voice of Women, 736 Bathurst Street, Toronto, Ontario, Canada M5S 2R4, (416) 922-2997.

For further information concerning the Innu struggle for their homeland, contact the **NATO Out of Nitassinan Campaign** through a
group working on this issue in your area, or through the Canadian
Peace Alliance.

PART ONE

PEACE

HISTORY

THE THREE PIECES in this section all contribute to the history of women's peace activism in Canada in the period up to World War II. Through an analysis of peace activism in the past, we can find the roots of questions and dilemmas that are still being vigorously debated today by peace activists and by feminist theorists. One such question concerns the relationship of feminism to pacifism. Not all feminists are pacifists today, nor were they in the past. Nor are all peace activists – male or female – feminists. Yet many would argue today (as do several contributors to this book) that all women are by their very nature more likely than men to support peace, and even more people – most notably many activists in the nineteenth and early twentieth-century women's movement – argued this way in the past.[1]

Women have been a part of the peace movements of Europe and North America since organized peace activism began in the nineteenth century. Women's organized peace activism in Canada goes back to the decades before World War I, as the articles by Thomas Socknat and Barbara Roberts demonstrate. The international peace movement has its origins among the English-speaking peoples in the period after the Napoleonic wars.[2] With the members of the Society of Friends as leaders, but with the collaboration of other Protestant groups, peace organizations emerged in the United States and Britain in the 1820s, and it was these Anglo-American groups that were responsible for organizing the international peace congresses of the mid-century decades.

Even by the mid-nineteenth century, a division between absolute pacifism, whose origins were primarily religious, and what Martin Ceadel has called "pacificism" – or a qualified pacifism – had arisen.[3] The latter group had divergent political views. There were liberal free-traders and early socialists involved in nineteenth-century peace activism.

Women were involved in this nineteenth-century peace activism from its beginnings, most often as members of male-dominated peace groups (the first all-woman peace group was founded in 1868), and it is interesting to note that female peace activists had, in the nineteenth century, difficulties within male-dominated peace groups that are similar to the problems that exist in the contemporary peace movements.[4] In the nineteenth century, women's feminist and reform activism was certainly connected to peace activism, but the international peace organizations were male-dominated and did not, as organizations, perceive any connection between the issues of feminism and the issues of pacifism.

As Thomas Socknat's paper explains, the earliest women's peace activism in Canada originated from within the Women's Christian Temperance Union and the National Council of Women of Canada. Some of the issues adopted by the Peace and Arbitration Committees of the National Council of Women – such as the campaign against war toys and the proposals to educate for peace – have obvious links with peace activism in our own period, and it is interesting that some leaders of the Canadian suffrage movement were also leaders in the peace activities of the women's groups.

The international network of peace activism that had developed before World War I faltered when war broke out. Many of those who had supported peace-related activities abandoned them as soon as their own nations became involved in the war. This was the case in Canada, and it was as characteristic of the women peace activists as it was of the men. Some women, like Nellie McClung and Flora Mac-Donald Denison, assumed an antiwar stance when war first broke out, but fell away from it and became supporters of Canada's "war effort," justifying their change of position by stating that the Germans were inherently more militaristic than the British, and therefore more responsible for the war.[5]

There are several general explanations for the fragility of the prewar peace movement, and some specific reasons for the fragility of women's pacifism. The nature of Canada's early twentieth-century women's movement has something to do with it. That movement tended to be characterized by a belief in woman's special nature, and to ground its claims for women's political and social equality with men more often by emphasizing the differences between men and women than by asserting their fundamental similarity. For the most part, Canadian women activists simply accepted prevailing notions about woman's separate sphere and about the identity between femininity and nurturance and used them as reasons why society needed women's special point of view. Historians have labelled the co-optation of femininity in the cause of women's activism "maternal feminism."[6]

As we have seen, much of the peace activity particularly associated with women in the period before World War I in Canada was generated by activists in the early women's movement. But just as their women's activism was characterized by a fundamental belief in gender differences, so was their peace activism. These activists claimed that women as mothers had a natural desire to preserve peace and had a special mission to fulfill in peace education.

The problem with this sort of pacifist sentiment, resting as it does on an acceptance of the values of femininity, is that it is easily undermined, because at bottom it defines women as supporters of men, and the role of supporter is particularily easily subverted in time of war. Women's opposition to war on behalf of their sons can quickly become women's support of the "war effort" when those sons become soldiers.

This transformation affected some of Canada's most prominent women peace activists during World War I. Randi Warne's provocative contribution to this section contains a valiant defence of Nellie McClung's behaviour during the war, but in the end Warne's paper demonstrates that McClung was peace-minded before World War I, as she was to be after it, but that during the war she supported the war effort. (Warne does, however, make an excellent case for the necessity of viewing this stance in the context of McClung's lifelong support for justice, humanity and a genuinely democratic vision of Christianity, and argues that there is little point in accusing McClung, who was never an absolute pacifist in any case, of "selling out.")

If women like Nellie McClung and Flora MacDonald Denison, for whom a commitment to peace was important, fell away from that commitment during the war, the majority of women activists in early twentieth-century Canada had never seriously considered the pacifist alternative. In Canada, as elsewhere, the main women's organizations sprang to the defence of the "war effort" and excoriated those women who did not do so, as both Roberts and Socknat make clear. But some Canadian women remained firmly committed to pacifism, even during World War I. Both Socknat and Roberts offer insights into the experience of the few women who opposed the war. Roberts's paper provides us with vivid portraits of two such women: Francis Marion Beynon and Laura Hughes. As Roberts's work on Beynon indicates, Beynon's analysis of the causes of the war was considerably more developed than that of either Christian or feminine pacifism. Beynon connected the causes of the war with economic factors, asserting that on both sides, war profiteers who had something to gain from the war were the real enemies of the ordinary people who were the victims of war.

The handful of Canadian women in public life who opposed the war had links to women of similar views in other countries. It is not surprising that the impetus for the organization of international women's resistance to World War I, which surfaced in 1915, came from U.S. women. In 1915, it was easier for the U.S. women to organize because the United States was still neutral in that year. Led by the social reformer Jane Addams, American women organized the women's peace conference held at The Hague in April, 1915, and the meeting that followed the war, in Zurich in 1919, which saw the founding of the Women's International League for Peace and Freedom.

Whenever wars occur, a clear perception of the meaning of violence and the right of minority expression are among the first casualties. For this reason, peace activism by women or men during World War I was muffled; governments silenced anti-war voices in countries on both sides of the conflict. After the war, however, the devastation it had caused inspired universal revulsion and a widespread determination to prevent future wars, and, in the 1920s, an optimism about the possibility of doing so. Thomas Socknat's paper describes the work that Canadian women did in the interwar years in a variety of peace organizations, the most radical of which was the Canadian Women's International League for Peace and Freedom.[7] Socknat's analysis, like Roberts's account of Beynon and Hughes, demonstrates that women who were active in this peace work most frequently came to it out of a commitment to a vision of society that was informed not only by pacifism but also by feminism and socialism.

In the 1930s, the Depression and the rise of fascism, with its accompanying threat of another war, brought new pressures and tensions to the Canadian peace movement, as it did to peace movements in other countries. Socknat documents the activities of the WIL women during this period, showing their affinity to the Co-operative Commonwealth Federation when it was established, and discussing their role during World War II, not often as opponents of the war, but as defenders of civil liberties in Canada, even during wartime.

All three contributions to this historical section demonstrate that while the voice of women speaking out against militarism and the evils of war has been a minority voice, it has nonetheless been an important part of the Canadian political landscape since the 1890s. These articles serve to remind us that the peace activism of our own period rests on a rich tradition, a tradition that has been all too often overlooked.

– D.G.

NOTES

1 Kay Macpherson, in her piece on the Voice of Women in this volume, makes it clear both that the vow was originally fuelled by maternalist peace activism and that, in her own case, her maternalism was transformed into feminism, largely through peace activism itself.

2 On the history of the international peace movement, see for example Peter Brock, *Pacifism in Europe to 1914* (Princeton, N.J.: Princeton University Press, 1972); *Pacifism in Britain, 1914-1945: The Defining of a Faith* (Oxford: Clarendon Press, 1980); and Sandi E. Cooper, "Women's Participation in European Peace Movements: The Struggle to Prevent World War I," in *Women and Peace: Theoretical, Historical and Practical Perspectives,* ed. Ruth Roach Pierson (London: Croom Helm, 1987), pp. 51-75.

3 See Caedel, op.cit.

4 For the first women's peace groups, see Cooper, op. cit., p.54.

5 On Denison see Deborah Gorham, "Vera Brittain, Flora MacDonald Denison and the Great War: The Failure of Non-Violence," in *Women and Peace: Theoretical, Historical and Practical Perspectives,* ed. Ruth Roach Pierson (London: Croom Helm, 1987), pp. 137-48.

6 On the Canadian women's movement, see the relevant chapters and references in Alison Prentice, Paula Bourne, Gail Cuthbert Brandt, Beth Light, Wendy Mitchinson, and Naomi Black, *Canadian Women: a History* (Toronto: Harcourt, 1988).

7 On the Women's International League for Peace and Freedom in Canada, see also Beverly Boutilier, "Educating for Peace and Co-operation: The Women's International League for Peace and Freedom in Canada, 1919-1929," unpublished M.A. Thesis, Carleton University, Department of History, 1988.

Nellie McClung and Peace

R.R. Warne

Why does war continue? Why do men go so easily to war – for we may as well admit that they do go easily? There is one explanation. They like it![1]

When I saw the first troops going away, I wondered how their mothers let them go, and I made up my mind that I would not let my boy go.... It was the Lusitania that brought me to see the whole truth. Then I saw that we were waging war on the very Princes of Darkness.... I knew then that no man could die better than in defending civilization from this ghastly thing which threatened her![2]

As popular wisdom would have it, Nellie McClung "sold out." McClung, the well-known feminist and social activist whom historian Catherine Cleverdon credits with almost single-handedly winning Canadian women the vote,[3] claimed in 1915 that woman suffrage would put an end to war.[4] Two years later, she has one of her characters say of World War I:

This is a holy war – holier than any of the crusades – for the crusaders went out to restore the tomb of our Lord, and that is only a material thing; but our boys are going out to give back to the world our Lord's ideals, and I know they are more precious to Him than any tomb could be![5]

What could occasion such a radical shift of ground? It is sometimes suggested that here, if nowhere else, McClung lacked the courage of her own convictions. When her eldest son, Jack, entered the army, maternal devotion triumphed over feminist certitude, leaving McClung in the unenviable position of having to qualify what had appeared to be her undying commitment to pacifism.

Such a reading of McClung is based upon two assumptions: first, that her later position, expressed in *The Next of Kin, Three Times and Out*, and her newspaper articles of the 1930s and 1940s, is in some way fundamentally inconsistent with the claims she makes in *In Times Like These*; and, second, more implicitly, that there is a normative feminist-pacifist position which McClung originally adhered to and then betrayed. The former assumption is based, I believe, on an incomplete reading of the McClung corpus. In the following pages I will explore two of McClung's works, *In Times Like These* and *The Next of Kin,* in an effort to show the consistency of McClung's view of violence and peace. While it is true that McClung came eventually to support the war effort, she did so late and reluctantly, not with the unambiguous jingoism Wendy Lill's 1984 play, *The Fighting Days,* implies. McClung was committed to effective action rather than pious abstraction; this pragmatic approach led her, in 1917, to support efforts for the war's early end as the lesser of two evils.

With regard to the latter assumption, I would simply suggest that a plurality of positions on pacifism may be morally defensible from a feminist perspective. As we will see, McClung ultimately rejects the dual-nature view of humanity which would allow a convenient dichotomizing of human character along the lines of "men rape; women nurture." While this is perhaps sociologically accurate, McClung rejects its ontological necessity. It is this belief that male behaviour *can* be changed which is at the very root of her feminist activism.

Finally, as McClung's many stories and novels show, she considered fighting legitimate in the service of justice. However, it is much less clear how McClung would approach the very real possibility of nuclear annihilation which informs current feminist reflections on strategies for peace. Given McClung's pragmatic, issue-oriented activism, one cannot simply extrapolate her past postion on war to discern her possible attitude to nuclear holocaust. It may well be that the realities of nuclear warfare necessitate a qualitative shift in our moral discourse on peace and war, such that all prior statements on the subject must be reconsidered in that light. By the same token, it is important to avoid committing the fallacy of presentism, in this case expecting McClung to espouse postnuclear attitudes in a prenuclear age.

In Times Like These (1915) is a collection of essays on a variety of subjects, many of them based on speeches delivered during 1914 Manitoba election campaign. McClung combines her passion for social justice, women's rights and temperance with a condemnation of "the war to end all wars." Drawing heavily on the dualistic biologism of

Charlotte Perkins Gilman,[6] McClung characterizes men as aggressive and violent. Paraphrasing Olive Schreiner, she states, "The masculine attitude toward life was: 'I feel good today; I'll go out and kill something.'"[7] This enthusiasm for aggression has, over the years, developed into what McClung calls "male statecraft," a materialistic, opportunistic approach to human and national relations in which life is cheap and gain is all.[8] The human cost of warfare is never considered, for "human life is cheap – to men – and of course there is always the Bishop crying: 'Let us have more!'"[9]

The price of war has always been paid by those least responsible: the poor, women and children. The cruelty, pain and sheer human loss of it has been obscured not only by the rhetoric of male statecraft, but by the very history children learn at school:

> History, romance, legend and tradition having been written by men, have shown the masculine aspect of war and surrounded it with a false glory and sought to throw the veil of glamour over its hideous face.[10]

Thus are new generations inculcated with an ideology of violence and conquest, a romanticized vision of what is in actuality

> the heartbreaking tragedy of war, which like some dreadful curse has followed the human family, beaten down their plans, their hopes, wasted their savings, destroyed their homes and in every way turned back the clock of progress.[11]

McClung's point in all of this is not simply to decry war, but to point out how it might be avoided in future. It is appropriate to remember here that, in the main, *In Times Like These* is a collection of campaign speeches, not a theoretical treatise. McClung used whatever she considered expedient to make her point and to convince her audience (*vide* her famous saying, "Never retract, never explain, just get the thing done and let them howl"). McClung's polarization of male and female character and her use of Gilman's biologism were part of that strategy. The "separate spheres" argument also held considerable sway, and if McClung could use a kind of Darwinist evolutionary theory to transform its biases to women's advantage, so much the better.

Nevertheless, McClung did not support a dual-nature view of humanity. Certainly, she believed that male dominance (Gilman's "androcentric culture") had skewed human development, that "the world, as created by men, is cruelly unjust to women,"[12] and that war is but that daily injustice writ large. Too, McClung felt that the counterbalance of women's perspective could fundamentally alter national priorities. She states quite plainly:

> No doubt, it is because all our statecraft has been one-sided, that we find that human welfare has lagged far behind material welfare. We have made wonderful strides in convenience and comfort, but have not yet solved the problems of poverty, crime or insanity. Perhaps they, too, will yield to treatment when ... men and women are both on the job.[13]

McClung is obviously convinced that women have a unique contribution to make to human culture, one which transcends male-defined roles of wife and mother inasmuch as it may confirm women's positive, self-articulated experiences of both. This is the logic of much of her argument for woman suffrage, and of her demand for a statecraft which is human, not merely masculine. However, it would be a mistake to conclude from this that she subscribed to a dualist anthropology. McClung believed that war, evil as it is, is not intrinsic to the male character. Rather, it is a social consequence of a biological accident made culturally normative.

McClung explains, "It is easy for bigger and stronger people to arrogate to themselves a general superiority,"[14] adding, "superior force is an insidious thing, and has biased the judgement of even good men."[15] The physical differences between men and women have been exacerbated by destructive notions of "femininity" to which both men and women who lack a sense of social responsibility subscribe.[16] It is one thing to observe that war has been a male prerogative; it is quite another to claim that it is a male imperative. McClung affirms the former and unequivocally rejects the latter.

> But although men like to fight, war is not inevitable. War is not of God's making [i.e., intrinsic to Creation] and, therefore, when enough people say it shall not be, it cannot be.[17]

This view of war as a crime committed by men is key to understanding McClung's later attitude to World War I. For McClung, there is no sense in turning your back on the criminal, or in repeatedly denouncing him for committing the crime. Rather, commission of crime demands two responses: (1) rehabilitation of the criminal and (2) changing the conditions which made the crime possible in the first place. Thus, as the war progressed, McClung did not waste her energies in castigating the government or the men who allowed the war to happen. Instead, she used its reality to fuel her argument for social changes which would prevent its recurrence. Chief among these was the equal inclusion of women with men in society's two main institutions, the government and the church. McClung did not ultimately polarize men and women. Instead she found in women's experience a spiritual and moral force which could educate men and offset a one-sided understanding of the world. That men in power had allowed and even encouraged war did not mean men were evil. Rather, the men in power could be likened to spoiled children who had gotten their own way for too long. Women would be a positive force in government, therefore, "for they have been dealing with bad little boys all their lives."[18] Ideally, both men and women would learn from exposure to the other's perspective, and work towards a world which integrated the insights of both in responsible mutuality.

However, at the time of the publication of *The Next of Kin* in 1917, one could only hope for such integration in a future world. The war had dragged on for three long years, with no end in sight. The glorious recruitment rhetoric of the heady days of 1914 (which McClung referred to as "this old drivel of the 'folds of the flag' ")[19] had turned into the reality of shattered bodies, broken lives and black-rimmed envelopes announcing death. McClung did not pretend to understand the reason for this continued horror. She had no theory to prove on the back of this human misery, no axe to grind about women's inherent moral superiority. Hers was an active response to the immediate situation. It was in this light that she wrote *The Next of Kin: Those Who Wait and Wonder,* a chronicle of the thoughts and experiences of the war's Canadian noncombatants.

In the Preface to *The Next of Kin,* McClung's shift in tone is immediately discernible. *In Times Like These* exhorts, challenges and outrageously rhetoricizes; *The Next of Kin* suggests and probes. McClung is no longer on the hustings, no longer "Our Nell," the media darling. The war had entered her life as it had thousands of others', and McClung the woman and writer was struggling to understand it. A meeting of a women's Red Cross Society in blizzardy Alberta had asked McClung to be their chronicler. After several women had told their stories McClung urged:

> Go on ... tell me some more. Remember that you women today made me promise to write down how this war is hitting us, and I merely promised to write down what I heard and saw.... I am not to be the author of this book, but only the historian.[20]

The Next of Kin must be read in the light of this claim. In *In Times Like These* McClung speaks in a single voice. In *The Next of Kin* she articulates the complexity of the war experience from a variety of perspectives. While her own understanding is always present (for example, the women in the Preface phrase their concerns in ways which echo statements in *In Times Like These*), her own perplexity is there as well. In presenting the reader with a kind of phenomenology of women's experience rather than a theoretical analysis, McClung has made a valuable, though overlooked, contribution to Canadian social history. More important, she has illuminated how ordinary people may react to war.

McClung is convinced that even in a "safe" land such as Canada, war is senselessly destructive. However, for McClung there is nothing so evil that some good may not come of it. *The Next of Kin* focuses on the transformation of the human spirit in times of trial; it likewise is concerned with the reform of human institutions in the service of peace. To focus on the former to the exclusion of the latter and thereby conclude that McClung came to regard war in a favourable light misreads both her text and her purpose, which was to offer understanding, comfort and hope. And as McClung considered work the best remedy for despair, she was quick to suggest specific practical tasks of social reform in church and government so that war might be avoided in future.

This said, it must be admitted that *The Next of Kin* contains statements which might well alarm committed pacifists (see the epigraph). After vilifying the German mind, she goes on to tell of her son's conviction that going to war can help save the British Empire.[21] If one wishes to turn McClung into a feminist icon, these are disturbing words indeed. In one fell swoop she seems to be repudiating her feminism, her pacifism, her objectivity and her inherent sense of fair play. Indeed, were McClung to have turned this cry of despair into a long-term position, such an assessment would be warranted; however, as I hope to show, it is not.

Certainly, it is tempting to try to explain away her lapses of judgment. But the fact remains that McClung was human. Faced with the slaughter of innocent women and children, in Belgium and in the sinking of the Lusitania, and with the increasing realization that her family, too, would be broken by war, she grasped for a justification. If *The Next of Kin* is read as a phenomenology rather than a treatise, McClung's outburst is an isolated moment of despair wherein perspective is completely lost. Undoubtedly, many of her readers would have had this experience themselves, and in including this episode in her text, McClung strengthens their identification with her, and thereby her political aims. "Conversion to the cause" was an underlying motive in all of McClung's writing, and she said whatever needed to be said to get the job done, even if it meant exposing her own human frailty.

The rest of the text repudiates much of McClung's cry of despair, specifically her condemnation of Germans. This is particularly evident in one of her concluding chapters, "The Believing Church." In the intervening chapters, McClung has regaled the reader with inspirational anecdotes full of humour and human interest, providing a political critique along with a kind of "how-to" manual for surviving the war emotionally. In "The Believing Church" she returns to the fundamental question of why there was war in the first place. Her analysis bears close examination, as it provides the foundation for McClung's later position on war, expressed in her syndicated newspaper column of the 1930s and 1940s. Too, it incorporates elements of her previous work and is therefore representative of McClung's thought as an integrated whole.

McClung begins by pointing out what she calls "the fallacy of hatred." Recalling her comments in *In Times Like These*, she states:

> The world's disease today is the withering, blighting, wasting malady of hatred, which has its roots in the narrow patriotism which teaches people to love their own country and despise all others.... We must love our own country best, of course, just as we love our own children best; but it is a poor mother who does not desire the highest good for every other woman's child.[22]

Thus, it is not that loving one's country is wrong; indeed, one of McClung's enduring themes is the glory of Canada, the "land of the fair deal." However, pride in oneself is no excuse for the abuse of others. While it is true that in general McClung considered the British Empire to be relatively benign, imperialism is not, and she showed little patience with those who felt the British Empire deserved to dominate the world.[23]

She further echoes *In Times Like These*[24] in pointing out that war proves nothing:

> blood-letting will never bring about lasting results, for it automatically plants a crop of bitterness and a desire for revenge

which start the trouble all over again. To kill a man does not prove that he was wrong, nor does it make converts of his friends.[25]

Granting that war proves nothing, how does it occur? McClung observes:

> That is the question which weary hearts are asking all over the world. We all know what is wrong with Germany. That's easy. It is always easier to diagnose other people's cases than our own – and pleasanter. We know that the people of Germany have been led away by their teachers, philosophers, writers; they worship the god of force; they recognize no sin but weakness and inefficiency. They are good people, only for their own way of thinking; no doubt they say the same thing of us.[26]

In this statement McClung's cry of despair is addressed and transformed. The problem of war is not specific evil nations, nor even evil men, although there are circumstances which encourage evil acts. The problem, for McClung, is "wrong thinking":

> Wrong thinking has caused all our trouble, and the world cannot be saved by physical means but only by the spiritual forces which change the mental attitude.[27]

McClung regarded her writing as one catalyst for this transformation. The main resource, however, is the church, which McClung excoriates for having

> failed to teach the peaceable fruits of the spirit, and has preferred to fight human beings rather than prejudice, ignorance, and sin, and has too often gauged success by competition between its various branches, rather than by cooperation against the powers of evil.[28]

She goes on, in this and subsequent chapters, to take the church to task on specific issues, notably denominationalism, militaristic hymns, an other-worldly "pie-in-the-sky" theology, meanness of spirit and failure to include women on an equal basis with men.[29]

The importance of McClung's Christianity for the cast of her feminist conviction deserves greater attention than it has received. For our purposes, it is important to note its implications for her position on peace and war. First, violence in itself is not evil. She states unequivocally:

All energy is good; it is only its direction which may become evil.[30]

Violence is acceptable for the purpose of self-defence; it is also allowable in the defence of those too weak to defend themselves. McClung's position is succinctly expressed by Pearlie Watson, the prototypical McClung character and the major protagonist of McClung's southern Manitoba trilogy, *Sowing Seeds in Danny, The Second Chance* and *Purple Springs*. Counselling her little brother about how to deal with a bully, Pearl tells him never to go looking for trouble, but if it comes, to meet it facing the right way – head-on. In glorifying war, in encouraging blind patriotism and in equating the Kingdom of God with a masculine military regime, nations and the church have gone "looking for trouble." They have also reaped what they have sown, to the immense suffering of the innocent and the powerless.

In enforcing hierarchy, the church has likewise allowed irresponsible but powerful men to let others bear the consequences of their disastrous decisions.

We have all wondered what would happen if the people decided one day that they would no longer be the tools of the man higher up, what would happen if the men who make the quarrel had to fight it out. How glorious it would have been if this war could have been settled by somebody taking the Kaiser out behind the barn! There would seem to be some show of justice in a hand-to-hand encounter ... but ... the exploding shell blows to pieces the strong, the brave, the daring, just as readily as it does the cowardly, weak or base.[31]

Finally, in discriminating against women, in contradiction to Christ's plain teaching of equality,[32] the church has essentially let the bullies run the schoolyard. It has abnegated its responsibility to this world by promoting an other-worldly, acontextual theology. She claims that the church must stop considering the minister as

a sort of glorified immigration agent, whose message is, "This way, ladies and gentlemen, to a better, brighter, happier world; earth is a poor place to stick around, heaven is your home." His mission is to make of this world a better place.... [33]

In short, the church has failed to teach people how to live peaceably and cooperatively, and it therefore bears much of the responsibility for the recurrence of war. This is true regarding nonbelievers as well, because the church has failed even to set an example of equity and fair play.[34] Whatever spiritual power it might have had is totally undercut by its patent failure to live up to its own ideals. A first step in remedying the situation would therefore be a return to Christ's teaching on the equality of women, allowing women to be ordained, and embracing this world as the proper focus for human spiritual energy.

In her articles written prior to World War II, McClung returns to the theme of Christian responsibility to teach peace. She was one of the few Canadians courageous enough to speak out against the internment of the Japanese, and in favour of Jewish immigration to Canada.[35] In her view, war was a crime and absolutely no justification for the commission of further crimes against others in the alleged service of national defence.

I have tried to show the need to examine McClung's position on war in the context of her work as a whole. The discussion focused on *In Times Like These* and *The Next of Kin* because it is in these two texts that McClung's alleged shift in thought occurs. McClung's brief outburst in *The Next of Kin* is atypical of her thought as a whole. The conclusion is borne out by McClung's later writing and her involvement in peace organizations and the League of Nations in the 1920s and 1930s. She wrote tirelessly of ways to avert war, but when it arrived, she sought to use its harsh reality as a resource for social transformation.

In assessing McClung's contribution to the ongoing conversation between feminism and pacifism, it is of utmost importance to recognize the qualitative shift in perspective which the possibility of total nuclear annihilation requires. McClung's attentions were geared to conventional warfare, not the potential destruction of the entire human race within minutes of a single decision. This being said, the question can legitimately be asked whether McClung can provide a resource for those whose feminist and pacifist convictions inspire them to social activism. For the perfectionist, for whom no exception is morally justifiable, McClung's contextual approach is clearly unsatisfying. For many others, however, McClung's work remains valuable in showing that there are no easy answers, no single villains or readily identifiable saviours in the human struggle for peace. As

McClung urged, we can recognize the conditions which foster conflict and work to change them, rather than spending our energies demonizing others and glorifying slaughter. In the end, there are no miraculous solutions; the hard work of peace is the responsibility of us all.

NOTES

1 Nellie L. McClung, *In Times Like These* (Toronto: University of Toronto Press, 1972), p. 15

2 Nellie L. McClung, *The Next of Kin: Those Who Wait and Wonder* (Toronto: Thomas Allen, 1917), p. 44 ff.

3 Catherine Cleverdon, *The Woman Suffrage Movement in Canada* (Toronto: University of Toronto Press, 1974), pp. 46-83.

4 McClung, *In Times Like These*, p. 15.

5 McClung, *Next of Kin*, p. 148.

6 *In Times Like These* is at time a virtual "cribbing" of Charlotte Perkins Gilman's 1911 publication *The Man-Made World: or, Our Androcentric Culture*. Gilman there argues that women are the "race-type," biologically given to the creation and preservation of the human species. Men are the "sex-type," analogous to drones in a beehive. Their inherent violence serves some long-term evolutionary purpose, but only within a female-defined culture can their destructive natures be contained. Our present world gives grim evidence of the effects of male dominance, which Gilman argues is an unwanted distortion of the natural cultural and biological order. A voracious reader, McClung often included, without attribution, the insights of other writers in her speeches, particularly if she felt the points they made packed a political "punch."

7 McClung, *In Times Like These*, p. 14

8 McClung picks up this theme in her syndicated newspaper articles of the 1930s and 1940s, in which she blames the vindictive Treaty of Versailles for the preconditions of World War II. In "Will the Women of Canada Consent to War?" (August 22, 1936), for example, she concludes her column as follows:

> There is nothing sacred about a bad treaty, made in anger. It was intended as a punishment, and that end has been accomplished, though the punishment fell heavily upon the innocent, as that sort of punishment always does. It was the common people of Germany who suffered, the clean, hard working, decent people; the same sort of people that we know here in Canada, our good German

neighbours – not the kaiser nor the warlords. They continued to eat regularly.

The people of Canada know these things, and if we fight Germany again it will be with a bad conscience. Wouldn't it be better to back down right now and be generous about it? It may not be amiss to remind ourselves that our religion is very clear on this point.

9   McClung, *In Times Like These*, p. 89.

10   *Ibid.*, p. 15.

11   *Ibid.*, p. 17.

12   *Ibid.*, p. 76.

13   *Ibid.*, p. 89.

14   *Ibid.*, p. 68.

15   *Ibid.*, p. 69.

16   *Ibid.*, p. 92 ff.

17   *Ibid.*, p. 15.

18   *Ibid.*, p. 89.

19   *Ibid.*, p. 55.

20   McClung, *Next of Kin*, p. 17.

21   *Ibid.*, p. 45.

22   *Ibid.*, p. 211.

23   See, for example, "Nellie's Way to Peace" (McClung Papers, Provincial Archives of British Columbia, Victoria, B.C., April 23, 1938).

24   McClung, *In Times Like These*, p. 17.

25   McClung, *Next of Kin*, p. 211 ff.

26   *Ibid.*, p. 213.

27   *Ibid.*

28   *Ibid.*, p. 214.

29   See *ibid.*, pp. 214-40.

30   *Ibid.*, p. 213.

31   McClung, *In Times Like These*, p. 17.

32   *Ibid.*, p. 69.

33   McClung, *Next of Kin*, p. 219.

34 See McClung, "Women and the Church" in *In Times Like These* and "The Last Reserves" in *Next of Kin.*

35 See, for example, "What Did We Learn in 1941?" on the Japanese question (McClung Papers, January 3, 1942) and "What of Jews in Canada?" (McClung Papers, April 27, 1940).

Women Against War, 1914-1918: Francis Beynon and Laura Hughes[1]

Barbara Roberts

IN TRADITIONAL HISTORICAL writing, Canadian women's reaction to the Great War was confined to sitting at home knitting socks, writing letters, and encouraging our brave boys to make the necessary sacrifice to ensure that this would be the war to end all wars. More recently, as women's history has become a popular field of study, some accounts show the tremendous contribution of Canadian women not only to the war effort, but to every aspect of economic, political and social life of that period. The sock-knitter and brow-soother has been replaced by the munitions worker, military enthusiast and patriotic clubwoman. But not all women saw the Great War as a noble cause. The patriotic militarist response of Canadian women was far from universal.

There was more than isolated resistance; there was a feminist-pacifist network, involving perhaps hundreds of women across Canada who were opposed to the war and worked to end it. Many were linked to the international feminist-pacifist network that convened the 1915 conference at The Hague, where women from belligerent and neutral countries met, worked out a peace plan and founded what would become the Women's International League for Peace and Freedom (WILPF), to which many of their granddaughters and great-granddaughters belong today.

This article explores the ideas, activities and methods of two Canadian feminist pacifists: Francis Marion Beynon of Winnipeg and Laura Hughes of Toronto.

Francis Marion Beynon was born between 1878 and 1884 into a strict Wesleyan Methodist farm family near Streetsville, Ontario. The family pioneered in Manitoba when Beynon was a child, but moved to Winnipeg in 1902. By 1908 Beynon, then in her twenties, was working in Eaton's advertising department.

Her sister Lillian Beynon Thomas was already a newspaper-woman. Francis Beynon was hired by George Chipman as women's editor of the *Grain Growers' Guide*, where she remained from 1912 to 1917, the period when the farm and suffrage movements were rising to their peak.[2]

Beynon believed that farm women had a crucial role to play in the movement for moral and social justice. In her writing, she linked women's equality and the vote with traditionalists' ban-the-bar and anti-brothel campaigns, with the farm movement's drive for economic justice, with rural concerns for health, schooling and hopes for a better life for the children, and with the social gospel and "good citizenship." Feminism, she believed, should not remain narrow and individualistic, but should become cooperative. By 1913 she was already one of the leaders of the Women Grain Growers network in the prairies.[3] Beynon saw women's experience of motherhood as a potential source of social reform. She urged a "new spirit of national motherhood," in which women would act not only if their own children were suffering, but on behalf of all children.

In gender-relations, family and suffrage questions, cooperation was her key principle. She wrote about the "new man" who was a friend and comrade to his wife and undertook a fair share of household and farm work. She praised men who were "willing to give up their special privilege in the interests of a square deal."[4] She rejected attacks on men as a class, and urged suffrage speakers to be as moderate as possible, avoiding promises that female suffrage would bring about the millenium. But she was a committed feminist and no toady: fuming over the inefficiency and indifference of a male Saskatchewan Grain Growers' Association official, she wrote Violet McNaughton,

> If anything would make a militant out of me it is the attitude of some men who make it so evident that they think any trumped up thing is good enough for the women.[5]

But she warned her network that "there is nothing to be gained by railing at men." Not only were they essential allies, but

> They are the product of conditions just as we are, and if they were not a thousand times better than the laws they have made our lives would be a veritable perdition.[6]

For her first few years as a journalist she was extremely popular with her readers, but during the war her feminist principles led her to express unpopular and radical antiwar views. She was part of the minority of the Canadian feminist movement who did not abandon their prewar pacifism to follow the call of flag and country. Like other feminist pacifists, she was shocked and chagrined that so many women, supposedly more peaceful than men, were fervent patriots and jingoists;[7] and that national motherhood became nationalist motherhood, viewing German "boys" not as other mothers' sons, but simply as the enemy.

Beynon's pacifism was strengthened rather than weakened by the war. She posed embarrassing questions about the consistency of principle, about the willingness of self-styled "patriotic" women's groups to practise democracy, and about the racism, hypocrisy, intolerance amd greed of the war lobby.

Like most feminist pacifists, Beynon saw the war as "illogical and barbarous." But her experience in the farm movement had given her an economic analysis. Preparedness had led to war, not to peace. In August 1914, she wrote that women's sons were being killed in order to "gratify the greed of gun-making corporations."[8] The money wasted on war, she said in 1915, could educate the entire population of Western Canada.[9] Obsession with the war effort meant indifference to moral and social problems and injustices; many prewar reformers had turned their backs on their commitments.

By 1916 those who dared criticize Ottawa's war policies were attacked by the daily press, by patriotic groups and even by church leaders. Beynon was not deterred. She maintained that Allied aims to so cripple Germany industrially and financially that she would never go to war again would create in Germans a desire for revenge and guarantee future wars. In 1916 she urged the Borden government to make a peace proposal, which she believed Germany was ready to accept.[10] She accused Canadian and British militarists of hindering socialist and suffragist efforts to promote a negotiated peace.[11] The causes of war, she believed, were economic and cultural: imperialism motivated by greed, and the jingo nationalism so carefully propagandized at every level of society by the militarists. Only by reconstructing the social order and the economy, and by moral and social regeneration, could this become the last war.[12] In the meantime, she urged in 1916, all governments should outlaw private profits in war production, and power should be taken away from monarchs and given to the people.[13] Under such circumstances, tsars, kings, kaisers and their general staffs could not manipulate populations into supporting wars which were against people's interests. She went on to attack the myths of nationalism and patriotism. More important than their countries of birth, the people of every nation had a common interest in peace, progress and social justice, and this could be a unifying force. Just as rulers and war profiteers on both sides had common interests, so did socialists and pacifists from every country.[14] This was not a war for democracy, she said; patriotism was a mask for the established order of injustice and exploitation.[15]

Indeed, democratic rights were severely curtailed in Canada. Whatever antiwar opinions the authorities had not censored or banned, the press and public opinion had effectively harassed and persecuted. Many Canadians who before the war had supported social, economic and moral reform now urged authoritarian, racist and undemocratic measures against all critics. Germany had been criticized for its authoritarian, undemocratic and militaristic social order; but human rights had ceased to exist for dissenters in Canada and Great Britain, which had become increasingly militaristic during the war, to the point that the similarities between the warring societies now seemed to outweigh the differences.

Women's groups had become militarist. Beynon, reporting from a conference of the National Council of Women of Canada, observed that nearly all the ladies attending were military enthusiasts. Some advocated military training for schoolboys, others preferred physical education; but each group claimed that its method would be more effective in preparing boys to be soldiers.[16] This war had claimed to be the war to end all wars, yet these leaders were preparing for future conflicts, not for a permanent peace.

Beynon was a fierce critic of Canada's 1917 conscription policy. She wrote that there should have been a referendum rather than a series of Cabinet orders; the draft should be applied universally to married as well as single men; Great Britain should have to renounce her imperial ambitions before Canadian men were conscripted to fight on her behalf; if there was to be equality of sacrifice, wealth as well as men should be conscripted.[17] She did more than write about conscription; she demonstrated against it, and was prominent in the anticonscription movement in Winnipeg, the centre of radical pacifist protest where the leaders included herself, J.S. Woodsworth, William Ivens and Fred Dixon.[18]

In early 1917, her columns focused on issues of treason and lasting peace. They were seditious, according to the standards applied by the authorities to other war critics. In Beynon's view:

Almost without exception one will find in the ranks of the most fervent patriots those men who are getting richer out of sweated labour and war profiteering ... and when they say it is disgraceful that those [workers] should refuse to be conscripted to fight for a way of living that means absolute misery for them, and more and more luxury for the capitalist, until the capitalists' wealth has first been conscripted, they are worse than hypocrites.[19]

Beynon believed that war would not occur if it entailed as much risk and sacrifice for the elite as for the ordinary citizen. She proposed a four-part plan to make future wars impossible.[20] Governments should agree that in case of war, all private property would be taken over by the state. As a preventive measure, there should be an international five-year media campaign for peace; any writer or editor of prowar articles during peacetime would face a five-year prison term. Governments should hold referenda on proposed wars: all men (regardless of age, wealth, occupation or health) voting in favour of war would be sent to the front. But, as she said,

None of these really sensible things will be done, because there is no profit in them for those who grow financially fat out of the slaughter of human beings.[21]

As her columns became increasingly frank, her popularity diminished and she received hostile mail and faced personal threats – even though a year later, in 1918, many, even a majority, of farm Progressives might be asking similar questions. Beynon's job was also threatened; the Press Censor may have warned her editor.

In mid-1917 she resigned and fled to New York, joining her sister Lillian Beynon Thomas and Lillian's husband A. Vernon Thomas, who had moved there in 1916 after he had been fired by Dafoe and Sifton's *Free Press* for his pacifist views.[22] She may have feared physical attack; at antiwar rallies she had attended, fellow activists had been roughed up or severely beaten, with the apparent approval of the authorities. Right-wing vigilantes, supported by leading military and business figures and by the press, staged brutal riots all over the West from 1917 to 1920. The feminist-pacifist heroine of *Aleta Dey*, her antiwar novel, died from a beating by patriots who opposed her leaflets and street-corner speeches.[23]

Her involvement in the Canadian antiwar movement did not end with her flight to New York. The associate editor of the *Grain Grow-*

ers' Guide, Mr. Weir, urged her to come back and help the anticon-scriptionists in the 1917 election; Beynon could "get a better hearing in the West than ever before." She replied that though she was ready to offer "any possible service to the radicals of my own country," she feared that her well-known "pacifist opinions would interfere with [her] usefulness." She felt herself to be more effective as a writer than as a speaker, so she remained in New York and sent columns to Canadian farm and labour papers.

Beynon saw the 1917 election as a "fight of democracy against Canadian militarism, Canadian capitalism, and the Canadian Press." The Borden government's disenfranchisement of alien men by the controversial Wartime Elections Act (which gave the vote to female relatives of men serving overseas, while taking it away from male Canadian citizens who had immigrated after 1902 from countries with which Canada was now at war) "created race hatred which will endure for generations."[24] She accused patriotic mothers and feminists like Nellie McClung of betraying their democratic principles by accepting a woman suffrage which gave only "British" the vote, and excluded the so-called "foreign" or "alien" women (for Nellie McClung had urged Borden to do this and told him all suffragists agreed).[25] After the election Beynon wrote sympathetically to Violet McNaughton, a fellow feminist pacifist, journalist, and farm activist from Saskatchewan. As Beynon had feared, the government victory was due in part to a "spirit of terrorism" that made everybody "afraid to come straight out and say where they stood."

> On the other hand, maybe if there had been more unselfish spiritual devotion on our side, it might have been responded to by the best elements among the people as it was in Australia [where conscription was defeated]. However that is easy enough to say at this distance and the fact remains that the worst possible blot has been put upon the page of Canada's history by the endorsation of the franchise act.[26]

Beynon's pacifism was allied to a feminist socialism (often criticized as illegitimate by male adherents of the Second International) which had not rejected its humanistic and radical utopian components. Her analysis was similar to those of other feminist (or socialist) pacifists, such as Crystal Eastman, Jane Addams, Catherine Marshall and, indeed, many of those who were then founding the Women's International League for Peace and Freedom.[27] Her pacifism seems to stem from three interconnected sources: her deep faith in the decency and wisdom of ordinary people, her religious convictions and her belief in democracy.

Francis Beynon was a thoroughgoing social democrat, extending her analysis to family and organizational behaviour as well as industry and politics. For her, democracy was "rooted in faith and faith in others is the rarest of human virtues." Parental and societal tyranny were based on lack of faith in the ability of others to make acceptable choices. In the midst of the 1917 crisis, she broadened her political analysis, revealing its consistency with her previous critique of power relations at the family level. Beynon's faith in maternal pacifism, the rationality of man, and human progress had been severely shaken by the war, but she still believed that ordinary people would make morally right choices if they had enough information. She blamed men's – and women's – militarism, racism and patriotic hysteria on systematic propaganda and ignorance of the facts rather than on inherent evil.[28]

Beynon and many of her pacifist colleagues were committed to the task of reshaping society to incorporate the spiritual in political life. "The only permanent conquest is a spiritual one," she concluded.[29] Her faith in democracy and in people was part of her "religious search," and vice versa.[30] She wanted to combine Christianity with a philosophy and method for radical social change. Rather than leading her to political quietism, her religious convictions impelled her into political controversy.

Beynon's antiwar columns were increasingly blunt as the war ground on. Her economic analysis became more detailed as more evidence of war profiteering accumulated. She was outraged by the increasing moral hypocrisy, injustice and suffering she saw around her. She was deeply hurt by splits in the suffrage movement, bitter attacks by former friends, and the death in the war of her betrothed.[31] In one of the last *Guide* columns she attacked the militarists' indifference to the human costs of the war and the "almost unbearable anguish" it caused.[32] Francis Beynon too helped pay those costs. She lost her home and career, and her faith in those prewar "fighting days" in which the fight was joyful because the cause was just, the Allies staunch and growing in number, and victory practically in sight.[33] A "woman's woman," as she described herself,[34] through the war she lost her community of sisters, when most of her women readers and colleagues opted for what she saw as the cause of hatred, greed and murder. She seems to have been a cooperative feminist of deep and well-thought-out Christian principles, gradually isolated, attacked and betrayed, but never surrendering her hope and courage.

Laura Hughes, born November 13, 1886, was the daughter of prominent Toronto educators and reformers James Laughlin Hughes and Ada Marean Hughes, and the niece of Sir Sam Hughes, a career soldier and Minister of Militia in charge of Canada's military effort during the Great War.[35]

Hughes had been exposed to political discussions since childhood, and was brought up to think she could make a contribution. Her father had given her a U.S. National Woman Suffrage Association lifetime membership (the Association's first) in 1905, shortly after her eighteenth birthday. Susan B. Anthony had sent Hughes copies of her memoirs and her multivolume history of woman suffrage, writing, "Canada wants a leader in the suffrage movement, and perhaps it is waiting for you to become such after you are thoroughly educated.... " As Hughes later explained, both her parents challenged her: "By goading and dares, mother and father were always spurring me on to some kind of activity." Her education was unconventional: "They counted everything from horse races to civic meetings as part of my education." In both her parents' and Sir Sam's homes, Hughes had met and discussed ideas and issues of the day with a constant stream of visitors. Her subsequent interest in peace issues was reportedly stimulated by her conversation wih one particular guest of Sir Sam's, an arrogant munitions manufacturer who informed her that despite the efforts of peace proponents, there would be wars whenever people like him wished them to occur. By her late twenties, Hughes was a seasoned hostess, a veteran of behind-the-scenes Ottawa political discussion and well trained for a lifetime of political activism.

In addition to her wartime WILPF organizing work, Hughes spoke to many women's groups and labour audiences on suffrage, factory conditions, war profiteering and exploitation of children. For example, she spoke to the Hamilton Women's Christian Temperance Union (WCTU) on the need for women's involvement in government, citing child labour and the nickel trust's shipments to Germany as abuses tolerated by the men in government.[36]

While she may have remained a middle-class reformist (as was said of her) on some issues, her pacifism was very radical indeed.

She told union groups that "capitalists were the cause of all the trouble, that Labourites must endorse the demand of the workers of Russia, Great Britain, France and the U.S. for a policy of no annexations and no indemnifications."[37] She charged that British church and government officials were part of an "international armament ring" which had prepared for war and continued to profit from sales to both sides during the war. By 1918 the Canadian government would use its War Measures Act to jail protesters and close down newpapers for similarly "seditious" utterances.

In April-May 1915, after the National Committee for Patriotic Service, the wartime umbrella Canadian women's organization, had refused the official invitation to participate in the international women's peace conference at The Hague, Hughes went as an unofficial delegate.[38] Upon her return she worked closely with Elsie Charlton and other feminist pacifists, mostly from the Toronto Suffrage Association and the Women's Social Democratic League, to promote the program of the International Committee for Permanent Peace (as WILPF was first known).[39] The Canadian branch of the Women's International Congress for a Permanent Peace (titles varied: it was also sometimes referred to as the Canadian Woman's Peace Party) was founded at a meeting at the Toronto YMCA in June 1915. The group considered nominating Julia Grace Wales as honorary president, "as she has done more for peace than any other Canadian," but later settled on Jane Addams. The group wrote asking Prime Minister Borden to consider the Hague resolutions in his eventual peace settlement proposal (but Borden's advisors responded, "There is certainly nothing practical about suggestions of this kind under present conditions"). Initially, some members of the Toronto WILPF group met monthly for study sessions and periodically for larger public meetings, inviting a variety of pacifist speakers: Chrystal Macmillan, WILPF cofounder and prominent British suffragist, spoke to a crowd of two hundred in October 1915. Despite the difficulties of working in a hostile environment, by June 1916 Hughes had written to the head office that she anticipated they were nearly ready to become the designated Canadian Section of WILPF (during the war there was only a provisional committee in Canada).[40]

Laura Hughes's associates included Dr. Margaret Gordon, president of the Canadian Suffrage Association and head of the Peace and Arbitration Committee of the Toronto Local Council of Women; Christine R. Barker, president of the Business Women's Club of Toronto, who resigned her office rather than support the club's war work; Harriet Dunlop Prenter, president of the Toronto Political Equality League, and a frequent writer and lecturer in the labour movement; Flora MacDonald Denison; and Alice Chown, the cousin of S. D. Chown, general superintendent of the Methodist Church.[41]

During the war, Hughes and her associates wanted to involve women from all areas of Canada in peace activities. Theirs was not a "stop the war movement," claimed Hughes and Charlton, but rather an attempt to ensure that there was never another war. The international WILPF program was in fact a stop-the-war movement, but it was not safe to promote it as such in the belligerent nations. Peace education was relatively harmless, especially if its purpose was couched in postwar terms.

In her personal correspondence with fellow WILPF members, Hughes went further. She saw the war as motivated and prolonged by profiteering, and sure to be repeated. Moreover, the war gave the powers-that-be an opportunity to tighten their control not only over the economy but over all aspects of society. Hughes saw the loss of civil liberties in the name of fighting for freedom as a long-term threat rather than a temporary wartime phenomenon. Laura Hughes provided an important link between Canadian WILPF members and the international movement. She provided information about where to get antiwar reading materials which could not be purchased in Canada. Urging feminist reformers to learn about international arms and strategic materials trusts, secret diplomacy and war profiteering, she said,

> If you can get a group of readers studying these books you will be doing good patriotic work, for the truth is always patriotic. And we must clean up at home before we start out to reform the world.[42]

On the local level, Toronto branch organizing was complicated by Laura's involvement in other activities and her absence due to out-of-town speaking engagements, periodic confusion on the part of various women over the allocation of responsibilities, and differences of opinion on how open they should be about their antiwar aims, in view of the tremendous hostility with which such activities were greeted. Although the problems were not unique to Canada (a similar divergence in viewpoints was plaguing the Australian sections), and WILPF headquarters took the line that several autonomous groups could coexist and cooperate, it seemed to be more difficult to do this in belligerent rather than neutral countries. As

Chrystal Macmillan commented in a letter to WILPF headquarters, the members of the "more advanced group consider[ed] that the others do nothing. The others think that only an educational line is possible." Harriet Prenter, who became the official WILPF contact, refused to use printed letterheads or distribute any literature other than material for the study of international relations. She may also have subverted some attempts by Laura's small radical study group to expand their activities. The extent of the activities of the Toronto women is as yet unclear; Prenter reported in the fall of 1916 that there were thirty members in the Toronto branch, two study groups were meeting, and Rose Henderson in Montreal had "fifty women ready to join a group." Yet Prenter was again enthusiastically announcing the imminent formation of a large Montreal group (among others), more than three years later. From the evidence thus far available, it appears that two overlapping subgroups, sometimes working more or less independently, sometimes collaboratively, were involved in different phases of WILPF work in Toronto during the war. Certainly in retrospect Hughes felt discouraged and frustrated by the failure to establish a solid and effective Toronto WILPF chapter, to the extent that in January 1920 she and Rose Henderson suggested that WILPF international headquarters ask the English WILPF to organize anglophone Canada as a subsection of the British chapter.[43]

Although Hughes's success in mobilizing effective antiwar sentiment was limited, her pacifist activities so embarrassed her uncle, Minister of Militia Sir Sam Hughes, that her "offered her a half-section of prairie land if she would give up her interest in peace work."[44] She carried out her WILPF correspondence from her parents' address. Ada Marean Hughes spoke to some of the same socialist women's groups with which her daughter was involved. And although James Hughes supported the war and was extremely proud of his son Chester (who enlisted against his mother's wishes and was killed in late 1915), he also supported his daughter's right to act on her beliefs.

Laura Hughes became second vice president of the Toronto Labour party. She had planned a speaking tour in late 1917-18 through Western Canada in response to invitations from that region, as a way to organize, inspire and unite labour and peace groups. These plans were cancelled by developments in her personal life. In December 1917 Laura Hughes married Erling Lunde from Edison Park, Illinois (a Chicago suburb), whom she had met that summer at the Second American Conference for Democracy and Terms of Peace. The local draft board accused Erling of shirking and sent him to prison for more than a year, after he claimed conscientious objector status. Hughes had their first child, Chester, while Erling was in prison; she was active in the CO prison release movement. Although she kept up her friendships and family ties and to some extent her peace and other political activities through visits home and correspondence, she was handicapped by distance. Until the early 1920s she continued to help organize Canadian branches of WILPF, but was increasingly preoccupied with her family and with local politics. Active in the U.S. WILPF and in farmer-labour and independent democratic politics, she became a well-known and highly respected political activist and educational and civic reformer in the Chicago area.[45]

Like her WILPF colleagues, Hughes believed that women's power would bring about profound social change. The WILPF grew directly out of the international feminist movement, which before the Great War had more than 11 million members in affiliated organizations. Hughes hoped that Canadian women would come to their senses and stop the war. Constraints of geography, scattered population and difficulties of communication would make the task of organizing a nationwide Canadian WILPF massive at any time. In wartime, public and official hostility to peace activities made it nearly impossible. Nonetheless, the hundreds of letters Hughes and Charlton sent out to women and to MPs between the fall of 1915 and late 1917, the dozens of speeches on the economic basis of the war, and all the other activities of the peace women did begin to bear fruit after the war. The national and international mobilization of women that she worked for did not take place until the 1920s. Nonetheless, Hughes and her WILPF colleagues in Canada and abroad helped to lay its groundwork.

What can we conclude about Francis Marion Beynon and Laura Hughes? Certainly they were courageous and committed. So were many of the "patriotic" women who were their close friends and associates before the war. Both Beynon and Hughes were activists, feminists, pacifists and socialists. It is no coincidence that Hughes and Beynon (and many wartime feminist pacifists) were socialists. Socialism gave them an understanding of the economic causes and consequences of war, and a deep suspicion of patriotic calls to sacrifice for the common good, which in fact sacrificed ordinary people to promote profits and power for rich men who ruled allied and enemy nations alike.

Socialism also expressed their vision, secular or religious, of a world based on feminist ideals of caring, cooperation and equality. Beynon was profoundly religious. Like many of her fellow pacifists, she saw socialists living out Christian ideals when most churches and churchgoers had abandoned them. Hughes, apparently more secular in inclination, saw feminist ideals abandoned in favour of hatred, profits and the rule of force; socialists who opposed the war at least held to ideals of equality and international brotherhood (and sometimes sisterhood).

Women's support for the Great War was not universal. The image of the patriotic clubwoman and sock-knitter is not fully representative of the experience of Canadian women. We need to know more about the relation between motherhood as an experience and maternalism, feminism and pacifism as ideologies and social movements. How have women's traditional values, and the emotional basis for them, become transformed into support for actions antithetical to the methods and goals of those values?

And finally, are these questions we ought to be asking also about men? In 1915 the mayor of San Francisco told an international peace conference of women that he had seen in the newspaper that morning a picture of a bedraggled European toddler, obviously alone, frightened and hungry, sharing the lunch of a soldier. The mayor then looked at his own eighteen-month-old son, well fed, well loved and happily playing at his feet. Nothing justified any child's suffering such experiences, he told the group, and that was why he wanted to try to stop the war. If we change the gender of the mayor, that reaction is recognizable as maternalist: generalizing from the desire to care for one's own children to caring for all children. The history of feminist pacifism has implications for the history of pacifists and nonpacifists, and of women and men.[46]

The story of those Canadian feminists who remained pacifist during the Great War has contemporary as well as historical significance. It is easy to work against war during peacetime. Working for peace during wartime is a different matter. These women's willingness to work for peace during the war was a mark of courage. Their contacts helped lay the basis for the flood of women into the peace movement of the postwar period, and their efforts provide an example for today's feminist pacifists attempting to avoid the Final War.

NOTES

1 An earlier version of this article was presented to the Annual Meeting of the Canadian Historical Association, May 1985, Université de Montréal. Another version was published by the Canadian Research Institute for the Advancement of Women. Special Publication No. 13, Ottawa, December 1985.

2 On Beynon's career see Anne Hicks, paper presented at Conference on Women in Manitoba History, January, 1988. See also Hicks's introduction to the reprint of *Aleta Dey* (London: Virago, 1988). Ramsay Cook, "Francis Marion Beynon and the Crisis of Christian Reformism," in *The West and the Nation,* ed. Carl Berger and Ramsay Cook (Toronto: McClelland and Stewart, 1976), p. 190, mistakenly says that the ad job was her first full-time job.

3 See Candace Savage, *Foremothers* (Saskatoon: privately printed, 1975), pp. 1-3.

4 *Grain Growers' Guide,* August 14, 1912; hereafter *GGG.* Unless otherwise noted, all *GGG* citations refer to her "Country Homemaker" column.

5 Francis Beynon to Violet McNaughton, December 29, 1913, McNaughton papers (hereafter VMP), Saskatchewan Archives Board, cited by Savage, *Foremothers,* p. 60.

6 Cook, "Francis Marion Beynon," p. 195; *GGG,* January 29, 1913.

7 Cook, "Francis Marion Beynon," pp. 196-97.

8 *GGG,* August 12, 1914; Carol Bacchi Ferraro, "The Ideas of the Canadian Suffragists 1890-1920" (M.A. diss., McGill University, 1970), p. 112. Cited hereafter as Bacchi, "Ideas."

9 *GGG,* November 25, 1915.

10 *GGG,* April 12, April 19, June 21, 1916; Bacchi, "Ideas," p. 113. See also Beynon's column reprinted by Violet McNaughton in *Saturday Press and Prairie Farmer,* July 15, 1916, asking if Great Britain should have been "crushed" for starting the Opium Wars in the 1830s.

11 *GGG,* July 26, 1916.

12 *GGG,* June 20, 1917; Cook, "Francis Marion Beynon," p. 199.

13 *GGG,* November 22, 1916.

14 Cook, "Francis Marion Beynon," p. 199.

15 *Ibid.,* pp. 197-98.

16 *GGG,* June 20, 1917.

17 *GGG,* January 20, 1917; May 30, 1917; June 13, 1917.

18 Thomas Socknat, "Witness Against War: Pacifism in Canada 1900-1945" (Ph.D diss., McMaster University, 1981), p. 125

19 *GGG,* June 13, 1917.

20 *GGG,* June 20, 1917.

21 *Ibid.*

22 Socknat, "Witness Against War," pp. 127-29. On being fired, see the case of Toronto schoolteacher Anna Held, who was harassed and forced to resign. She would not sing the "hate verse" (verse 2) of "God Save the King": see *Canadian Forward,* January 25, 1918, pp. 2, 8.

23 Francis Marion Beynon, *Aleta Dey* (Toronto and London: C.W. Daniel, 1919).

24 *Winnipeg Voice,* December 7, 1917.

25 *GGG,* December 27, 1916. See also McClung's close friend and colleague Lillian Beynon Thomas to Violet McNaughton, December 21, 1916, criticizing McClung's request. She said that the organized suffragists of Manitoba wanted no limitations on the federal franchise. vmp A1 E18.

26 Beynon to McNaughton, January 11, 1918, VMP A1 D1. On Violet McNaughton, see B. Roberts, "Why Do Women Do Nothing to Stop the War? Canadian Feminist Pacifists and the Great War," Special Publication No. 13, Canadian Research Institute for the Advancement of Women, Ottawa, December 1985.

27 See Anne Wiltsher, *Most Dangerous Women: Feminist Peace Campaigners of the Great War* (London: Pandora, 1985); Blanche Wiesen Cook, ed., *Crystal Eastman on Women and Revolution* (New York: Oxford University Press, 1978); Gertrude Bussey and Margaret Tims, *Women's International League for Peace and Freedom 1915-65* (London: George Allen and Unwin, 1965); Marie Degan, *The History of the Women's Peace Party* (Baltimore: Johns Hopkins, 1939); Jane Addams, Emily Balch and Alice Hamilton, *Women at the Hague: The International Congress of Women and Its Results* (New York: Garland, 1972); Jill Liddington, "The Women's Peace Crusade: The History of a Forgotten Campaign," in *Over Our Dead Bodies: Women Against the Bomb,* ed. Dorothy Thompson (London: Virago, 1983); Jo Vellacott, "Antiwar Suffragists," *History,* October 1977; Lela Costin, "Feminism, Pacifism, Internationalism and the 1915 International Congress of Women," *Women's Studies International Forum,* Fall 1982.

28 Hicks, "Francis Beynon."

29 *Ibid.*

30 *GGG,* November 22, 1916; December 27, 1916; January 3, 1917.

31 Hicks's deduction from scattered hints in Beynon's columns, and information from family members.

32 *GGG,* July 11, 1917.

33 The phrase "those fighting days" is from her "Country Homemaker" column, *GGG,* January 1, 1913. Wendy Lill's hit play of that title, based on *Aleta Dey* as well as on the facts of Francis Beynon's biography, convincingly portrays her views and deeds, together with the opposition she faced from her readers, the general public and her fellow feminists during the war.

34 *GGG,* December 17, 1913.

35 For Laura's parents, see *Canadian Who's Who,* 1910, p. 111, and Henry James Morgan, *Canadian Men and Women of the Time* (Toronto: Wm. Briggs, 1912).

36 In Australia, where women had the vote, zinc mines had been nationalized. She urged Canada to do the same with nickel, pointing out that the mine owners were selling it for use in Krupp guns which then killed Canadian soldiers: "Urges Women to Work Hard for Franchise," *Hamilton Herald,* December 15, 1916; see also "Factory Act Not Enforced," *ibid.,* March 23, 1917. Although the organization was not named the Women's International League for Peace and Freedom until the 1919 postwar conference, I have used the WILPF name throughout to minimize confusion.

37 *Canadian Annual Review,* 1917, pp. 433ff. Hereafter *CAR.*

38 For the official Canadian refusal, Adelaide Plumptre to Jane Addams, April 15, 1915, WILPF Papers, University of Colorado at Boulder. But see Emily Murphy's sympathetic reply and request to be kept informed, Murphy letters April 1915, Chrystal Macmillan to Mrs. William Thomas of Chicago (who forwarded material to Murphy), January 25, 1916, WILPF papers.

39 Socknat, "Witness Against War," p. 103.

40 On WILPF's later history in Canada, see Thomas Socknat's paper in this volume, "Educating for Peace and Co-operation: The Women's International League for Peace and Freedom in Canada, 1919-1929," and Beverly Boutilier, "Women and Peace in Interwar Canada: The Case of the Women's International League for Peace and Freedom," unpublished Master's Thesis, Department of History, Carleton University, 1988.

41 On Margaret Gordon, see Bacchi, *Ideas,* pp. 115, 119 and biographical appendix; on Christine Baker see CAR, 1915, p. 350; on Harriet Prenter

see Bacchi, *Liberation Deferred? The Ideas of the English-Canadian Suffragists, 1877-1918* (Toronto: University of Toronto Press, 1983), pp. 122-23, and Boutilier (op.cit.), Chapter 3; for Flora MacDonald Denison, see Deborah Gorham, "Vera Britain, Flora MacDonald Denison and the Great War: The Failure of Non-Violence," in *Women and Peace: Theoretical, Historical and Practical Perspectives,* ed. Ruth Roach Pierson (London: Croom Helm, 1987), pp. 192-221; on Alice Chown see Socknat, "Witness Against War," pp. 103-8; Alice Chown, *The Stairway* (Boston: Cornhill, 1921); Diana Chown's reissue of *The Stairway,* (Toronto: University of Toronto Press, 1988).

42 Hughes to Zoe Haight, August 12, 19[16], ZHP A5.4: WGGA.

43 One of the early circular letters from Laura Hughes on behalf of the Toronto members of WILPF (mimeographed, to "Dear madame") explained how they had urged Prime Minister Borden to press the Hague proposals for a permanent peace on the British goverment during his overseas tour (in fact, he would commit himself to Canadian conscription and German defeat). This letter was attached to a handwritten one, Hughes to McNaughton July 12, 19[16], that McNaughton sent to Irene Parlby. Julia Grace Wales, born 1881 at Bury, Quebec, earned her B.A. at McGill in 1903 and her M.A. at Radcliffe. She taught for decades in the English Department of the University of Wisconsin. In the early months of the war, she drafted a plan for "continuous mediation without armistice," proposing that the United States convene an international commission of neutral nations. The Hague Conference adopted a version of the plan, and sent delegates on missions through Europe, asking governments to cooperate. The scheme foundered when President Wilson refused to convene the commission. For details of her life and the mediation plan, see Walter Trattner, "Julie Grace Wales and the Wisconsin Plan for Peace," *Wisconsin Magazine of History,* Spring 1961. For the Hague Conference and subsequent activities, see "Report of the International Congress of Women, The Hague, 1915; President's Address, Resolutions Adopted, Report of Committees Visiting European Capitals" (Women's Peace Party, n.d.); Lela Costin, "Feminism, Pacifism, Internationalism and the 1915 International Congress of Women"; Jill Liddington, "The Women's Peace Crusade: The History of a Forgotten Campaign," in Jane Addams, Emily Balch, and Alice Hamilton (comps.), *Women at the Hague: the International Congress of Women and Its Results.* For Ottawa's response to the WILPF proposal, see Page, "Canadians and the League of Nations," p. 30. On conflicts, see WILPF office secretary to Chrystal Macmillan, August 1, 1916, discussing Laura Hughes's letter received June 19, 1916, and on Prenter's plans see Chrystal Macmillan to Aletta Jacobs and Rosa Manus, November 15, 1916. Chrystal Macmillan to Aletta Jacobs, November 12, 1915, describes her organizing discussions

with the Toronto women, and mentions her meeting with NCWC women and her WILPF lecture. See also Prenter to Emily Balch, August 25, 1919; Laura Hughes Lunde to Emily Balch, November 7, 1919, and February 25, 1920, for differences of opinion about leadership and how to proceed in the wartime setting. See also Boutilier, op. cit., Chapter 3.

44 Laura Hughes Lunde to Zoe Haight, August 9, 1919, with a marginal note by Violet McNaughton dated November 1959, in ZHP A5.4: WGGA.

45 Laura Hughes Lundes to Zoe Haight, August 9, 1919. ZHP A5.4: WGGA (Women Grain Growers' Association correspondence). See also Carol Bacchi, *Liberation*, pp. 122-30. I am indebted to Chester Lunde and Anne Lunde for information on Laura Hughes Lunde.

46 See May Wright Sewall, *Women, World War, and Permanent Peace* ([San Francisco: John Newbegin, 1915] New York: Hyperion Press, 1976). These are the proceedings and background of the International Conference of Women Workers to Promote Permanent Peace held in San Francisco in 1915, in conjunction with the Panama-Pacific International Exposition.

For Peace and Freedom: Canadian Feminists and the Interwar Peace Campaign

Thomas P. Socknat

IN THE SPRING OF 1931 the Canadian section of the Women's International League for Peace and Freedom sponsored an international conference in Toronto. There, on the campus of Victoria College, Canadian and American feminists assembled for a historic group photograph – a visual record of the women's network during the interwar years. Clustered around Jane Addams, the matriarchal figure of the women's peace movement and honorary president of the organization's international section, were Agnes Macphail, president of the Canadian section; Lucy Woodsworth, Canadian secretary; Anna Sissons, president of the Toronto chapter; and Alice Loeb, Toronto women's rights and labour activist. In all, at least three generations of women were captured by the camera and preserved as evidence of a feminist challenge to their society as well as to what has become accepted historical interpretation.

Canadian historians, including feminist scholars, have tended to dismiss the interwar years as a time of little consequence in feminist history.[1] According to this "accepted" version, the first wave of Canadian feminists coincided with the liberal reform movement at the turn of the century, becoming almost inseparable from the campaign for woman suffrage. The wartime attainment of that single objective, the franchise, appeared to satisfy feminist demands, and as women retreated to their traditional roles as mothers and homemakers, the struggle to actually liberate women was deferred until well after the Second World War. This delay, it is argued, occurred because the early women's movement was dominated by so-called maternal feminists, those who adopted a limited gender-oriented social outlook rather than genuine feminism – the advocacy of sexual equality – and also because women generally failed to pursue political power beyond their suffrage victory. Both judgments are as unfairly harsh as they are misleading: they devalue the groundbreaking contributions made by early feminists and obscure the highly politicized activities of Canadian women during the interwar years.

Some feminists actually did assume political offices, mainly on the local and provincial levels, but the majority, still barred from the inner circles of power, sought another route to achieve their political goals. As Veronica Strong-Boag has recently acknowledged, feminism "survived into the 1920s and 1930s as much more than what could be found in the stubbornly male world of elite politics."[2] Once they gained the right to vote, feminists merely altered rather than ceased their activism. In particular, their disillusionment with the First World War gave rise to a new wave of feminism which was based on a radical critique of society and which, in the following two decades, found its major expression in the campaign for peace and social justice.

I

The active association of Canadian women with the peace movement began in the context of progressive reform during the late nineteenth century. Nearly all reform groups endorsed the search for world peace and order through the rational practice of international arbitration and mediation. Canada's women's groups were no exception, beginning in the 1890s when the Dominion Women's Christian Temperance Union (WCTU) established a peace and arbitration department with the avowed purpose of moulding public opinion "to believe that arbitration and reconciliation are better for a nation than war and conquest."[3] After the Boer War the department accelerated its work, and by 1904 it was joined by a similar peace and arbitration committee within the Canadian National Council of Women under the direction of Ada Mary Brown Courtice, WCTU activist and Quaker wife of the founder of the Canadian Peace and Arbitration Society, the first secular peace organization in Canada.[4]

After eight years of difficult, frustrating work, Courtice enjoyed a limited sense of achievement. Although the national peace committee represented only thirteen of twenty-five local councils, it had persuaded libraries to collect peace literature and had collected more than two thousand signatures for a world peace petition. The Canadian Peace and Arbitration Society itself also enjoyed the active support of women and included among its executive directors Dr. Margaret Blair Gordon, president of the Toronto Suffrage Association.[5]

Gordon's prominence in the peace movement generally reflected the sympathy of other suffragists.

But the more radical feminists of the day, such as Flora Mac-Donald Denison, Toronto journalist and president of the Canadian Suffrage Association, went further and argued that the ability of women to effectively combat militarism and foster peace depended solely on their achievement of full political freedom.[6] Rather than an end in itself, the enfranchisement of women was viewed as a practical, preparatory step towards a restructured society based on equality and justice.

Pacifists and feminists were in agreement, therefore, on the need for sweeping changes in societal attitudes and values, such as replacing nationalism with internationalism. In particular, they attacked the militaristic conditioning of Canadian boys through the practice of cadet training in public schools and the sale of war toys. Before they were able to arouse public opinion, however, their educative campaign was interrupted by the Great War.

The war proved to be one of the greatest mobilizing forces among Canadian women. Despite earlier assumptions about their pacifistic nature, nearly all women's groups endorsed and supported the war effort in some manner. Indeed, it was through war work that women proved their patriotism and were rewarded with the vote. But the war also proved to be an important watershed in the development of a more radical feminist-pacifist alliance. A small but vocal minority opposed the war by equating it with gender and class exploitation by a militaristic patriarchal state.

The feminist hope of uniting women against war received an important boost in the spring of 1915 when a planned meeting at The Hague of the International Suffrage Alliance was replaced by the International Congress of Women, or Women's Peace Conference as it became known. Women from around the world discussed plans for ending the war and established an International Committee for Permanent Peace with the goal of creating branches in their home countries.[7]

Although Canada's major women's organizations rebuffed the invitation to attend the congress as "untimely peace propaganda," at least one Canadian, Laura Hughes of Toronto, attended as an unofficial delegate.[8] Upon her return home, Hughes joined with Elsie Charlton, Alice Chown and others in the Toronto Suffrage Association and the Women's Social Democratic League to found the Canadian Women's Peace Party, a branch of the Women's International

Committee for Permanent Peace (later renamed the Women's International League for Peace and Freedom).[9] It was the first instance of an all-women peace society in Canada.

Hughes hoped that similiar branches would be organized in every province, and to that end she utilized the existing suffragist network in distributing antiwar literature and developing pacifist contacts across Canada. Outside Toronto, she was most successful in attracting the interest of western feminists, including Saskatchewan suffragists Gertrude Telford, Zoe Haight and Violet McNaughton as well as Gertrude Richardson of Swan River, Manitoba, and Lillian and Francis Beynon of Winnipeg.[10]

Midway through the war, therefore, a feminist-pacifist network had begun to take shape, but there was little formal organization. Nevertheless, all of the women involved, from Hughes to McNaughton, had roots in the suffrage campaign; they became increasingly radical and pacifist as they found their feminist goals frustrated by the war. What sustained them as wartime pacifists, however, was not just their feminism but an overall radical critique of society. They were in basic agreement that the only path to peace was through a complete restructuring of society on a foundation of economic justice and social equality.

It was a new feminist ethic, a blend of feminism, pacifism and socialism, that became the guiding light of the women's movement in the postwar era.

II

The Women's International League for Peace and Freedom (WILPF) was the only pacifist organization to have survived the war in Canada. As such it exercised a leading role in reviving the peace movement during the 1920s. In this campaign the WILPF women were successful in enlisting the active support of like-minded men, but the WILPF itself remained an all-women organization. As feminists they advocated gender equality, but that did not mean they wanted women to emulate the male standard, perceived as aggressive, violent and militaristic, but rather to develop a new social norm incorporating maternal values. The WILPF, therefore, represented a politicized challenge to traditional values already weakened by postwar disillusionment. Although they largely remained aloof from Canada's traditional political parties, mainly because they were not entirely welcome, the women attracted to the new movement were highly political and certainly not nonpartisan as some observers have suggested. Indeed, the WILPF feminists were primarily socialists of one type or another – sympathetic to labour demands and the cooperative ideal.

Employing both a class and gender analysis, they also recognized the importance of family limitation in freeing both the working class and women from social and economic enslavement. Of course, the issue of birth control was also linked to the prevention of war because it would not only deprive generals of their recruits but also eliminate any necessity for wars to limit the world population.[11] Thus, the WILPF emerged as one of the earliest proponents of birth control in Canada.

The blending of feminism, pacifism and socialism was clearly evident in the new WILPF branch founded after the war in Vancouver by its first president Lucy Woodsworth and its secretary Laura Jamieson.[12] By 1921 Jamieson had succeeded Woodsworth as president, quickly becoming the most prominent and influential pacifist in western Canada. A graduate of the University of Toronto with a B.A. in philosophy, Jamieson had been a leading proponent of suffrage and a Canadian delegate to the League of Nations in 1920. She was also a socialist, as were her WILPF associates Helena Gutteridge, an activist on the Vancouver Trades and Labor Council, and Dorothy Steeves, a future CCF politician.

As president of the Vancouver branch, Jamieson took the lead in fostering a new dynamic approach for the WILPF that involved educating the public to accept new ideas, values and social priorities. In 1923 Jamieson organized the British Columbia tour of Margaret Sanger, the outspoken American birth control champion, and helped rally Vancouver's feminists, socialists and progressives behind the creation of the first Canadian Birth Control League.[13]

Despite such gender-specific concerns, Jamieson was mainly devoted to the cause of world peace. Through her initiative the Vancouver WILPF branch cooperated with other civic groups in sponsoring public lectures on peace, a peace library, peace pageants and an annual international fair during armistice week.[14] Jamieson thought of peace not only as the absence of war but as a new way of life built on a truly cooperative social order which would allow for the peaceful release of tensions and thus fulfil human needs without recourse to social violence and war. In her opinion, this pacific spirit was already visible in the international friendship and cooperation of women in the WILPF, but its wider acceptance demanded a radical social and economic reconstruction. Peace would only be assured, she maintained, when the cooperative spirit of peace-loving peoples replaced the aggressive, competitive spirit of the capitalist economic system.[15] It was an idealistic faith, not necessarily in the nature of women but in the promise of cooperation. Throughout the 1920s Jamieson promoted her ideas in journals and public lectures. Whether expressed through speeches or poetry, her message was clear. The path to peace lay

Not merely in national prosperity, but in the happiness and contentment of citizens;

Not merely in the assertion of rights, but in the willing assumption of duties;

Not in spendid isolation, but in courageous co-operation;

Not in arrogance and disdain of other peoples, but in sympathy, love and understanding;

Not in treading again the old ... blood-stained pathway which ends inevitably in chaos and disaster but in blazing a new trail along which other nations will follow, where wars shall be no more.[16]

Jamieson hoped that Canada would blaze such a trail. When she spoke of peace as the extension of the western cooperative idea to international affairs, farm women on the prairies were increasingly attracted to the peace campaign; by the mid-1920s several local chapters of the United Farm Women of Alberta had become affiliated with the Vancouver branch of the WILPF.

One of Jamieson's earliest and most important disciples was Violet McNaughton, the Saskatoon suffragist who had already been attracted to the WILPF during the war. As the women's editor of the *Western Producer,* one of western Canada's most widely read farm newspapers, McNaughton popularized the cooperative spirit of pacifism and became a regular propagandist for the WILPF.[17]

Despite the imaginative and energetic approach of Jamieson and McNaughton in the West, the original WILPF branch in Toronto remained the leading exponent of a feminist-pacifist-socialist activism. After the wartime departure of Laura Hughes, several members, including Harriet Dunlop Prenter, had maintained close contact with the labour movement – a tradition continued by the socialist feminists who exercised postwar leadership, including Alice Loeb and Rose Henderson.

Alice Loeb was a perennial figure in the campaign for peace and social justice throughout the interwar decades. As president of the

Toronto WILPF chapter in the 1920s she helped organize a broad range of support for the No More War Movement and placed pacifist resolutions before labour meetings. A member of the World League for Sexual Reform, Loeb was also a tireless birth control propagandist.[18] In 1927 she chaired at least one of Emma Goldman's lectures on planned parenthood at Toronto's Hygeia Hall and ensured that Goldman, the exiled American anarchist and feminist who had taken refuge in Toronto by the late 1920s, became a frequent speaker at WILPF events.[19]

Rose Henderson, another WILPF stalwart, was first attracted to radical politics in England. A Dublin-born daughter of the manse, she was well educated, having received a Ph.D., and was a member of the British Labour Party. In 1911 Henderson emigrated to Montreal, where she was active for the next eight years in social work, in the establishment of juvenile courts in Canada and in the advocacy of old age and mothers' pensions. During the war she became active in labour politics and the movement for a broad labour party as in Britain.[20]

By 1920 Henderson moved to Toronto, where she not only continued her involvement in socialist politics and child welfare but became an active member of the WILPF, representing the Canadian section at several international conferences – at The Hague in 1922 and at Vienna in 1936.[21] She was also a frequent lecturer on the economic causes and human costs of war and its exploitation of women and the working class. While the working class supplied 93 percent of the army, its blood "coined into profits on the battle-fields," she argued, working women were used to do the "meanest work." "In munition, garment, and packing factories, they toiled incessantly, doing the work of men, but receiving 'women's pay.'" But, following the example of the international labour movement in attacking the evil causes of war, British, Canadian and American women were marching towards a united front, "a league of mothers that will encompass the world and wipe war forever from the earth."[22] Although Henderson emphasized the maternal nature of women and their desire to protect children from war, her radical challenge was unmistakable: In order to abolish war, its economic causes, hatched within capitalism, had to be uprooted. It was up to women, the "mothers of the world," to become martyrs in that cause, "prepared to suffer as much in the cause of peace as they were willing to suffer in the cause of war."

Of course, Henderson did not speak for all women interested in preserving international peace. More traditional women's organizations with reactivated peace committees, such as the WCTU, the National Council of Women and even women's missionary societies, steered a safer course by promoting the League of Nations as the greatest hope of averting another war. The League of Nations Society of Canada itself received the enthusiastic support of spokeswomen such as Winnifred Kydd and Mary McGeachy, and by the late 1930s it was headed by Cairine Wilson, Canada's first woman senator.[23] But other women, still uncomfortable in such a male-dominated organization, preferred all-women groups such as the Women's League of Nations Association, founded in 1927 by Alice Chown.

A suffragist and wartime pacifist, Chown has been described as "almost a parody" of the reform age; indeed she took up a variety of causes.[24] After the war she moved to New York to try her hand as a writer but became involved in trade union and communitarian activities instead. By the mid-1920s she had joined the staff of Commonwealth College, a workers' school in the Arkansas Ozarks, where she taught English composition and ran the cooperative store.[25] In 1927, her attention once again turning to world peace, Chown returned to Toronto. Through her Women's League of Nations Association she attacked imperialism and promoted the spiritual unity of all people as the basis for world peace, enlisting the support of a small group of Toronto churchwomen.

Although Chown on the one hand and the National Council of Women on the other broadened the base of women's peace activism, the more radical feminists were attracted to the WILPF, mainly because they shared the feminist-pacifist-socialist ideas of Henderson, Loeb, McNaughton and Jamieson. Drawing on an economic analysis of war and idealized assumptions about the maternal nature of women, they came to see peace as synonymous with their agenda to eliminate class exploitation, enhance the equality and freedom of women and protect future generations.

III

One of the most intractable problems in building a national feminist-pacifist network was organization. By the early 1920s the WILPF had attracted only a few women, mainly in Toronto and Vancouver, but there was little, if any, coordination between the two groups. Canadian women did not respond quickly. In fact, support for the WILPF, and the peace movement in general, did not really gain momentum until mid-decade, after the fourth international congress of the WILPF in Washington in 1924.

Attended by representatives of twenty-two nations, the Washington conference attracted a sizeable delegation from Canada that included Lucy Woodsworth of Winnipeg and Agnes Macphail, the first woman member of the Canadian House of Commons and a staunch WILPF supporter.[26] The Washington meeting proved to be an important occasion for Canadian feminists: it allowed them to make valuable contacts in the international women's network, increased their political experience, and helped popularize the WILPF at home. With that last goal in mind, Macphail invited the European delegates to include Canada in their tour of North America.

In June the much-heralded train dubbed the "Pax Special" pulled into Toronto carrying the distinguished delegation of twenty-five women including German feminist Lida Gustava Heymann; Marcelle Capy, editor of the radical French feminist magazine *La Vague*; and Lady Claire Annesley, British activist in the No-Conscription Fellowship. Following advanced publicity in Toronto newspapers, the WILPF delegation received an enthusiastic reception in Massey Hall.[27] Although there was some noisy opposition in the press to the presence of women from Austria and Germany, the visit of the international feminists heightened Canadian interest in the peace movement. As Lady Annesley concluded, "at least we have got the people of North America to think about peace and by the enthusiasm that has greeted our delegates we feel sure there will be an increased activity for the cause."

Increased pacifist activity there was. For the WILPF specifically, the second half of the decade proved to be a time of growth and expansion, mainly because of an organizational drive launched by Laura Jamieson in 1925. Since there was no real national organization, Jamieson took it upon herself to serve as the Canadian WILPF secretary. She then designated the Vancouver branch the national office, began distributing promotional literature and, by the fall of 1927, embarked on a speaking tour through western Canada.[28]

When it came to planning activities, Jamieson displayed the same energy and innovation. In 1928 she coordinated the various peace observances of several women's groups and the League of Nations Society in Vancouver into a one-day peace conference during armistice week.[29] The conference was effective, and the idea soon spread to other cities. In April 1929 a similar conference was staged by the newly organized WILPF branch in Winnipeg. Violet McNaughton's peace group in Saskatoon followed in June with an even more ambitious program that featured talks by Jamieson and J.S. Woodsworth, among others. The one-day peace conferences were immensely popular: They not only mobilized support for peace and facilitated interaction between groups but also became occasions for the crystallization of thought and the revitalization of commitment. Moreover, their adoption on a regular basis during armistice week exemplified the commanding influence of Laura Jamieson and the WILPF in the resurgent peace movement.

An even more significant event occurred in 1929 when Agnes Macphail, Violet McNaughton and Laura Jamieson represented Canada at the sixth international congress of the WILPF in Prague, Czechoslovakia. The presence of a Canadian delegation representative of three regions of the country was symbolic of both the growing influence of the WILPF in Canada and the desire for closer cooperation between the various Canadian branches. In Prague, the Canadian delegates discussed future plans for peace work at home and agreed that the time had come to organize on a national basis.[30] The three women returned fully inspired by their international experience and hopeful that a stronger WILPF could be built in Canada. As acting Canadian secretary, Jamieson began to circulate monthly WILPF newletters in which she reiterated the plea for unity.

Within a year the move to national coordination of the WILPF was completed with the formal organization of a Canadian section with official branches in Toronto, Winnipeg and Vancouver and affiliated groups on the prairies. Vancouver remained the national headquarters, probably because Jamieson was maintained as the Canadian secretary. Other national officers included Agnes Macphail as president, Lucy Woodsworth as treasurer, and vice-presidents from each of the five provinces with WILPF representation: Ontario, Manitoba, Saskatchewan, Alberta and British Columbia. McNaughton headed a publicity committee; Alice Loeb chaired a committee on militarism. A committee on education was directed by Beatrice Brigden, the socialist feminist and leading birth control advocate from Brandon, Manitoba.[31]

In their brochure the Canadian feminists claimed their aim was to "unite women of all countries, and of all parties and classes, who are opposed to war, exploitation and oppression." Although their agenda included the usual support for the League of Nations and the principle of arbitration and conciliation, its major provisions concerned the education of Canadian children. They hoped to ensure that teachers were properly instructed about the League "so that our youths may learn to solve international problems by peaceful and constructive methods." They also proposed that a university course in international relations be offered in each province, along with the creation of appropriate libraries and international scholarships. This could be accomplished easily, they insisted, if the Canadian government would show its good faith in the Kellogg Peace Pact by financing the preparation for peace as it had the preparation for war. The formula they suggested was one dollar for peace for every hundred dollars spent on military preparedness. Another suggestion called for the creation of peace activities that would catch the imagination of children and make peace as interesting as war.

Above all, however, the WILPF's primary objective was the elimination of militarism in education. Their central target was the glorification of the military and war in Canadian school textbooks. They condemned books which stressed the events of wars more than their causes, or admiration for military prowess instead of cultural and scientific achievements. They did not object to the study of war as long as it was branded a primitive means of settling disputes. They demanded that the militaristic bias of textbooks be replaced with lessons on the prevention of war, international good will and the economic and spiritual unity of all people.[32] The issue appeared to come to a head at the end of the decade when the Toronto branch sponsored an independent survey by fifty-seven history teachers of all history books used in Canadian schools.[33] The committee report concluded that between 17 and 30 percent of the content of most of the books was devoted to military history, but since it provided no evidence that a militaristic bias prevailed throughout the books, the Toronto Board of Education refused to act. Defiantly, the WILPF women continued to demand a revision of textbooks in order to reorient Canadian society towards peace.

Their other favourite target, and the one which aroused the most interest and debate, was cadet training in the schools. The WILPF protests were publicized in the *Western Producer* by Violet McNaughton and registered in the House of Commons by Agnes Macphail. "Why," she asked in one speech, "should we take our boys, dress them in uniforms and teach them to strut along to martial strains with their foolish little guns and swords at their sides?"[34] Macphail's lurid description of schoolboys being sent to a bloody slaughter caused a public outcry, but the WILPF persisted in its campaign.

What they proposed as an alternative was proper instruction in physical education. According to a 1927 report of their education committee, however, even physical training programs had come under military influence.[35] The WILPF found that three-fourths of all instructors of physical training courses at teacher training institutions were officers of the permanent militia. In Ontario only men with a cadet instructor's certificate issued by the Department of Militia and Defence could be granted certificates as specialists in physical culture by the Ontario Department of Education.

Finally realizing they needed more direct politcal influence, the Toronto WILPF adopted a new tactic – encouraging more of its members to run as candidates for the board of education. Although several women, including Rose Henderson and Ida Siegel, were successful, once on the board it was not easy to persuade the other members, many with imperialist sympathies and military memories, to abolish the cadet system.[36] But they finally achieved that goal in 1931 after Ida Siegel, member for Ward Four, publicized the practice of rewarding teachers financially according to the number of cadets in their classes, which in turn resulted in favouritism being shown to cadets over other students. The cadet program was disbanded temporarily.

The campaign to abolish cadet training and to revise school textbooks had absorbed most of the energy of the WILPF until the more urgent question of international disarmament took centre stage. In 1930 disarmament became the theme of the annual peace conferences held across the country, and WILPF groups began circulating the "International Declaration of Disarmament," a worldwide petition initiated by Lord Robert Cecil, joint president of the League of Nations, with the hope of consolidating public support of the International Disarmament Conference scheduled to commence at Geneva in February 1932.[37] Like most pacifists of the time, the WILPF women shared the optimistic view that they could improve the conference's chance of success by rallying public opinion to its side; they threw themselves into the petition campaign, ultimately collecting approximately 500,000 signatures.

As another preparatory step towards the disarmament conference, the Toronto branch hosted a special international conference or "summer school" at the end of May 1931. It was held at Wymilwood, the women's union of Victoria College, under the direction of the new president of the Toronto branch, Anna Sissons, wife of Professor C.B. Sissons, J.S. Woodsworth's cousin. Organized around the theme "The Economic Basis of Peace," the conference featured talks by Jane Addams, the WILPF's titular head, and Emily Balch, president of the U.S. section. Agnes Macphail, president of the Canadian secton and a member of the League of Nations disarmament committee, chaired the main discussion on disarmament.[38] Drawing feminists from Chicago, Cleveland, Detroit and seven Canadian cities, the conference was the first of its kind in Canada and certainly an important achievement for the Canadian WILPF. Through it, and through the petition campaign, the Women's International League for Peace and Freedom generated enthusiasm not only for disarmament and the peace movement in general, but also for the organization itself.

For the next few years the WILPF reaped the harvest of this increased popularity. The Edmonton peace group, under the leadership of Nellie McClung, had already become a full-fledged branch of the WILPF, increasing the number of Canadian branches to four, as well as the peace groups in Brandon, Regina, Saskatoon and Calgary.[39] Violet McNaughton helped the Moose Jaw peace group affiliate with the WILPF in 1931, and by 1937 the feminist writer Laura Goodman Salverson had organized two new groups in Jasper and Edson, Alberta.

As a national organization, however, the WILPF was still loosely structured and had been in a state of transition since Laura Jamieson had stepped down as national secretary in 1931.[40] Although Lucy Woodsworth had temporarily assumed her duties, making the Winnipeg branch the new national headquarters, by mid-decade it was increasingly evident that a stronger national organization was necessary if the WILPF was to be effective. In 1936 McNaughton and Lila Phelps of Winnipeg agreed, and the following year the Winnipeg branch hosted a national conference.[41] The Winnipeg meeting drew the leading WILPF feminists from across Canada: Anna Sissons from Toronto, Laura Jamieson from Vancouver, Mary McConkey from Edmonton, Laura Goodman Salverson and Rachel Coutts from Calgary, Mrs. G. Hartwell and Mrs. G.W. Hutchinson from Regina, and Beatrice Brigden, Lucy Woodsworth and Mrs. F. L. Lloyd from Winnipeg. The delegates passed various resolutions endorsing issues ranging from birth control to peace. Most important, they chose a new national executive headed by Anna Sissons. The national WILPF conference was the culmination of more than two decades of painstaking work in organizing a feminist-pacifist network in Canada.

IV

Meanwhile, the WILPF women had other rows to hoe during the 1930s, especially since the severity of the Depression had underlined the urgent need for radical social change. The economic collapse directly challenged their feminist-pacifist-socialist beliefs and drove them to more direct political involvement. Although the WILPF activists had always planned to accomplish their goals through the democratic political process, it was not until the Co-operative Commonwealth Federation (CCF) was formed that they found an acceptable political home. The WILPF feminists came to view the CCF as a political extension of their own movement, and there was much cross-fertilization between the two groups.[42] In fact, the WILPF groups were an important nucleus of CCF support and helped ensure that women's issues were raised in the new party.

In British Columbia, WILPF women such as Helena Gutteridge, Dorothy Steeves and Laura Jamieson were in the vanguard of the movement. Jamieson was particularly active in the Vancouver section of the League for Social Reconstruction and joined a cooperative, mainly composed of the unemployed in Burnaby, because she believed "co-operative associations were the intermediate steps between the present order and the socialist state."[43] As a juvenile court judge she officially remained undeclared until 1938; a year later she joined her WILPF colleague Dorothy Steeves as a CCF member of the British Columbia Legislature.

In Calgary Rachel Coutts and her sister Marion Coutts Carson actively promoted the CCF, as did Beatrice Brigden and Lucy Woodsworth in Winnipeg and Alice Loeb, Mary Ramsay, Maud Robinson, Gwenyth Grube and Rose Henderson in Toronto.[44] By 1933 Loeb had become literature secretary for the party in Ontario, and in 1934 Henderson ran as a CCF candidate for her seat on the Toronto Board of Education, an example later followed by other WILPF women such as Grube.[45] But Henderson and Loeb went further: by 1936 they had become leading figures in the Toronto CCF Women's Joint Committee, a short-lived feminist group which aimed to address social problems affecting women, especially those pertaining to the family, and to help train CCF women for political leadership.[46] The committee also helped sponsor a Mothers' Day peace program as Henderson, Loeb and WILPF women across the country officially wedded their feminism and pacifism to democratic socialism.

The political activity of the Women's International League for Peace and Freedon was not, however, limited to the CCF. Through the wider peace movement the WILPF cooperated with a variety of liberals and leftists, including communists in the Canadian League Against War and Fascism (later the League for Peace and Democracy), a united front organization headed by A. A. MacLeod. Almost every WILPF group in the country either cooperated with or directly affiliated with MacLeod's League as it successfully staged peace rallies, torchlight parades in support of the Spanish republicans, and protests against the persecution of European Jews.[47] In May 1936, for instance, the Toronto WILPF helped fill a crowded Maple Leaf Gardens to hear the French General Georges Pouderoux, a proponent of the World Peace Congress, explain why "war is not inevitable!"[48] For political novices it was an exhilarating educational experience. New international issues, such as the plight of Jewish refugees and the boycott of Japanese goods, also captured their attention.

The WILPF's association with the united front, however, was short-lived. As in the CCF, opposition arose to working with the communists. The acrimonious debate, which persisted well into the war years, centred on the apparent failure of communists to respect democratic procedures and the WILPF commitment to nonviolence. Although united in common cause, for instance, the Women's Department of the Communist Party of Canada had openly criticized the liberal pacifism of WILPF, and once the left increased its support for the international brigades in Spain and armed resistance to fascism, the leftist-pacifist alliance began to fall apart.[49] By 1937 the Toronto WILPF branch had broken its affiliation with the League for Peace and Democracy and the national executive warned other WILPF groups to do the same.[50] For the rest of the decade the Women's International League for Peace and Freedom remained pacifist – committed to reduced military spending, refugee assistance, the boycott of Japanese goods, and, above all, to the CCF's neutralist foreign policy. Despite their sympathy for radical change, it was through the CCF and democratic socialism that Canada's feminist pacifists sought to realize their political objectives.[51]

V

Not unexpectedly, the Second World War was an immense challenge to the survival of the Women's International League for Peace and Freedom. On the one hand, the WILPF was weakened as an effective champion of women's issues. As in the previous war, Canadian women discovered that it was through war work that they could best achieve such goals as increased employment opportunities and improved child care.

On the other hand, the WILPF's pacifist basis was seriously undermined. Many Canadians in the peace movement had already abandoned pacifism for the fight against fascism and, after a heated debate at the beginning of the war, even the CCF reversed its traditional neutralist policy. In a similar crisis of conscience the WILPF reverted to a quasi-pacifist position. It allowed Agnes Macphail to support the war while remaining the group's honorary president. Mary McConkey, an outspoken supporter of the war effort, also remained active in the Edmonton branch.[52] Generally, however, the WILPF's pacifist front was maintained, mainly because of the sensitive leadership of its wartime executive in Toronto: Anna Sissons, president, Ida Siegel, treasurer, and Alice Loeb, secretary.[53]

In September 1939, when the Canadian Parliament met in special war session, so did the WILPF executive. Its aim was to draft an official response to the war and to offer guidance to its members. The resulting statement assured pacifists that their past efforts had not been futile but had actually produced "a distinct lessening of hate" between peoples if not between governments. The WILPF had been on the right course – always urging the removal of the causes of war, particularly the economic rivalries that bred international hatred, and always standing for a social order founded on justice. Blame for the war was cast on governments that failed to follow the WILPF's lead. Canada and Great Britain were particularly criticized for not properly supporting the League of Nations and for helping to "arm Germany right up to the eleventh hour," thereby ensuring that Canadian boys would be "killed with bullets tipped with Canadian nickel." At the same time, however, the WILPF realized that it could not be indifferent to the war's outcome, especially since the democratic rights of common peoples in Britain, France and Canada appeared to hang in the balance; to that end it endorsed an allied victory.[54]

What, then, was the proper wartime response for WILPF women? In confronting this question Laura Jamieson proposed a positive course of action. Rather than sulk in frustration, she argued, the WILPF should use the war as an even greater opportunity to get more women involved in working for a peaceful, just world.[55] Canadian women could cooperate in international relief and reconstruction schemes. At home they could help preserve democracy by defending fundamental civil liberties such as the rights of free speech and assembly as well as freedom of conscience. The WILPF executive agreed, and ensured that the Women's International League for Peace and Freedom continued to work for peace, not by opposing the war but by protecting democratic freedoms in Canadian society.

Throughout the war years, therefore, the WILPF women were absorbed in humanitarian and civil libertarian work. They refrained almost entirely from criticizing the war or doing anything that might have brought their fragile "pacifism" into question. It was a much lower profile than that of the 1920s and 1930s.

VI

During the interwar years the Women's International League for Peace and Freedom was an important outlet for feminism in Canada; it mobilized women with a radical vision of a more just society. The women attracted to the WILPF also shared a number of personal characteristics. Although there were a few Jewish women among them, the great majority were white, Anglo-Saxon, Protestant and middle-class. Many were also British-born. Their average age was between thirty and forty years, which means they were born around the turn of the century and matured during a time of increased agitation for women's rights. It is no surprise that they emerged from the suffrage campaign.

They were also fairly well educated; some had university degrees. Like most educated women of the day they sought gainful employment, and a few entered male-dominated professions such as medicine and law. Others chose more traditional "maternal" careers, becoming teachers or entering some type of social work, including a variety of services in charity organizations, social settlements and the trade union movement. Perhaps most striking were the Canadian feminists who developed careers as journalists and writers – positions which allowed them an influence far beyond their numbers. Indeed, it was through the power of the pen that they successfully developed a national feminist-pacifist-socialist network.

Above all, the WILPF women harboured radical ideas in politics and in religion; as they broke out of traditional moulds some women gravitated towards labour churches, theosophy and Bahaism. A few others would probably have agreed with Laura Goodman Salverson's verdict that all religion was a "garden plot of fancy ... an escape from the difficulties of human relationships and social obligation" – the very problems feminists tried to confront and resolve in a nonviolent manner.[56]

Some women, such as Violet McNaughton, had been converted to pacifism as early as the Boer War, but for most it was the First World War experience that made pacifism part of their radical creed. Subsequently, through the Women's International League for Peace and Freedom, Canadian feminists spearheaded the interwar campaign for peace and social justice. Their aim was to restructure society so as to reflect a new degree of compassion, economic justice, gender equality and nonviolence. As a step in that direction they sought to change Canadian social attitudes through educational campaigns, conferences and public demonstrations. Gradually they were drawn more directly into politics, mainly to the CCF, in the belief that a democratic socialist government would expedite their objectives. But it was the WILPF itself that offered these women practical political experience – chairing routine meetings, drafting resolutions, coordinating a national apparatus, attending international conferences – and helped prepare them for political offices, from seats on school boards to provincial legislatures.

Throughout the interwar years, therefore, Canadian feminists in the Women's International League for Peace and Freedom hoped to secure peace and promote feminism by actively seeking substantial change on a variety of fronts, but, in a society conditioned to remember men in newspaper headlines and value victories at the polls, not to mention those on battlefields, they have largely remained hidden from historical scrutiny, little more than curious, determined faces in old photographs.

NOTES

1 For instance, see: Carol Bacchi, *Liberation Deferred? The Ideas of the English-Canadian Suffragists, 1877-1918* (Toronto: University of Toronto Press, 1983) and John H. Thompson with Allen Seager, *Canada 1922-1939: Decades of Discord* (Toronto: McClelland and Stewart, 1985). This essay is written partly in response to the challenge posed by Sylvia Van Kirk in "What Has the Feminist Perspective Done for Canadian History?" in *Knowledge Reconsidered* (Ottawa: Canadian Research Institute for the Advancement of Women, 1984).

2 Veronica Strong-Boag, "Pulling in Double Harness or Hauling a Double Load: Women, Work and Feminism on the Canadian Priaries," *Journal of Canadian Studies* 21 (Fall 1986), pp. 32-52. See also: Veronica Strong-Boag, " 'Ever a Crusader': Nellie McClung, First-Wave Feminist," in *Rethinking Canada*, ed V. Strong-Boag and Anita Clair Fellman (Toronto: Copp Clark Pitman, 1986); Joan Sangster, *Dreams of Equality: Women of the Canadian Left, 1920-1950* (Toronto: McClelland and Stewart 1989); Veronica Strong-Boag, "Peace-Making Women, 1919-1939," in *Women and Peace*, ed. Ruth Roach Pierson (London: Croom Helm, 1989).

3 *Report of the Convention of the Dominion Women's Christian Temperance Union*, 1896, pp. 56-59.

4 Terry Crowley, "Ada Mary Brown Courtice: Pacifist, Feminist and Educational Reformer in Early Twentieth Century Canada," *Studies in History and Political Science*, 1980, pp. 76-114.

5 Thomas P. Socknat, *Witness Against War: Pacifism in Canada 1900-1945* (Toronto: University of Toronto Press, 1987).

6 Flora MacDonald Denison, *War and Women* (Toronto: Canadian Suffrage Association, 1914), p.6. For more on Denison see Deborah Gorham, "Flora MacDonald Denison: Canadian Feminist" in *A Not Unreasonable Claim: Women and Reform in Canada 1800s-1920s*, ed. Linda Kealey (Toronto: The Women's Press, 1979), pp. 47-70.

7 Gertrude Bussey and Margaret Tims, *Women's International League for Peace and Freedom 1915-1965: A Record of Fifty Years Work* (London: George Allen and Unwin, 1965); Anne Wiltsher, *"Most Dangerous Women": Feminist Peace Campaigners of the Great War* (London: Pandora, 1985).

8 *Mail and Empire* (Toronto), April 23, 1915, p.9; Socknat, *Witness Against War*, p.55.

9 Saskatchewan Archives Board, Saskatoon (SABS), S.V. Haight Papers, file A5.8, Elsie Charlton and Laura Hughes circular letter, n.d.

10 For more on the wartime pacifists see: Barbara Roberts's contribution to this volume and her "'Why Do Women Do Nothing to End the War?' Canadian Feminist-Pacifists and the Great War," Canadian Research Institute for the Advancement of Women, Special Publication No. 13, 1985; Socknat, *Witness Against War*, Chapter 3; Ramsay Cook, "Francis Marion Beynon and the Crisis of Christian Reformism," in *The West and the Nation*, ed. Carl Berger and Ramsay Cook (Toronto: McClelland and Stewart, 1976).

11 See, for instance, Angus McLaren and Arlene Tigar McLaren, *The Bedroom and the State: The Changing Practices and Politics of Contraception and Abortion in Canada, 1880-1980* (Toronto: McClelland and Stewart, 1986).

12 SABS, McNaughton Papers, A1. E95 (2), Laura Jamieson, WILPF circular letter, March 26, 1931; Public Archives of Canada (PAC), J.S. Woodsworth Papers, MG 27, III C&, Vol. 2, Woodsworth to Hattie, August 25, 1921.

13 McLaren and McLaren, *The Bedroom and the State*, pp. 59-60.

14 SABS, McNaughton Papers, A1. H32 (1), Women's International League for Peace and Freedom, Vancouver branch, pamphlet, n.d.

15 Laura Jamieson, "International Peace Is World Objective of Organized Women," *Western Producer*, November 24, 1927, p. 14; Socknat, *Witness Against War*, pp. 106-7; Donald Page, "Canadians and the League of

Nations before the Manchurian Crisis" (Ph.D. Thesis, University of Toronto, 1972).

16 Laura Jamieson, "Canada First," *Canadian Trade Unionist,* October 21, 1926, p. 2.

17 SABS, McNaughton Papers, A1. E95 (1), McNaughton to Jane Addams, October 4, 1926, p. 2.

18 Socknat, *Witness Against War,* pp. 107-8; McLaren and McLaren, *The Bedroom and the State,* p. 163 n. 13.

19 Interview with Kay Morris, Toronto, November 1986; interview with Elaine Melhuish Sefton, Toronto, November 1986.

20 Martin Robin, *Radical Politics and Canadian Labour 1880-1930* (Kingston: Industrial Relations Centre, Queen's University, 1968), p. 220; *The Canadian Who's Who* Vol. II, 1936-37 (London: 1937) p. 497.

21 SABS McNaughton Papers, A1. E52, Laura Jamieson to McNaughton, October 20, 1924; Women's International League for Peace and Freedom, Toronto branch, newsletter, July 1936.

22 University of Toronto, Thomas Fisher Rare Book Library, Kenny Collection, Rose Henderson, "Women and War" (circa 1926), pp. 5, 15-16.

23 Socknat, *Witness Against War,* Chapter 3.

24 Ramsay Cook, *The Regenerators: Social Criticism in Late Victorian English Canada* (Toronto: University of Toronto Press, 1985) p. 232.

25 Queen's University Archives (QUA) Lorne Pierce Collection, 200IC, Box 15, Alice Chown to Edith Chown Pierce, November 28, 1926, and Alice Chown memorial card, 1941; *Globe and Mail* (Toronto) March 3, 1949, p. 4. I am indebted to Diana Chown for specific information concerning her great-aunt.

26 SABS, McNaughton Papers, A1. E52, Laura Jamieson to McNaughton, October 20, 1924; Bussey and Tims, *Women's International League for Peace and Freedom,* p. 39; Margaret Stewart and Doris French, *Ask No Quarter* (Toronto: Longmans, Green, 1959), pp. 140-41.

27 A. F. Key, "Women's International League for Peace and Freedom: In Interview," *Christian Guardian* June 18, 1924, pp. 11, 22; *Evening Telegram* (Toronto), June 6, 1924, p. 15.

28 SABS, McNaughton Papers, A1. E95 (1), McNaughton to Jane Addams, October 26, 1927.

29 *Ibid.,* A1. E52 (2), Laura Jamieson, "How Did the Peace Conference Turn Out?" *Church Review,* n.d., p. 8.

30 *Ibid.*, A1. E95 (1), Agnes Macphail to McNaughton, March 1, 1929, and Laura Jamieson, WILPF newsletter, September 7, 1929.

31 *Ibid.*, A1. H32 (1), Women's International League for Peace and Freedom, Canadian section, pamphlet. For more on Brigden see: Beatrice Brigden, "One Woman's Campaign for Social Purity and Social Reform," in *The Social Gospel in Canada*, ed. Richard Allen (Ottawa: National Museum of Man, 1975), pp. 36-62. By 1930 ten thousand Canadians subscribed to the international organization's *Pax International.* Page, "Canadians and the League of Nations," p. 387.

32 Page, "Canadians and the League of Nations," p. 384.

33 Isa M. Byers, *Report on the Canadian School History Textbook Survey Committee* (Toronto: Women's International League for Peace and Freedom, Toronto branch, 1931).

34 As quoted in Stewart and French, *Ask No Quarter*, p. 88.

35 *Military Training in Canadian Schools and Colleges* (Toronto: Women's International League for Peace and Freedom, Toronto branch, 1927).

36 SABS, McNaughton Papers, A1. E95 (2), Women's International League for Peace and Freedom, Canadian section, January 19, 1931; interview with Ida Siegel, Toronto, February 5, 1976.

37 SABS, McNaughton Papers, A1. H32 (1), Women's International League for Peace and Freedom, Toronto branch, newsletter, April 1931; the Women's League of Nations Association, headed by Alice Chown in Toronto, was also behind the disarmament petition. Women's League of Nations Association to Women's Church Societies, March 1, 1931 (courtesy of Diana Chown). For more on the support of the National Council of Women and other women's groups see: Socknat, *Witness Against War*, pp. 129-30

38 SABS, McNaughton Papers, A1. E95 (2), Women's International League for Peace and Freedom, "Preliminary Programme of an Institute on the Economic Basis of Peace."

39 *Ibid.*, A1. E95 (4), M. Cousineau to McNaughton, October 15, 1934; McNaughton to Anna Sissons, November 13, 1934.

40 *Ibid.*, A1. D34, Jamieson to McNaughton, July 3, 1932.

41 *Ibid.*, A1. E95 (4), McNaughton to Lila Phelps, April 22, 1936; Minutes of the Organization Conference, Women's International League for Peace and Freedom, Canadian section, Winnipeg, June 1-2, 1937

42 Thomas P. Socknat, "The Pacifist Background of the Early CCF," and Joan Sangster, "'Women and the New Era': The Role of Women in the Early CCF, 1933-1940," in *Building the Co-operative Commonwealth Federation: Essays on the Democratic Socialist Tradition in Canada*, ed.

J. William Brennan (Regina: Canadian Plains Research Centre, 1984), pp. 57-98.

43 SABS, McNaughton Papers, A1. D34, Jamieson to McNaughton, July 13, 1932.

44 *Ibid.*, A1. E95 (4), Women's International League for Peace and Freedom, Toronto branch, newsletter, July 1936, Rachel Coutts was an Alberta public school teacher. She and her sister Marion had been active in the Calgary branch of the Dominion Labour Party. Both sisters had been members of William Irvine's Unitarian church. Anthony Mardiros, *William Irvine: The Life of a Prairie Radical* (Toronto: Lorimer, 1979).

45 University of Toronto, Thomas Fisher Rare Book Library, Woodsworth Memorial Collection, Box 10, Alice Loeb File; Gerald Caplan, *The Dilemma of Canadian Socialism* (Toronto: McClelland and Stewart, 1973); interview with Gwenyth Grube, Toronto, 1986).

46 John Manley, "Women and the Left in the 1930s: The Case of the Toronto CCF Women's Joint Committee," *Atlantis* 5 (Spring 1980), pp. 100-117; Sangster, "Women and the New Era," pp. 88-89.

47 Socknat, *Witness Against War*, pp. 163-65; Provincial Archives of Ontario, A.A. MacLeod Papers, League for Peace and Democracy agenda of events; interview with Virginia MacLeod, Toronto, March 30, 1976.

48 Georges Pouderoux, *War Is Not Inevitable!* (Toronto: Canadian League Against War and Fascism, 1936); interview with Ida Siegel.

49 Joan Sangster, "The Communist Party and the Woman Question, 1922-1929," *Labour/Le Travail* 15 (1985) pp. 46-47.

50 SABS, McNaughton Papers, A1. E95 (4), Report of the Canadian Women's International League for Peace and Freedom, National Convention, June 1937.

51 Although she was not active in the WILPF during the 1930s, Alice Chown also came to see the CCF as the "only hope" for Canada. QUA, Lorne Pierce Collection, Box 15, Alice Chown to Lorne Pierce, circa 1935.

52 PAC, C.B. Sissons Papers, MG 27, III, F3, Vol. 5, Mary McConkey to Anna Sissons, June 17, 1940.

53 *Ibid.*, Women's International League for Peace and Freedom, Canadian section, slate of national officers, 1942.

54 SABS, McNaughton Papers, A1. E95 (5), Statement of the WILPF Executive, September 1939.

55 *Ibid.*, Laura Jamieson, "Women and the Present War," n.d.

56 Laura Goodman Salverson, *Confessions of an Immigrants' Daughter* (copyright 1939, reprinted Toronto: University of Toronto Press, 1981), p. 377.

PART TWO

THINKING
ABOUT PEACE

In THINKING ABOUT the issue of peace, Dorothy Smith takes on the maternal essentialists who believe "women are spontaneously averse to war because of their biological orientation to life." An essentialist view of women's "natural" pacificism creates a theoretical impasse for feminists. If women are by nature "peace-makers" and men "war-mongers," no possible change awaits us.

In her analysis of "gender, power and peace," Smith describes war as "a vast technological and managerial enterprise" which suppresses the community's consent. The large-scale global economy fuels wars with armaments and is supported by a network of researchers and intellectuals. This "strange world" of military management, a world organized by "texts" rather than concrete particulars, is sustained by "the culture of masculinity," a learned, not biologically determined, consciousness about the world. Structured hierarchically, this culture depends on the repression of "the other" – women and homosexual men. Women peace activists provide the possibility of strong new voices to interrupt and transform "the abstractions of the patriarchal structures of power" with a consciousness of community and the interrelated particulars of being in the world.

Moving the discussion of war to a different cultural arena and the repression of a different "other," Kim Echlin's travel narrative presents a tragic drama which plays out the terms of Smith's theorizing. Her moving account of an ocean voyage, a discovery and a loss opens this anthology to a history far from Canadian shores, and constructs a painfully instructive story about the relation between cultural imperialism, the development of nuclear weapons and the abstract bureaucratized military manoeuvring which destroyed a people's everyday life. An expert in native storytelling, Echlin focuses her analysis on the U.S. testing of nuclear weapons and the exploitation and suffering of the people of the Marshall Islands. She traces the cultural transformation of Marshallese storytelling from creation myths to accounts of "jellyfish babies." Echlin points out how death and mutilation are the underside of American public relations huckstering in the shape of mushroom-cloud cakes. The invention of the "bikini" is a bizarre reminder of the invasive character of militarism not only into our everyday lives but also in the social construction of gender itself.

Novelist and critic Donna Smyth outlines the contemporary "language of war." Tracing the rhetoric of the right wing, she describes how the "militarization of language is matched by the increasing militarization of society." "Macho warriors" and a set of marketplace values organized by competition rather than consensus characterize this process. Citing the violent rhetoric of military magazines, Smyth traces the same rhetoric in nonmilitary advertising. In this world where women become "Real Women" and men are warriors, we ignore these correspondences at our peril.

One new cultural form which dramatizes Smyth's thesis is the popular action / adventure novels produced by the Canadian publisher Harlequin Books. "Packaged and promoted to become a regular staple of the modern man's cultural diet," these novels are part of a flourishing "paramilitary consumer industry," writes Sandra Rabinovitch. "Antisocial" and individualistic, these macho warriors perform their daring feats in a fictional world where "war never ends." The cynicism of this popular cultural form is underlined in Rabinovitch's analysis of the appropriation and transmutation of the "feminist" into a parodic reactionary "action / adventure heroine." Drawing on the insights of psychoanalysis and cultural theory, Rabinovitch points towards the cultural coordinates and structures of thought which underline the violent mythmaking of these fictional Rambo-style characters.

– J.W.

Gender, Power and Peace

Dorothy E. Smith

EARLY IN THE WOMEN'S movement, in the effort to expose the arbitrary bases of inequality, we emphasized the sameness of women and men. More recently we've returned to an exploration of gender difference, which I will relate here to issues of peace and war.

But I begin with the experience, common to us all, of a major and growing gap between our everyday lives and our power to control the political and military organization purporting to defend them.

The twentieth century has seen a new bureaucratic and technological organization of kingdoms of death: the Holocaust, the firebombings of Tokyo and Dresden, the atomic bombing of Hiroshima and Nagasaki, the Vietnam war, the ongoing endemic localized wars and the military repressions, the war of a military against its own people.

War today is a vast technological and managerial enterprise that does not require the consent of a people. The executive of the United States committed its military, its resources and its people to a war in Vietnam without having to consult or mobilize the American people. The United States prepares for and wages wars, directly or by proxy, all over the world without involving its people actively. New technologies and the new methodologies of organizing war reduce the dependence of military and political leaders on the mobilization of a whole people to fight, hence reducing their need for a people to consent to war.

For us in Canada, these effects are intensified because of our military and economic relation to the United States. But we share with people in the United States the problem that we are always having to react to what has already been set in motion in the places where "they" rule. According to polls, more than 84 percent of the Canadian public favours a nuclear freeze. We did not choose nuclear armament; we did not choose the escalation of nuclear confrontation; we did not choose that our country would be a site for Cruise missile trials; we did not choose that Litton would manufacture components of missile guidance systems. We don't get asked; we react.

Our reactions do make a difference, of course, but by definition we are reacting to things that are already in place and have become taken for granted. Unless there's a crisis, such as Reagan's escalation of nuclear confrontation with the Soviet Union, we tend to tuck the problem away at the back our minds and concentrate on more immediate issues – child care, unemployment, reproductive choice, free trade. Do our protests and demonstrations influence the ongoing course of disarmament negotiations? Yes, but we have to do a lot to win even a little.

I think this organization of power is directly sustained by patriarchy, in particular by a culture of masculinity that is essential to its operation, even its existence. I'm not talking, however, about any special virtue or peaceableness of women or any innate biological disposition of men to jump into airplanes and drop bombs on people. Such notions don't stand up when we explore the immensely complex organization of the kingdoms of death and their everyday routine character as paid work.

Wars today involve large-scale complex organization. Even when they still look like the old-style small bands fighting with one another, there are bigger powers behind the scenes. Wherever there is war, whether the bigger political powers are involved or not, the participants include the manufacturers of armaments, who are now deeply embedded in the organization of the global economy. In 1985 the overall value of the international flow of armaments was $1 trillion. It increased 80 percent in constant prices between 1960 and 1980. Wars and preparation for wars require a vast and complex industrial organization producing not only weapons, but guidance systems, plutonium, uranium, missiles, missile silos, airplanes, warships, submarines, military emplacements, underground shelter systems, airfields, supercomputers, communications and information-processing technologies, and much more. War is now both a major factor in international trade and essential to the functioning of the major capitalist economies.

So military organization is tied into a vast investment of capital, a vast organization producing and selling armaments. And both military activity and production for military uses consist of organization, management and communication of technologically advanced modes of repression, intervention and spying. There is an intellectual and scientific research establishment serving Star Wars, serving the strategies of nuclear confrontation, serving the military need for information control and cybernetics. One-third of the scientists in the United States are funded by the military.

People go to work for this vast complex as they go to work at any other job. People who work for armaments manufacturers have jobs that are organized in such a way that workers can't easily relate what they are doing to the end product, someone's death, probably the deaths of many; they don't have to consent, care about, want, that death. People who do the strategic thinking about nuclear confrontation with the Soviet Union use a language that makes death and suffering invisible.[1] Doing a good job earns them a good living, perhaps good career prospects. They aren't fighting because their own survival and the survival of the people they care about are directly threatened – they aren't fighting at all; they're doing a job. And even in the Vietnam War military managers did their best, through quotas and incentives, to make killing and dying as close to an industrial organization as they could.

The routine workings of this complex aren't powered by instincts of aggression. Killing isn't picking up your spear, your helmet and your shield and leaving your tent as Achilles did to confront Hector on the plains of Troy. This complex of power has a peculiarly abstract organization. Think of the strategists walled up in the Pentagon or hidden in a basement of the White House. Do they gallop around the field of battle as Wellington did to see directly what was going on, to give orders and encouragement directly, risking their own lives in doing so? They do not. The world they know is mediated by texts, maps, statistical information – texts that are products of other texts based on forms and instruments and readings and measures and records. Beyond the directly military, there are the powers and decisions organized in relation to other types of texts – balance sheets, statements of assets, evaluations of returns on investments and figures on a monitor registering fluctuations of the stock market or the fluctuating price of the dollar on the world currency market. And wars and rumours of wars are heard via text and telephone, not as the sounding of trumpets, the clash of weapons, the cries and screams.

It is a strange world to live and act in. Men (and women) go to work for organizations that serve other goals and objectives than theirs as private individuals. Power, activity and goals are vested in forms of organization separating themselves from particular individuals whose work brings them into being. Individuals exercise power and intiative not as individuals, but as participants in organizations. How is it that people find it convincing? How is it that this net of texts is held up as a reality? How can people act as if an organizational world put together on texts is real, more real than actual people – and so make it a reality in its consequences for them?

It is the culture of masculinity that sustains this. The world of military power, of military enterprise, of the production and marketing of weaponry, and of the scientific and technological apparatus servicing these is dominated by men. Men learn to identify certain ways of thinking and feeling relating to other men and to women as properly masculine. These sustain men's faithful participation in this organizational world by disconnecting what men do on the job from their relations with particular others, with themselves as situated and feeling people, with a specific place and time.

Men have been specialized to function within this specialized organization of consciousness. Their training becomes a basis for a personal expansion of powers within professions or bureaucracies. Men learn, as women generally do not, the hierarchies of achievement and the politics of advancement. Relations of desire, fellowship, reward and punishment are structured to fit the impersonal process of large-scale organization, creating an identity between the individual and the organizational objectives of expanding power. An insider describes how the masculine culture of engineering identifies personal desires and relationships with organizational objectives:

Unlike manual labour, managerial work is a personal obligation. The 'responsible boss' assumes he is indispensable; and he lives for his work. As Tom describes, there is an ambiguous extension of 'work' into 'social life' – winning contracts, repeating gossip, reaffirming the masculine culture of the engineering world. For the aspiring careerist, it is as important that he be able to perpetuate the conversation, as it is that he display his competence 'on the job'.[2]

Masculinism teaches men relationships with other men that bind them into the organizational world of games played on paper and monitors. Here's one description from the paper world of banking:

An uncommon degree of intellectual perspicacity and personal daring was required for the job, and Curtis had both qualities in great measure. To instantly weigh the complex effects of rates of exchange, tax possibilities and investment risks – such as the potential for revolution in a foreign market – and a host of other technical factors demanded a clear understanding of the subtleties involved, as the numbers both had a truth of their own and were the ever-shifting abstraction of innumerable human tendencies. Moreover, those tendencies were personified by whoever was across the negotiating table from Curtis: another man or group of men (and only men) – colleague, antagonist, advisor, perhaps all three. One had to weigh him as well, constantly gauging the odds, calculating that hundredth of a percentage point around which millions of dollars turned, establishing trust, and, yes, dominating this other man, because that was how successful deals were made: men in scarcely distinguishable brown or gray suits weighing glances, unconsciously registering tiny shifts in tone of voice, building confidence and fear, then striking at the exact moment. Curtis derived a positive thrill from such transactions, which compensated him for much and was undoubtedly far more important to him than actual money; and he was very good at what he did.[3]

Consider that in this game, people's livelihoods are being negotiated. Consider this as a paradigm for arms negotiations, or for the jockeying of different armed services for weaponry, or any other context in which such organizational play goes on. Consider this world which is created to be independent of the actualities into which its effects, its decisions will penetrate.

Through such means men's personal achievements become means to purposes not their own but vested in organizations – government, military, corporate, and so forth. To those scientists who worked at Los Alamos in the making of the atomic bomb, there came a moment of truth. They had joined the project excited by its creative intellectual possibilities and by the propects of working with some of the most talented physicists of their generation. When bombs were dropped on Hiroshima and Nagasaki, they learned that they had been part of purposes alien to their own.

The culture of masculinity has a special interpretation of rationality. Beyond reason, it requires being sealed in a world put together on paper or on monitor. According to this culture, it is rational to estimate the proportion (millions) of the U.S. population that could die in a nuclear war without destroying the country's social structure, but it is not rational to take into account the fear that my children, my lover, my friends, will likely be among them. The culture of masculinity relies on "hard facts." Hard facts are facts in texts. They are measured, added up, subjected to statistical analysis. They are "objective" – more real than actual people and how I feel about them. They have to be looked at, faced up to, dealt in. They have the authority of power vested in texts. They displace the soft (female) world. They displace and subordinate the actual experience and lives of actual people. Hard facts were cited in the Atomic Energy Commission's decision to allow testing of nuclear weapons in Nevada to continue, even though children living downwind of the test site were already getting sick and beginning to die.

> Despite the downwinders' worries, the A.E.C. remained adamantly opposed to changes in the test series, according to now-declassified commission records. "I think this will set the weapons program back a lot, to go to the Pacific," said Commissioner Libby at the A.E.C.'s Feb 23 1955 meeting. "People have got to learn to live with the facts of life," he continued, "and part of the facts of life are fallout."[4]

Masculinism says "men don't cry." They are able to make the hard, the rational, decisions that have real-world consequences for others. (Commissioner Libby didn't have to live with the facts of fallout; his children weren't dying.) When Nixon and Kissinger planned the illegal invasion and bombing of Cambodia during the Vietnam War, the readiness of Kissinger's aides to develop the practicalities of their plan was viewed by Kissinger as an exercise "separating the men from the boys." The culture of masculinity separates the individual from his conscience, his qualms and his sense of shared humanity.

The culture of masculinity also organizes subordination. Beyond the relations of ruling, public fantasies such as the Rambo image of the male body as incarnate will and desire transform ordinary individual male powerlessness into the transcendent power of the patriotic project "America." Such fantasies, embodied again recently in the figure of Colonel "Ollie" North – the clean-cut mafioso of the Reagan mob – secure the consent of the powerless to the marauding American empire. Similar fantasies of transcendent male power create the soldier as instrument of purposes that aren't his. At his hearing Lt. William Calley, leader of the massacre at My Lai, said:

> I killed no human beings that day at My Lai. I didn't do it as a person. I did it for the United States of America, my country. We didn't go there to kill human beings. We went to kill an ideology.[5]

This is the shabby inverse of Don Quixote's mad but noble chivalry, attacking not windmills seen as giants, but actual people seen as ideology. Lt. Calley is / was a man subservient to a mythology that veiled in its banal trappings his uses to powers and purposes not his own.

Women represent what must be denied if the textual world, the organizational world, in which these men act, is to prevail over people's ordinary good sense and care for others. The culture of masculinity is a form of repression. It depends, just as a game does, on the ability of the players to believe in it, to exclude distractions, to exclude the actualities of the world outside the game. Its strenuous morality has its demonological flip side. As well as its outer enemy, the "commies," it has its inner enemies, the feminine and the "fag." In basic training, the U.S. marine learns to name his fear, his feeling for others, his reluctance to inflict pain or death, his weakness, as characteristics of the other, female or fag, the antitheses of men. What in him might impair his capacity to kill on command is repressed.[6] Women and homosexual men destroy the proper relations of hierarchy and undermine morale, says a Rear Admiral of the Canadian Fleet. The culture of masculinity at all levels organizes men's subservience to ends and objectives for the most part concealed from them and not in any case their own.

The feminist critique of patriarchy has these relations of hierarchy as its historical site. Women are still largely marginal to the relations of ruling. As individuals and in view of what we share with other women, we are situated differently from men in the world we share with them. Generally we still have a more intimate relationship to children. Generally we are more preoccupied with local and familial relationships. Generally the work of caring is still ours. Even the few among us who are implicated in the relations of ruling are less wholly claimed by the seductive possibilities of power, if only because that power is so rarely granted to women.

Women don't hang back from wars when what we care about is directly engaged. Women have fought and fight now in revolutionary wars. We have no special virtue. Our special relation to the struggle for peace comes at this particular time in these specific historical circumstances. Our work at home, in families, in relation to children, locates us still, whether as individuals or through what we share with other women, outside the abstracted and textual organization of ruling powers, in particular places, in relation to actual other people – people we know and have known. The rupture that the culture of masculinity creates for men between their private and local selves and the objectified world of power doesn't exist in the same way for us. We have the strongest sense of the actuality of our local lives: of how time has knitted together our lives with those of our parents, our lovers, our children, our friends, our neighbours; of an everyday / everynight world that our work has built. We can see our own hands very concretely in what is around us. I do not celebrate this local and particular world per se, for it can be mindless and entrapping. But it is firm ground for our sense of what a human world is.

As women have been silenced, this everyday / everynight actuality has also been silenced. As we have been deprived of authority, so has the world of our work as women. The repression of the actualities of our lives sustains the abstractions of the patriarchal structures of power. In our fight for peace, we break the barriers against admitting our experience to full political discourse; it is our business to transform that discourse, to make an entirely new voice heard, to break down the fragile citadels of masculinity. As one woman writing of her commitment to the struggle for peace at Greenham Common said:

> Ultimately, the essential thing about us as human beings is not what political system we live under, or what we achieve in world terms, but the ties of affection that bind us to those we love, *and* the respect and sympathy we have for those whom we know to have the same ties, the same needs – wherever they might live.[7]

NOTES

1 See Carol Cohn, "Sex and Death in the Rational World of Defense Intellectuals," *Signs*, Summer 1987, pp. 687-718.

2 Andrew Tolson, *The Limits of Masculinity* (London: Tavistock, 1977), p. 126.

3 Joel Kovel, *Age of Desire* (New York: Harper Colophon, 1982), pp. 42-43.

4 From Howard Ball, "Downwind from the Bomb," *New York Times Magazine*, February 9, 1988, pp. 33-42.

5 Quoted by Osvaldo Bayer, "Forgotten mass murderers live a good life," *The Guardian*, May 11, 1988, pp. 10-11.

6 Barbara Roberts, "Phallusies of Sociobiology: A Feminist Critique," a paper presented at the Annual Meetings of the Western Anthropology and Sociology Association, Brandon, Manitoba, 1983.

7 Bel Mooney, "Beyond the Wasteland," in *Over Our Dead Bodies: Women Against the Bomb*, ed. Dorothy Thompson (London: Virago, 1983), p. 13.

Island Sacrifices[1]

Kim Echlin

It comes, it goes, that is how all Majal stories begin. Long, long
ago there wasn't any land at all, only ocean, and the god Lowa
looked down through a hole in the clouds and said,
mmmmmmmmm, and all the islands appeared.

SETTING OUT for Micronesia was a chance. It began one hot afternoon in a tiny art gallery on the north coast of Oahu. I was talking to
a young artist who told me that in the Marshall Islands the oral tradition is still alive. On a whim, in search of stories, I took the last of my
money and bought a plane ticket to a place I'd never even seen on
the map. Once I got there I heard traditional stories, yes, but also I
heard the most fearsome myth of our time – the tale of atomic
destruction. I want to tell you this story. I cannot tell it with integrity
if I do not also tell you that my father had a fatal heart attack while I
was out sailing on a coconut ship in the Pacific. I had to go home to
my own encounter with death, to assume my new place in the world
as the next generation. I was not ready.

But we grow into roles that we are not always ready for, searching
to hear our internal voices. They have grown distant and seek to be
heard. They spin out each of our personal stories and weave into the
memory of our people. What will our memory be?

Chernobyl, Hiroshima, Nagasaki, Muroroa, Bikini: a litany of
sacrificial temples to the god of our age. It began one morning in
Almagordo, New Mexico. From the Bhagavad-Gita, "I am become
death, destroyer of worlds," spoke Robert Oppenheimer, and then
bombs were dropped, weapons were tested, power plants were
bought, sold and traded all over the globe. In Hiroshima, 78,000 dead,
69,000 injured; in Nagasaki 30,000 dead, 25,000 injured; thousands
irradiated in Nevada, French Polynesia, Micronesia, the Ukraine;
how many unknown? Continued weapons testing by Russia, America, Great Britian, France, China, India. Nuclear power plants in Canada, India, the United States, Africa, Germany, England, France, Russia, Asia.

Only forty years ago American navy ships sailed into a tiny atoll called Bikini, way out in the Pacific. Translators for navy officials knew no word for "bomb" in the Majal language, so they told the islanders that they had a powerful new god they wanted to bring to the island. That is how the testing began. It comes, it goes.

▲

The flight from Honolulu to Majuro, district centre of the Republic of the Marshall Islands, takes only five hours, but the plane flies westward and crosses the International Date Line into tomorrow. Looking down through the thick damp panes of the small airplane, all I could see were whitecaps rolling over the ocean for thousands of sea miles, not a ship or island in sight, only endless rolling ocean.

As the plane descended I looked down to see a string of tiny islands curved round a blue lagoon. We circled and plunged for the landing, coasting close over the surface of the waves as if we would dive into the sea. But then, bump, we landed, engines screaming, on the hard ground. I stepped out of the plane into the hot trade winds, seven degrees north of the equator, and wondered how I got there.

Clutching my little bag, I looked around, lost. A fat, smiling Majal man leaning smoking on a tinny taxi gestured me to get in. He let out the clutch and we jerked onto the rough road. I did not know where I was going, only that he must know where it was. By the side of the road I saw a little girl squatting in the shade holding a scruffy chicken. She raised her eyebrows at us, and the smiling Majal man pulled to a stop so she and the chicken could get in beside me. We drove through coconut groves along the beach and drew up to a dusty strip of cement and tin buildings – a supply store, some little shops, a bank, two little eating places. The girl with the chicken got out and I sat waiting. Finally the driver gestured me out too, pointing to a crumbling cement building tucked in behind. I guessed this was the hotel.

The place seemed empty. After a while, a young woman came out from behind a closed door holding a big ring of keys and led me to a room. I threw my bag on the bed and escaped from the stifling room, the tedious whirling of the fan and the silent peeling wallpaper back onto the street.

I arrived on a Sunday. Wandering along a road near the ocean I heard the thin nasal warble of Christian hymns. A cluster of white gravestones shone bright in the hot sunlight against the blues of sea and sky. I slipped into the back of the church. Everyone smelled good there together, warm and flowery, their hair rubbed shining with coconut oil and hibiscus, men on one side, women on the other, little children sitting in white and flowers in front of the preacher, who stood behind the altar in a flowing white gown. Their voices warbled praise for a baby born under a star. At the end the preacher strode down the centre aisle and the congregation tumbled out behind him like a wave, gathered round waiting to ring the church bell. I followed, and standing just outside their circle I looked at the bell. It was an old torpedo hung upside down and fixed with a clapper.

The preacher rang the torpedo and the ringing floated away in the howling trades over the ocean. Then everyone drifted off. I left too, and a group of smiling children ran after me shouting, *"Riballe! Riballe!"* Then their mothers called and they turned to go home.

Riballe means "clothes wearer" and is used for all strangers on the islands. It comes from long ago when missionaries kept a box of clothes at the back of the church and insisted that people dress themselves before they entered the house of God. Then, each time the people left, they undressed, put the clothes back into the box and went naked and smiling into the sunlight.

Micronesia lies between Hawaii and Japan in the north Pacific. There are two thousand islands spread over about 3 million square miles of ocean. But the total land area is only about seven hundred square miles. The Marshalls are the atolls to the east. No one knows where the people came from. Polynesia? Asia? But they have lived in the islands for a thousand years.

An atoll is living coral growing on the rim of an ancient sunken volcano. It seems to float just above the waves like a crescent moon fallen from the sky. There is no fresh water in the Marshalls – only rainwater and coconut milk called *ni* to drink. And nothing can sink roots very deep into coral, so there is coconut and pandanus and arrowroot to eat. The people are as at home on the shifting ocean as on these tiny bits of land. On outrigger canoes they learned to sail thousands of miles navigating by the stars and a complex knowledge of wave patterns. Little boys sat at the feet of ancient navigators deep into the night memorizing the turning sky. During the day, the old men dropped the children into the ocean and taught them to feel the movement of the waves on their skin. They set pails of water in the canoe and taught them to watch the ripples on the surface. Waves coming from the east are called *buntokrear* and waves crossing are called *kalibtak*. The old men tie twigs together with shells, elaborate maps marking the wave patterns and islands. They point out the birds – that one means land; that one is an ocean bird who flies out over the sea. The sacred navigator holds the memory of the people and wears a thousand details of the ocean like a bracelet in his mind. The precious beads of land belong to the women. Women gathered coconut and dug arrowroot and cooked in deep earth ovens. They cut pandanus from the trees and twisted and sucked its juices through their teeth. Everything was given from the mother. There is an expression in Majal language: Mother our only mother, father and father of other. The land was passed from grandmother to mother to daughter and they kept it clear and swept off the graves of the ancestors. And the old stories tell how the woman Loktanur gave the secret of the sail.

You know, long ago Loktanur's nine sons had a canoe race. Whoever first reached Je Island, where the sun rises, would be the *irooj* – the leader. And Loktanur stood on the edge of the water with all her big bundles and called out to her eldest son, "Tumur! Take me aboard!"

But Tumur didn't want her and her bundles and shouted back to her, "Go with my other brothers!"

So said each son she called to, until finally the youngest, Jebro, stopped and took her aboard.

"Jij! How can I paddle against the wind with all that stuff!"

Then Loktanur unrolled her bundle and lifted a sail, the first sail of woven pandanus leaf. She showed Jebro how to sail off wind and into wind, *kabbe* and *bwabwe,* on and on to the edge of the northern sky. And you can see him still, you know, up there in the distant sky, turned away from his brother Tumur. Why? Well, that is another story....

The people lived according to their ways for a long time. But in 1825 a Russian circumnavigator called Kotzebue marked these islands on a map and wrote that they were uninhabited. In the nineteenth century, Germans discovered the islands again and claimed them. Then the Japanese came and began trading for copra – dried coconut. And American missionaries sailed by looking for souls. But at the time the atolls were still so far away that the ships came maybe once, maybe twice a season, and for a while the people continued to fish and tell their stories.

▲

I learned that for three dollars a day I could sail from Majuro to the outer islands on a coconut ship called the Micro-Chief. They didn't know when she would sail; they were still loading supplies. They said just to wait at the hotel. I went back to my bed that night and lay looking through the open window at the stars above the ocean. I was falling asleep when I felt something jump on me and scramble away. I sat straight up in the darkness. There was nothing between inside and outside. Two green eyes blinked at me from the corner of the room. A cat had jumped through the window.

When people don't understand powerful phenomena they infuse them with supernatural powers.

After Hiroshima, Nagasaki and the first Pacific tests, the popular imagination in America seized the image of nuclear power and began to transform it. In New York enterprising minds decided to paint crucifixes with radium paints so they'd glow in the dark. The young women in the factory painted their own teeth so they would glow in the dark too. In Tennessee, scientists amused themselves by making golf balls with a cobalt 60 core, blindfolding the caddy and making him find the ball with a geiger counter. A revealing bathing suit was called the bikini because the effect of the flesh it bared was comparable to the effect of nuclear blasts on the Pacific atoll. Spike Blandy, commander of the first Bikini Island test shot, threw a celebration at the Army War College Officers' Club in 1946 and was photographed with his wife for the *Washington Post* society page. They are cutting a huge cake of angel-food puffs moulded into the shape of a mushroom cloud.

Newspaper reports of the Bikini testing hailed the event with the optimism and reverence usually reserved for a saviour. War-weary Americans perceived the weapons as their hope against more war, more suffering, more loss. For many the bomb was apocalyptic power, beyond their understanding. The bomb became distant and godly. No one was responsible for it.

▲

When the Americans arrived at Bikini in 1946 to begin their twelve-year testing program, the first job was to move the islanders. They brought in Navy DUKW boats that had the jaws of sharks painted on the bows and could sail right up on shore. The commodore ordered helicopters, and there were crews of scientists and filmmakers to record the event. A photographer described their arrival in a *National Geographic* article, July 1956.

FAREWELL TO BIKINI

About the middle of February, 1946, modern civilization suddenly overtook the natives of Bikini Atoll in the Ralik Chain of the Marshall Islands.

These brown people had progressed to using kerosene lanterns and a few imported steel hand tools, introduced by missionaries. Thanks to the Japs and our own armed forces, they were familiar with many kinds of airplanes, but ships were something that passed far at sea if at all.

A few could read and write their simple language, and Juda, the local chief, could speak and understand a little English. The outside world they knew little about, and cared less.

Then the U.S. Navy decided that Bikini was the place to test the atomic bomb, and almost overnight the natives found themselves in the Atomic Age.

The first inkling the Bikinians had of this was the arrival of Commodore Ben H. Wyatt and his staff to gain their consent to the test and to arrange for their evacuation to safety on another island in the Marshall group. After much discussion, Juda arose and spoke for his people. He signified that they would be happy to cooperate.

It took only ten days to arrange the move. The people loaded supplies onto the naval ships, and in the evenings went aboard to watch Roy Rogers and Mickey Mouse projected on the afterdeck of the Navy ship Sumner. They had never seen movies or typewriters or microphones before. The day of departure the Bikini people conducted a ceremony at the graveyard to honour the ancestors. They cleaned the headstones and decorated them with flowers; they sang and promised they would return. The Navy asked permission to film the ceremony. The crew had trouble with the sound equipment and asked the people to do the ceremony again in order to get a better take. Then everyone gathered up the last of their things, got on the Navy ships and sailed away. Before it was over, the American testing agenda would span twelve years with sixty announced atomic and hydrogen bomb tests. The Bikini people would never go home.

▲

It seemed an eternity waiting for the Micro-Chief to sail. I walked the length of the atoll twice a day. I swam. I slept. My ship didn't leave on Tuesday or Wednesday or Thursday. In the islands you wait for shipments, wait for winds, wait for currents. There are a thousand things to wait for. But I was restless and impatient. I didn't know how to wait.

I met a man who had just returned from the outer islands, where he had been taping people's accounts of the nuclear testing. The worst test was in 1954. It was called Bravo, a fifteen-megaton hydrogen surface detonation that shot a fireball of intense heat up at a rate of 300 miles per hour, with 100-mile-per-hour winds at the edge that rocked Bikini's quiet lagoon like a typhoon. Winds carried the radioactive cloud over Ailinginae, Ailuk, Bikar, Likiep, Rongelap, Rongerik, Taka, Wotho, Utirik, Jemo and Mejit, all inhabited islands, some as far as 275 miles to the east. A Japanese fishing boat called the Lucky Dragon was also in the area. Some of the Majal people thought the white ash fallout was mosquito poison and collected it in their rain barrels. Their fish turned yellow and everyone began to get sick. Two days later Navy officials evacuated them. Sitting in the shade of a palm tree I listened to their stories on the tape recorder. The first speaker was a middle-aged woman. In the background we could hear the rushing ocean and the roar of the island generator and children playing and laughing.

I was on Rongelap in 1954 and heard the explosions and saw the sky turn red. During this time I was cooking food for the children – it was still dark and the whole sky changed colour. Later something fell down on us, like white rain, and made the water in the wells turn yellow. The next day an airplane came to check our island and then the next day a ship arrived to take us away.

When we arrived on Kwajalein we started getting burns all over our bodies and people were feeling dizzy and weak. At that time we did not know if we would ever return to Rongelap and we were afraid. After two days something appeared under my fingernails and then my fingernails came off and my fingers bled. We all had burns on our ears, shoulders, necks and feet, and our eyes were very sore.

There were many problems with the women and many

forms of *jibun* – miscarriage. We gave birth to jellyfish babies. My older sister had a baby like a crab and another woman had a baby with no arms. Another woman had a baby without a skull. We were afraid to feed them. We were afraid the white rain was in our breasts and milk.

I was afraid to return to Rongelap in 1957 but they said it was safe, only don't eat the coconut crab. When we ate the arrow-root it burned our mouths and everything we were used to eating had changed colour. We did not understand at that time what the poison was....

One account was by the island magistrate, who had dealt often with the Atomic Energy Commission. His voice was deep and even and grave. There was no sound behind him; even the ocean was quiet. The tape turned and crackled.

I was sitting with a man from the AEC just before the Bravo test and he stuck out the tip of his finger in front of me and said, "Your life is about that long, John."

When I asked him what he meant he explained that they were setting off a new bomb on Bikini soon. I said why didn't they move my people and he told me there was no order from Washington.

On the morning of the bomb I was awake and drinking coffee. I thought I saw what appeared to be the sunrise, but it was in the west. It was very beautiful, red and green and yellow, and I was surprised. A little while later the sun came up in the east and then something like smoke filled the sky and a strong hot wind like a typhoon swept across my island. All the people heard a great explosion. And the powder began to fall.

They took us off the island and we were sick. The AEC took my son Lekoj and two other children to New York for their thyroid problems. In 1972 they noticed that the white-blood-cell count of my son was very low. They took him to Honolulu for blood transfusions and Dr. Conard told me that he would be all right. Then they notified me to go to Washington, where they had taken my son. I arrived at the hospital and saw that his condition was very serious and that he was very weak. I will never forget being in Washington with my son – I have never felt such sadness in all of my life. He died a day later from leukemia.

On and on that afternoon we listened to the voices of the people

telling their stories. The sun was getting low in the sky when someone came by and told me the Micro-Chief would sail in a few hours'
time. After all my waiting I felt suddenly afraid to go. I did not want to
leave the island. I did not want to sail out alone upon the ocean.

▲

The Micro-Chief sailed out of the lagoon under a full moon. I stood
on deck amid all the bundles and chickens and copra sacks and
watched until the land disappeared. We chugged out into the open
sea.

Every morning I got up early and went up on deck to watch where
the ocean meets the sky. On mornings when we reached an island I
would stand on the first deck watching the sailors unpack the hold
with a crane. They liked to flex their shining arms and grin up at me.
The wealthy islands took lots of supplies – tinned foods, Coca-Cola,
clothing – but the small ones took only a few cardboard boxes – sail-
cloth, nails, marine paint. These small islands sent back large burlap
sacks of dried coconut to trade for money.

Twenty days at sea. Thirty days at sea. On board ship there is
nothing to do. The whole world looks blue. The Majal people have a
word for something like crazy that means "too much sky in your
head." When we're anchored at an atoll I go ashore. The sailors hold
the flat-bottomed punt for me. It is called a boom-boom for the
sound it makes slapping on the waves. I jump down from the deck
onto the supplies and ride over the reefs to the sandy coast. Every
chance I get I walk the small islands and watch the people working
and resting in the shade of their low thatch huts, cooking in deep
earth ovens, rubbing their white canoes and cleaning their fish. It is a
strange pleasure to be here in this world so strange to me – sky and
winds and sea. I do not know where I have been or where I am
going.

The children follow me, calling *Riballe! Riballe!* Once I went
swimming and got stung by a blue jellyfish. They all laughed because
everyone knew it was the wrong season for swimming; it was
jellyfish season. My legs were red and swollen with poison and a
child scrambled up a palm tree and brought me down a coconut to
drink. A Majal woman from the ship called Neibor came over and I
asked her what the children were giggling and chattering about. She
said, "They are just discussing that the best cure for jellyfish sting is to
pee on it, but no one has the courage to offer."

On the smallest islands the people are still curious about *riballe*, but on most islands the people are accustomed to strangers. Many Majal people were the subject of an Atomic Energy Commission study for twenty-two years. Twice a year scientists and doctors from the Brookhaven Institute visited the contaminated people, testing them with machines, collecting their urine, finding thyroid disease, leukemia, miscarriages and deformed babies, physical and mental disorders. The Majal people provided invaluable data on the effect of radiation poisoning. The Brookhaven study, a thick document of scientific language, is a masterpiece of prose which reports and disclaims at the same time.

A TWENTY YEAR REVIEW OF MEDICAL FINDINGS IN A MARSHAL-LESE POPULATION ACCIDENTALLY EXPOSED TO RADIOACTIVE FALLOUT

1. Background
A. The Accident
The testing of nuclear devices in the Marshall Islands (see Hines), beginning with Operation Crossroads at Bikini in 1946 and ending with the moratorium in 1958, did not result in significant radiation exposure to personnel or fallout contamination outside the test area except in one case. On March 1 1954, the detonation from a tower of a thermonuclear device, Bravo, in the Castel Series of tests at Bikini resulted in a serious fallout accident. The yield was about 17 megatons, considerably greater than expected, and an unpredicted shift in winds in the upper atmosphere caused the radioactive cloud to drift over and deposit fallout on several inhabited atolls to the east....

The exposed people were evacuated by planes and Navy ships within about two days and taken to Kwajalein.... Complete removal of the radioactive contamination from the skin and hair required many cleansing procedures, the coconut oil used on the hair was particularly retentive....

The report includes photographs of two brothers taken over twenty years of study. One boy had been away from his island visiting relatives and so was uncontaminated and an excellent control. He becomes stronger and taller in each photograph, while his brother's height is stunted due to a thyroid condition. They stand naked, year after year, holding dated cards to show their comparative rates of growth. In the early pictures they are smiling broadly. By the end their faces are grave as they stare into the camera. In each photograph two strips of black tape discreetly cover their genitalia.

▲

One morning aboard the Micro-Chief I noticed that the sun rose on the other side of the ship. We were circling back to an island called Ebon and then to Kili in the north. The Majal woman, Neibor, was going home to Ebon to see her mother. Neibor had been to school in America and had not been home for four years. We walk the deck in the evenings arm in arm and the last night before we reach Ebon we make a feast. We eat crab and drink soda and suck pandanus and even open a tin of oranges. But we're too stifled below in the cabin so we go out on deck and see an old, old man called LaKebol. I have seen LaKebol squatting there on the deck many days, always watching the horizon. Neibor tells me he was a great navigator.

As we walk by she begins to talk to him and we squat down. They start telling stories. Neibor has learned lots of jokes in the United States and she likes a song about a ding-a-ling. The old man laughs and tells us a Majal story about Edao. Edao is a funny one, always sailing around, tricking people just to laugh, creating new things. They say that Edao made Majuro. He tricked a powerful *irooj* into trading away his fastest outrigger for a heavy old *koa* boat that wouldn't float, and when they started to chase him he threw the atoll of Majuro in the way. Old LaKebol told lots of stories that night.

You know, a long time ago people didn't have necks ... until the day Edao thought he'd like to trick an *irooj* and he turned himself into a coconut tree. The *irooj* wandered by looking for a drink and he stuck his head into the hollow of the tree to get some rainwater, but the hole was really Edao's ass! Snap! Edao squeezed it shut and the *irooj* had to pull and pull until he got a long, long neck. Finally Edao let go and ran away. That's why we have necks, you know.

After that I went and squatted beside LaKebol almost every evening. I learned to wait. We'd watch the sun go down and the stars rise and he told me many, many things those long nights on deck. How the world began and where the sunrise came from, about demons who run on the reefs at night and great sea expeditions led by his father, about drifting lost and thirsty on the ocean until the navigator finds the right waves.

I close my eyes now and see the glow of the starboard light tracing shadows where the wind and sun had carved deep creases into his old face. I see the sparkle of his eyes under the stars.

I asked LaKebol about the first foreigner on his island and he said, "I do not know about first, but first I saw was when I was one small boy and those men of Japan were fighting those men of America. One man of Japan on our island heard they lost their war and he crawled under a coconut stump, took off his boot and with his own toe shot himself through his head. *Jij!*"

After the Second World War was over and the Marshall Islands were officially an American protectorate, the nuclear testing began.

▲

When questioned about the ethics of nuclear testing in the Marshall Islands, Henry Kissinger commented, "There are only five thousand people out there – who gives a damn!"

▲

The Micro-Chief's hold was almost empty. We had sailed the southern route: Jabwot, Ailinglaplap, Namorik, Jaluit, Mili, Ebon. Our last stop was Kili.

Kili is different from every other place we had visited. It is an island, not an atoll, and has no lagoon. Without a lagoon the people cannot sail or fish because the waters are deep and wild. It is difficult to get supplies in and out of Kili because the waves are rough. Often in the past the supply ship has had to sail by without stopping, and the Kili people have had to wait.

We anchor well off the island. An electric tension passes through the sailors on the Micro-Chief. They don't flirt and flex their arms. They say the island is inhabited by bad spirits. A few years ago a captain on another coconut ship lost his leg in an outboard motor when they capsized trying to get the boom-boom into Kili. Who could live in such a place?

Kili has traditionally been uninhabited. But when the Americans discovered that the Bikini people could not go back to their contaminated island they moved them here. All the other land was taken.

And they did not need to fish or sail because they had lots of compensation money. And they did not want to settle anywhere because they wanted to go home, to their atoll, to the graves of their ancestors.

We stay only a few hours at Kili because the waves are coming up. Kili people live in American-made tin houses and negotiate for money. Compensation to the ex-Bikini people who now live on Kili is in the millions of dollars. At one time a resettlement program projected over a six-year period was to cost $3 million. By 1969 the islands were cleared of nuclear test debris and scrub vegetation. The top two inches of Bikini's topsoil were removed and pandanus trees planted. But radioactivity was in the food chain, particularly in one of the staples, the coconut crab. The project was abandoned.

I stop in a little restaurant for a drink and ask for *ni*, coconut milk. A laughing man pats his belly and says, "We too fat to go up coconut tree. You drink Coca?"

We are hurried back to the Micro-Chief. One load of supplies remains. The men try to swing them down to the boom-booms heaving on the waves. We stand helplessly on deck watching the sea grow wild and high. The Bikini people stand helplessly on Kili shore watching the battle. The captain decides it is too dangerous. They put the supplies back in the hold, pull up anchor and slowly chug northward towards Majuro. Another supply ship will bring the boxes back in six months. I stand on deck a long time watching Kili disappear into the waves.

That night I go and squat beside LaKebol. He too came from Bikini, but he won't live on Kili. He says he must live where he can sail. That night was the last night he told me stories. He told me the story of his people.

My father lived one long life. In his day they said on Bikini that our spirit Librojka always protect our island from all other powerful demon. When those men of America came they told us they are bringing one big demon. In those days we have no word for bomb. But we know Librojka is most powerful and will kill all demon so we say, "All right! Stop talking, we will move."

But we never go home. We move first to one island, not enough coconut, then another island, not enough room, then Kili, no lagoon for fishing.

And I say, enough! Enough drifting lost at sea. And I sail back alone to Bikini to see what happened there. I sail all alone and find our island and our graves all fallen over. The graves have not been swept. Our coconut trees have double heads and big ships of America lie rusting in our lagoon. I walk and walk and find the west side of Bikini gone. My home is disappeared into the sky, my mother's land and my wife's land all gone, no land to bury me, no land to return to after sailing, no land to call my home.

My people are lost at sea and they have taken down their sail. They drift and they've given up. They no longer look for their island. All right! Some say America will pay them more money so they don't work but wait for pay. Some say they are sick from poison so they don't make life but wait to die. My people have lost all happiness to sail. And no one to say, "All right! Enough of this drifting westward. Let us tack back and see what we find."

No one to captain.

Myself, I know only this. My work on this world is not to worry about poison. My work is to find God. If our life is short, let us hurry to find God. Twenty-eight years now and those people of Bikini are still there waiting on Kili. And many of those older men and women have already died and their bones are buried on that little island far away from home.

So you see for yourself, hear my word: Look for God now. Never mind what others say and stay free from all things that tie you to this world. Those *riballe* brought us light. But I'm afraid they have turned away from God in pride of their own knowledge and strength. Be aware to follow no one into darkness.

Twenty-two years now I watch that first man among those doctors, Dr. Conard. He comes to test my people and take their blood. And I know many of our men want him to pay them for their blood. And I watch him walk fast down a road to west end and come back walking fast to east end. And many times he passes me where I sit under my house and waves to me and says, "*Yokwe*, hello!" And I say to myself – maybe he's afraid I want him to pay me for something. That is why he hurries. And I'm thinking I want to ask him to come and sit here and I'd ask him would he like to hear our story of Loktanur and how she gave us the first sail. Because I notice that Loktanur is the name of his ship. Who knew to paint her name upon the bow? So

promise me now you'll tell our story of Loktanur and say any-
time he need to test my blood it is all right. It will always be all
right with me.

▲

It comes, it goes.

The Micro-Chief sailed back to Majuro and a message waiting for
me. I left those islands as suddenly as I'd arrived, carrying away a
thousand stories. In Majal tradition they always see you off. They say,
"Ships come and go but sometimes people never come back."

I do not know where I am going, where I have been, only I
remember my father sent me off, go, go, be free, then stood shoulders rounded wistful smile waving god be with you au revoir, caught
behind thick panes of airport glass.

So those people of Majuro took me to the airport and put flowers
around my neck. In the old days they used to tie young coconut
leaves to the mast of the ship and wade around the outrigger chanting to the god of navigation. I turn to say goodbye in the forever part-
ing moment, not knowing if I will ever feel the other again. Loktanur
rising. Night stars and sea winds speaking all.

*The oral accounts of the effects of the nuclear testing have been
adapted from a series of translated interviews by Mr. Glenn Alcalay
of Rutgers University. The stories of LaKebol have been adapted from
stories gathered, translated and published by General Knight in* Man
This Reef, *Micronitor Press, November 1982. To order this book, write
to P.O. Box 14, Majuro, Republic of the Marshall Islands 96960.*

NOTES

1 An abridged version of this essay was first published by *Canadian
Forum*, August / September 1986.

Getting Tough and Making Sacrifices: The Language of War in the 1980s

Donna E. Smyth

THE MILITARIZATION OF language, both verbal and visual, in the 1980s reflects and manifests a new fusion of high technology, mass media culture and the ideology of the New Right. International in nature, this phenomenon includes Great Britain and Canada, but its driving and shaping force comes from Reagan's America. Reagan was a president who cited, approvingly, movies such as *Rambo* and *Rocky IV* as manifestations of the American psyche and who, at the same time, promoted the Strategic Defense Initiative (Star Wars) as the high-tech answer to Mutual Assured Destruction (MAD), the doctrine of deterrence symbolized by nuclear parity between the United States and the Soviet Union. *Rambo*, the movie, and Star Wars, the strategy, mark the ends of a continuum. On the one hand, a new rhetoric of war dominates economic and political discussions on what politicians call the "high ground." On the other hand, this rhetoric is transformed into hard-core war pornography in such publications as *Soldier of Fortune, Gung Ho, New Breed, Eagle* and *American Survival Guide*. In strategic defence journals, such as *International Defense Review* and *Nato's 16 Nations*, it surfaces in the soft-core porn of the weapons ads which play on the correlation between military power and macho sexuality. The blatant nature of these messages is matched on a more general public level by the transformation of public discourse into political propaganda.

In Canada, the 1984 election of the Mulroney government signalled more changes in public and foreign policy than most voters realized. Mulroney's evident infatuation with Reagan climaxed in the first so-called Shamrock Summit in Quebec. Among other things, the summit marked the signing of the Quebec Memorandum, which committed Canada to modernizing the DEW Line ("Distant Early Warning" radar stations in Canada's arctic) in a joint venture dominated by American interests, policy and money. In that same year, when Canada was declared "open for business," then Defence Minister Robert Coates set up the first tour of Pentagon officials to teach

Canadian businessmen how to procure more defence contracts with the United States. Since that time, the Mulroney government has consistently promoted an industrial-military base in Canada modelled on the American one and intimately related to American defence needs. Mulroney's campaign promise of "jobs, jobs, jobs" has turned out to mean defence-related jobs in areas like the Maritimes where there is such a high level of unemployment that workers feel they have no choice when the only job in town is liable to be building weapons or weapons components.[1]

At the same time as the country's economy is becoming more militarized and more dependent on the United States, the domination of American mass media culture is increasingly obvious. Rambo videos and their clones and Rambo toys and dolls are widely available. So are the war pornography magazines. Their impact on Canadian culture appears more diffuse and less concentrated than in the United States, but the same images and language are inside our heads and must influence our perceptions and behaviour. It is imperative, then, to understand the genesis and significance of these phenomena in the country which the Prime Minister calls Canada's "best friend."

The 1981 election of Ronald Reagan marked the coming of age of the New Right in America. High-profile ideologues such as Jeane Kirkpatrick, former U.S. ambassador to the UN, and George Shultz, U.S. Secretary of State, moved from the background of the political arena in such groups as the Committee on the Present Danger to the foreground in positions of power within the Reagan administration. Committed to the extermination of communism, they abandoned any pretence of wanting peaceful coexistence in the world. Their motivation is to make the United States the supreme politico-military power in the world. In early 1981, Richard Pipes, Reagan's Soviet expert, said: "Soviet leaders would have to choose between peacefully changing their Communist system ... or going to war."[2] From that point on, the Pentagon's Defense Guidance Plans have included the premise of fighting and winning a protracted nuclear war.[3]

The problem is that such a premise is politically unpopular. To be rendered palatable to a public that fears nuclear war, it must be seen as the natural conclusion of a certain view of the world. The public must be trained in this view and trained not to feel fearful because some sacrifices are necessary. In a 1981 interview with Robert Scheer, Charles Kupperman, former defence analyst for the Committee on the Present Danger, described how his view of nuclear war differed from that of Physicians for Social Responsibility: "What they [the Physicians] are talking about is a very individual thing, but I'm concerned about the survival of this nation, and the preservation of our freedom and independence. At some point, as it has been the point in the past, people have had to fight and die to preserve our freedom and independence. Of course it bothers me that any American has to give his life." Kupperman goes on to summarize his view succinctly: "Nuclear war is a destructive thing, but it still is in large part a physics problem."[4] To achieve this goal, the ideologues have "enhanced" far-right values by enshrining them in intellectual respectability, in terms of both language and institutions. In this intellectual climate, universities and "think tanks" become the generating ground for a transformative grammar quickly adopted by politicians and the media."

Among groups in Canada disseminating and lobbying for right-wing views, the Fraser Institute is probably best known in intellectual / academic circles, while the National Citizens' Coalition (NCC) is most politically prominent. Among other causes, the NCC champions Star Wars to the extent of placing ads in American papers reading:

"Thank You. Stand fast ... without your defensive umbrella, Canada could have become the Afghanistan of the north. Your country's generosity is unparalleled in human history. In a world where 91 countries are ruled by dictatorships, the United States is a beacon of life, freedom, and hope."[5]

The coalition models many of its techniques on American right-wing tactics and has met with the Heritage Foundation and High Frontier, the group which spawned Star Wars evangelist General Daniel O. Graham, who toured Canada to persuade this country to participate in Star Wars. In a reverse flow pattern, the Lyndon LaRouche Jr. group in the U.S. has made attempts to recruit Canadian farmers in Saskatchewan and has set up the Consolidated Agriculture Movement Incorporated (CAM Inc.) to push its views in Canada.[6]

Suddenly the public hears phrases such as "getting tough" and "making sacrifices" coming at us from all directions. These phrases are generated by the neoconservative model of "the market" and of competition where the toughest survive and the weakest go to the wall as the necessary "sacrifices." In this fierce, late-twentieth-century version of Darwinian survival of the fittest, being "aggressive," "bold" and "tough" are equated with being realistic and being victorious. This militarization of language is matched by the increasing militarization of society. The Americans have gotten "tough" with the Soviets and "tough" on terrorists. Civilian sacrifices have to be made economically to support this militarization, and civilian sacrifices have to be made in the event of a war, whether conventional or nuclear. For example, Irving Kristol, self-styled American neoconservative philosopher, writes in an essay on the role of NATO in Europe that the Americans have to be prepared to match the Soviets at the conventional military level "just as they have shown themselves prepared to make the sacrifices necessary to match us at the nuclear level."[7] In another essay, Kristol makes the ambitions of the New Right perfectly clear:

> ... we [the Americans] are simply not a sufficiently active presence in the world, at either the politico-military level or the ideological. The two do go together – otherwise, one's claim to the future is empty rhetoric.[8]

Written in 1982, the essay is called "The Key Question: Who Owns the Future?" In a parallel with the commodities market trading in "futures," the future itself becomes a commodity to be owned by the most successful entrepreneurial nation which maintains its ownership, its "divine right," by military power.

In an article on American think tanks, Gregg Easterbrook picks up the metaphor, apparently without irony: "In politics, words are map co-ordinates that show on whose territory a battle is being fought."[9] In this New Right map of the world, everything is perceived as a commodity or a battle. There is no middle ground for discussion or negotiation. Values are clearly and simplistically defined: us versus them, the free world versus the communist world, the empire of good versus the empire of evil. On the "high ground," this is transformed into discussions of entrepreneurship using words like "spirit," "vision" or "sacred trust."[10] The twin "thrust" of economic free enterprise and defence is mirrored in the title of the green paper on Canada's foreign policy: *Competitiveness and Security.*[11]

The effective enshrining of this ideology requires an Enemy. If the public and the mass media are to receive the correct message, demonization and dehumanization of the Other are essential. In a speech supporting Barry Goldwater's nomination at the 1964 Republican Convention, Ronald Reagan said:

> We are at war with the most dangerous enemy ever known to man.... The guns are silent in this war but frontiers fall while those who should be warriors prefer neutrality.[12]

In 1982, Kristol wrote an article called "Understanding the Soviet Mafia":

> We know that the Soviet leaders are – to borrow Ben Wattenberg's pellucid phrase – "liars and thugs."
> ... if you wish to understand the Soviet political system and the people who inhabit it, you could make an excellent beginning by going to the movies and seeing *The Godfather* and *The Godfather, Part II.*[13]

Canada and the other Western industrialized countries follow the American lead in defining Soviets as The Enemy. This is reflected in our military alliances, especially NORAD and NATO, both dominated by American policy and interests. It is reflected in mass culture by the popular assumption that anyone doing peace work, especially on the streets, must be a communist. The second popular assumption is that, without these military alliances, we'd all be speaking Russian.[14] Consequently, it is somewhat confusing when the Americans suddenly declare that there is another form of The Enemy whose name is Terrorist. In 1986, The Terrorist becomes, briefly, Gaddafi, "the mad dog of the Middle East." The world is told that Gaddafi has to be "punished," has to be "taught a lesson." The civilian casualties of the American bombing raid on Libya are necessary sacrifices. At home, the Canadian and American public is warned that some civil liberties may have to be sacrificed in order to prevent terrorism.

In this political climate, the word "warrior" assumes a new potency: we hear of cold warriors, star warriors. The macho warrior image ranges from Rambo to Edward Teller, architect of American nuclear policy and one of the prime proponents of Star Wars. The hard-core war pornography of magazines such as *Soldier of Fortune* features ads for all kinds of warrior "survivor" weapons as well as for "mercs" (mercenaries). SOF is the classiest act of these military fantasy magazines and is subtitled "The Journal of Professional Adventurers." One firearms ad reads: "When your life is on the line, you leave nothing to chance" and "In a world of compromise, some men don't."[15] The editorial in the 1985 anniversary issue focuses on Tom Hayden and Jane Fonda's role in protesting the Vietnam war:

> Hayden and Hanoi Jane have never been the pair to let patriotism or any other honorable emotion stand in the way of treason or disrespect to the people who fought while they fiddled around the world supporting the enemy or wringing crocodile tears from the liberal community....

We'd much rather have a sister in a cathouse than a brother
who coughs up even one penny for this travesty [a proposed
monument to Vietnam protesters to match the one being built
for the Vietnam vets, now reconstituted as heroes in the current
American revision of that period of their history].... [16]

Eagle ("For the American Fighting Man") and *Gung Ho* ("The Magazine for the International Military Man") are more blatant and
violent. They feature on-the-spot re-creations of "action" in the hot
spots of the world where mercenaries and right-wing-backed guerrillas are on the front line, warriors fighting communism. An article in
Eagle is called "Sucking Hell in Nicaragua"; the same issue has a story
on small arms, "Mad Dog Killers" of the F.D.N.," and the blurb reads:
"With cia leftovers and what they can take from the enemy The
Nicaraguan Freedom Fighters are winning against the best the
Soviets can throw at them."[17] The subscription ad for *Eagle* reads:

FIRE MISSION! You're a Grunt, or you were a Grunt, or will be a
Grunt – and you want a connection to that raw, raunchy, randy
world of Violent Combat Action.[18]

Obviously, this is a direct appeal to men who, in their ordinary
lives, never come anywhere near "the action" except in their fantasy
lives. Presumably, seeing themselves as military adventurers is their
substitute for direct sexuality. The boot camp chant summarizes it all:
"This is my rifle / This is my gun / One is for killing / The other's for
fun."[19] When he says "gun," the recruit slaps his crotch. Along with
New Breed and the survival-type magazines, all these publications
feature how-to articles on hand-to-hand combat, defence, and guns
and knives for the ordinary citizen to use in his "violent" society. The
myth of society's violence is a useful one; if "it's hell out there," the
individual must be violent in order to survive. In the United States,
every man must have a gun, and his home becomes a mini-fortress
buttressed by security systems and guard dogs. Individual "toughness" is incarnate in the macho myth heroes of mass culture of the
1980s as portrayed by the likes of Stallone, Schwarzenegger and
Norris. The war-porn publications review these actors' movies in
great detail. The following is a sample of the style:

New Breed Screen Heroes: "Kicking Red Butt on the Silver
Screen".... although there are more stuntmen than actors, movies like this will help bring American pride back to our youth.[20]

"The pride's back" in the Plymouth ads in more conventional magazines too. On TV it can be seen in the romanticization of the American National Guard commercials in which the man leaps into the fighter plane while hearing, in voiceover, the laments of his wife and children who want to get on with ordinary life and do not understand that he is out protecting them. At the end of the ad, the Enemy planes turn back and a male voiceover says: "The bear has turned away." The Soviet bear has been defeated by the National Guardsman who, in reality, never picks up anything more romantic than a rifle. Of course, considering the American male's attitude towards rifles, the simple conventional weapon should have been enough. The ad and others like it represent the level of propaganda being directed at the American public by their own government. American pride depends on American warriors, economic or military. Fighting for freedom is equated with fighting for capitalism. In 1984, in an address to the United Nations, Reagan said "there's an increasing realization that economic freedom is a prelude to economic progress and growth and is intricately and inseparably linked to political freedom." He described "our open advocacy of freedom" as the "engine of human progress."[21] In the war-porn genre, "freedom fighters" range from Afghanistan to Mozambique to Angola to Nicaragua. These warriors are on a personal crusade which mirrors the larger one articulated by Reagan and his star warriors. Both types are obsessed by weapons – better and more accurate machine guns, antitank guns, planes, helicopters, missiles and bombs.

Ordinary defence review and military magazines geared to professional military and academic strategists feature phallic ads for Fire It and Forget It Weapons, missiles, planes, etc. They proudly display cluster bombs with their "bomblets," the deadly little children designed to rip flesh which are released by the mother-bomb.[22] These weapons become an intricate part of the consumer's psyche and reinforce an identification and confusion of male genitals with weapons.

The warrior regards nonwarriors as nonmen. Even a desire to negotiate with the Soviets is seen as "appeasement." Robert Scheer quotes the Committee on the Present Danger: "The Soviet military buildup of all its armed forces over the past quarter century is, in part, reminiscent of Nazi Germany's rearmament in the 1930s."[23] Verne Orr, the U.S. Secretary of the Air Force, in a 1984 address to the Air Force Association, warned of the dangers of "raising a generation of negotiators and appeasers, a generation of Neville Chamberlains who think they can acquire peace through capitulation and without strength."[24] Anyone who opposes military solutions becomes an appeaser and a pacifist. "Pacifist" becomes a dirty word, just as it was during the world wars. In fact, right-wing speakers frequently accuse pacifists of causing World War II.[25] This rhetorical confusion usurps any ground for opposition. Thus, a politician like Reagan had the temerity to quote Gandhi and other great leaders of nonviolent protest as if they shared a common political view.[26] The warrior co-opts "peace" language for his own purposes: "we do not build bombers to win wars; we build bombs to prevent wars," and "We established the first peace academy in America on the banks of the Hudson at West Point, New York, in 1802 and we call it the U.S. Military Academy." He boasts about "the willingness of the public to sacrifice a substantial part of their taxes to keep America strong."[27]

One month before the Gorbachev-Reagan summit in Geneva, the Heritage Foundation issued a new manifesto which spelled out that "any arms control accord with the Russians would be regarded as a betrayal equivalent morally to a Munich-style appeasement."[28] The Heritage Foundation published, in 1980, *Mandate for Leadership*, a 3,000-page document presented to Reagan's transition team soon after he was first elected. They, like the Committee on the Present Danger, are dedicated to spreading an ideology which they describe as "responsible conservatism" around the world. Their seed money came from Joseph Coors, the beer baron, and their corporate donors include The Chase Manhattan Bank, Mobil Oil, Fluor Corporation of California, Gulf Oil (Chevron), Reader's Digest Association, Smith-Kline Corporation and the Amway Corporation.[29]

The connections behind the New Right in America begin to sound eerily like the connections between fascism and big business before and during World War II.[30] What the rhetoric does, however, is to substitute Soviet totalitarianism for Nazi fascism while, at the same time, appropriating the fear of fascism for its own ends. The New Right in Canada uses the same tactics and is busy cultivating similar connections.

When the world belongs to the macho warrior, what happens to women? The New Right's answer is clear enough: women become Real Women. The warrior requires the ideology of the family and women in their proper place. Who would he defend, if he didn't defend women and childen? Kristol, for instance, becomes apoplectic about women being integrated into military service:

And then there have been the absurd attempts to fully "integrate" women into our services, so as to please the more militant and more radical women's libbers [women can contribute
from "noncombat" positions, "mainly at home"].... The notion
of "fighting women" is bad enough. (The Israelis tried it and
quickly gave up.) But fighting Mothers?[31]

The irony is, of course, that, under the conditions of modern warfare, women and children are on the front line while the warriors are
in their radiation shelters or their nuclear submarines. In the event of
a nuclear war, we will all be victims, but women, children and nonmilitary males will die first.

In the world of the warrior, victims are necessary sacrifices. Star
Wars is being constructed to protect American missile sites, not civilian populations. War pornography substitutes weapons for women
as the objects of desire and excludes women from its discourse. In
this masculine world, the only women who are accepted are those
who become like men, like the "Iron Maiden," Margaret Thatcher, or
those who promote the traditional role of the "power behind the
throne," like Diana, Princess of Wales. First ladies, like Mila Mulroney, are becomingly feminine and helpless and support their warrior
husbands on all fronts.

The new rhetoric of war permeates every aspect of our lives and
keeps us, as a public, in a constant state of "prewar" tension. In such
a state, we are vulnerable and easy to manipulate. Herman Kahn's
book title, *Thinking the Unthinkable* [about nuclear war], passes into
common usage; "to nuke" becomes a verb in everyday conversation.
We are conditioned to live with terror by repetition and rhetoric. This
rhetoric masks the reality that we are being conditioned to make
sacrifices of our lives and ourselves so that the warrior's world pros-
pers and flourishes until it eventually destroys itself and us with it.

*Author's note: Since this article was written, Canada's White
Paper on Defence has been published. It promotes a militarized
economy, an increased defence budget (including the purchase of nuclear-powered submarines) and uses warrior rhetoric and American strategic analysis throughout. See, for
example, Chapter 3: "The Military Threat." The military integration of Canada with the United States is, of course, intimately linked with the economic integration proposed under
the Mulroney-Reagan "Free Trade" deal.*

NOTES

1 In June 1986, the three Maritime provinces were competing with each other to attract Litton Systems, an American branch plant, in their latest expansion of their industrial-military expansion in Canada. Litton won, in conjunction with Oerlikon-Buhrie of Switzerland, the LLAD (Low Level Air Defence) contract from DND and must build a new plant in the Maritimes as part of that contract. The Nova Scotia provincial government is also lobbying to have Thyssen, a West German company, build an arms manufacturing plant in Cape Breton. Pratt and Whitney, another American branch plant which received $333 million in grants under the Canadian DIPP (Defence Industry Productivity Programme) between 1969 and 1985, is already located in the aerotech development park outside Halifax.

2 Robert Scheer, *With Enough Shovels: Reagan, Bush and Nuclear War* (New York: Vintage Books, 1983) p. 8.

3 *Ibid.*

4 Scheer, p. 183, p. 185.

5 Nick Filmore, "The Right Stuff. An Inside Look at the National Citizens' Coalition," *This Magazine* 20, no. 2, June / July 1986, p. 9.

6 Terry Punch, "They're Back," *Briarpatch* 15, Issue 10, December 1985 / January 1986, p. 81.

7 Irving Kristol, *Reflections of a Neoconservative* (New York: Basic Books, 1983), pp. 251-52.

8 Kristol, pp.255-56.

9 Gregg Easterbrook, "Ideas Move Nations," *The Atlantic Monthly*, January 1986, p.80.

10 *Ibid.*

11 *Competitiveness and Security: Directions for Canada's International Relations,* presented by The Right Honourable Joe Clark, Secretary of State for External Affairs (Ottawa: Minister of Supply and Services, 1985).

12 Quoted by Dan Caidwell, "U.S.-Soviet Political Relations: A Regional Assessment," *AEI Foreign Policy and Defence Review* 5, no. 2, March 1985, p. 7.

13 Kristol, p. 271.

14 These observations are based on the writer's personal experience during years of peace activism when the first question one is asked on the street is usually: Are you a Communist? In popular perception, dissent from official policy is subversive. Having to learn to speak

Russian is, of course, one of the slogans on the Lyndon Larouche kiosks in airports across the country.

15 *Soldier of Fortune: The Journal of Professional Adventurers*, August 1985, p. 13.

16 Unsigned editoral, SOF, August 1985, p. 12.

17 These articles appear in *Eagle for the American Fighting Man*, September 1985.

18 *Eagle*, September 1985, p. 77.

19 Cited by Donna Warnock in "Patriarchy is a Killer: What People Concerned About Peace and Justice Should Know," in *Reweaving the Web of Life: Feminism and Nonviolence*, ed. Pam McAllister (New York: New Society Publishers, 1982), p. 22.

20 Review by Major Larry B. O'Brian in *New Breed*, March 1986, p.58.

21 "Address to the United Nations. U.S. and U.S.S.R. Negotiations," *Vital Speeches of the Day*, Vol. LI, no. 1, October 15, 1984.

22 See random sample of ads taken from *International Defense* and *NATO 16 Nations*.

23 Scheer, p. 37.

24 Verne Orr, U.S. Secretary of the Air Force to the Air Force Association, 1984 National Convention, Washington, D.C., "Let's Set the Record Straight: National Defense is Bipartisan," *Vital Speeches of the Day* VI, no. 2, November 1, 1984, p. 35.

25 For example, Harvie Andre, ex-Associate Minister of Defence, Canada, during a public panel on "The Military and the Public: What We Know, What We Should Know," held in Halifax, N.S., on March 7, 1986, made a statement to this effect.

26 *Vital Speeches of the Day* LI, no. 1, October 15, 1984, p. 7.

27 Orr, p. 36.

28 Arthur Gavshon, "The Power and Influence Behind America's Right," *Manchester Guardian*, December 1, 1985, p. 9.

29 *Ibid.*

30 Charles Higham, *Trading with the Enemy: An Expose of the Nazi-American Money Plot 1933-1949* (New York: Dell, 1983).

31 Kristol, p.259.

Shootout on the New Frontier: The Return of the Warrior[1]

Sandra Rabinovitch

Life is a competition, and I am a competitor.... I will fight the battle, spill the blood, smear myself with it, and stand at the bar of judgement.... It is the way of the world. It is the ultimate disposition. Stand ready ... The Executioner is here.[2]

IN A BLAZE OF high-tech glory, the warrior has returned to capture the popular imagination. His brawny image leaps boldly from the bookstands, brandishing sophisticated weaponry that reflects his links to a flourishing paramilitary consumer industry. Like the screen's Rambo and Commando, the new paperback hero is a "legitimate savage" who operates outside the sanctioned justice system, using violent means to worthy ends. He's the mythic American hero outfitted in new armour, the focus of a literature that glorifies aggression and elevates male animal courage into a cult.

The field of battle might be anywhere, the target any man. But at bottom, in the deep living heart of things, it was all the same war, everywhere.

Civilized Man, the builder, versus Savage Man, the destroyer.

It was a war with roots in Cain and Abel, branches in Biafra, Belfast, Vietnam. War everlasting, yeah.

Mack Bolan had signed on for the duration, and while strength – while life itself – remained, he would continue the fight.[3]

Mack Bolan, the Executioner, is the leader of this new breed of fictional heroes. His never-ending war against organized crime, international terrorism and other evils of contemporary life has earned him millions of devoted fans worldwide. The Executioner and his brothers-in-arms on the bookstands – among them the Destroyer, the Penetrator, the Butcher, the Survivalist, Death Merchant, the Doomsday Warrior and the Warlord – are compelling figures of fantasy in this booming area of the publishing industry. The fantasy is one of ultimate power, and its appeal is stronger than ever: at least sixty men's adventure series, featuring both the "lone wolf" avenger and the increasingly popular heroic ensemble, currently fight for followers in a highly competitive market.

Although action / adventure fiction springs from a long tradition of heroic literature – with roots, as well, in the pulp detective novel – as a publishing phenomenon it is relatively young. World War II veteran Don Pendleton created the Mack Bolan character in 1969, at the height of conflict over the Vietnam war, in a deliberate attempt to dignify the American fighting man. The first Executioner title became an overnight bestseller and spawned a host of imitators. But it wasn't until 1981, when Toronto's Harlequin Books acquired the Executioner series and began publishing action / adventure under its Gold Eagle imprint, that the category really became big business. With the romance publisher's well-developed marketing muscle behind the books, action / adventure soon began to compete with more established, respected categories such as mysteries and science fiction. Now every major mass-market publisher is getting into the action.

Just as Harlequin-style romance novels have found their way into women's homes and hearts through direct marketing and drugstores or supermarkets, with free copies often slipped into bridal packs or boxes of detergent, men's action / adventure series are packaged and promoted to become a regular staple of the modern man's cultural diet. From the bold image on the cover to the requisite heroic stunts, the product holds no surprises. Many writers for hire may contribute to a series under a single pseudonym, so consistency of style is vital: like the hero himself, the writing tends to be lean and tough, with an emphasis on so-called unflinching realism. The successful action / adventure line often develops a cult following, which publishers encourage with promotional events and giveaways: Mack Bolan reader conventions, newsletters and bumper stickers, for example. Spinoff series inevitably follow. Fans can subscribe to a direct-mail bookclub, collect and swap titles in their favourite series, and seek out the backlist at major chain and second-hand bookstores.

Hoping to tap into the paramilitary market, publishers advertise in consumer magazines such as *Soldier of Fortune* and *Guns & Ammo*, as well as military publications. New York's TOR Books co-publishes an action / adventure series with *Soldier of Fortune* itself. Toronto's Gold Eagle features a "weapon of the month" on some of its inside covers, and sponsors the awards for the National Survival Game – the popular new "adult recreation" of capture-the-flag in camouflage. Promoting a survival ethic, the paramilitary consumer industry appeals to the modern warrior with guns, combat clothing and paraphernalia, survival training, adventure experiences and fantasy. Whoever he may be, today's warrior / consumer is equipped for every contingency. In the United States – action / adventure fiction's largest market – book sales are highest near military installations, but publishers claim their readership covers a broad cross-section in terms of age, social standing and education. Even if the typical reader is not actually a soldier or veteran, or engaged in some paramilitary activity, in fantasy he's prepared to take charge and fight back.

Action / adventure fiction embraces a number of readily identifiable subgenres – the mercenary series, the antiterrorist series, the urban vigilante series, Vietnam stories, and the hugely successful "survivalist" or post-nuclear holocaust series – each with its own conventions. In looking for that special "hook," publishers have turned increasingly to the news, and to issues of contemporary concern. The stories feature a volatile mix of fantasy and reality: the more fantastic they are, the more they seem to play into the very real fears and frustrations of their readers. The rise of terrorism, the escalation of the arms race, the deterioration of Soviet-American relations and the revival of the Cold War have all charged this literature with a certain plausibility – and provided fodder for the publishing industry.

> The war goes on, and it justifies itself. The terrorists must be opposed, the cannibals destroyed – and the civilizers left in peace. Today, there is simply too much at stake for a man with hands and eyes to turn away....
> There's a proverb that says that blood cannot be washed away with blood. For all I know, that may be true. Sometimes it takes a cleansing fire.[4]

With a style as direct and persuasive as advertising copy, and with content as reliable as corn flakes, action / adventure fiction delivers what it promises. But inevitably the question arises: what values are these stories selling? The producers of this fiction claim that the books provide a healthy fantasy outlet for violent impulses and renew an abused American patriotism. The revenge fantasy in which the American hero strikes out against injustice and corruption both at home and abroad serves, as well, to validate the experience of U.S. Vietnam veterans – a form of "belated active mastery," in Freudian terms, to compensate for the collective blow suffered by the American people. But social critics argue that this form of fantasy exploits the conflicts men face in today's society, fuelling political paranoia and encouraging a reactionary sensibility.

The books claim to support so-called old-fashioned American values. Mack Bolan, for example, has surrendered what he terms "the three F's of the good life: friends, family, freedom" to "the three B's: bullets, bombs and blood."[5]

> This Executioner waged his war everlasting because he valued life. He was raised with the American ideals of peacefulness and respect of human life....
>
> To believe in something is one thing, Bolan knew; to be willing to die for something is the true measure of commitment and a life lived large to the last heartbeat.
>
> This Executioner knew no other way.[6]

Beneath the surface of the text, however, the values of action / adventure are closely identified with those of the American right wing. The hero combats the advances of Communism and the threat of the "foreign other" both near and far. His action team may include men of colour, but they are carefully established as homogenized Americans, resolute in their support of the hero. When the mercenary hero's mission takes him to foreign lands, to lead or perhaps to liberate people of other races, his flamboyant success invalidates the collective power of the people themselves: the visiting white god steps in to save the faithful. Action / adventure fiction serves to confirm white American superiority and promotes individual as opposed to collective action. The message of the books is essentially antisocial: in their vision of the world as a war zone, they celebrate a very bitter kind of individualism.

> This was a specialty war.... a job for a loner, without support, a guy who knew every way and every wile, a guy who could stride through rivers of blood to kill again and again ... and be willing to take his lumps in that final judgement of the universe.[7]

Popular culture's lone crusader has links to the culture hero of mythology, who journeys to the underworld, the primeval world, following the classic pattern of separation, initiation and return. But in action / adventure fiction, that corrupt jungle world exists all around us. The new hero's battleground is the urban wilderness, from which there can be no return: his triumph brings no moral redemption. And so in book after book, the war never ends. The relentless sameness of the stories, their heavy-handed repetition of themes and deliberate lack of psychological resolution, reflect the malaise in contemporary culture: the feelings of impotence and alienation that characterize post-World War II "corporate society." The hero's isolation is romanticized in an exaggerated form of "rugged individualism"; but the overblown ideal of masculinity celebrated in the genre addresses a sense of loneliness and confusion. Toronto cultural critic Varda Burstyn[8] describes the new warriors as

> atoms in the void, unconnected to any organic community, unable to form relationships of any resonance or vitality, always and only their weaponry, shooting in an empty universe.... The men in these books are men who are helpless and lost in this world, phenomenally angry at this world, and so strike out in an almost infantile way against the social conditions that gave it rise.

Adrift in an indifferent society, the alienated individual turns for reassurance to traditionally male virtues of cunning, bravery, strength and purpose. Action / adventure fiction reflects back to him an image of extraordinary potency. Mack Bolan's motto is "Live Large, Stay Hard"; he's a "penetration specialist." In the world of the novels, killing becomes the ultimate expression of personal power: violence is highly charged, eroticized, in long graphic scenes of emotional release.

> Knees bent, holding the Stoner with its heavy 150-round ammo box in both hands, Bolan spun in a semicircle, his index finger holding down the slim metal of the trigger against the rear of the trigger housing. The weapon bucked and spasmed in his hands, only his powerful wrists and forearms keeping the muzzle down. The big guy found target after target.[9]

The hero is violence incarnate: in a kind of Zen state, a state of perfect unity between man and weapon, he realizes himself in the moment of battle. This is the "action" of the adventure, the thrill the reader is after. This cult of phallic weaponry and male virility – one of the genre's most prominent features – speaks to a very beleaguered sense of male identity, an imperilled masculinity. As Varda Burstyn comments,

The virtual equation of the phallic hero with the weapon itself suggests that men are so angry and so frustrated that the only appropriate metaphorical vehicle for their wish fulfillment, in terms of a better identity, is one that is utterly violent.

The aggressive action celebrated in the fantasy suggests that there can be simple solutions to complex social problems. But even more important than the action itself is the moral context in which it occurs. The action / adventure story maintains clear-cut ethical and political standards. Rape, torture and other acts of brutality may be described in lavish detail – a kind of sly pornography, in which the reader imaginatively plays the dual role of villain and victim – but it is the hero's absolute condemnation of these atrocities that sparks his revenge. The enemy with whom such degeneracy is inevitably associated can assume many different guises: the Mafia, the Russians, the Nazis, the Iranians, the CIA, bureaucracy and government at all levels, from all parts of the world. Just as the hero is a warrior without roots, the enemy is essentially amorphous:

> The Executioner had come to realize that he was fighting a holy war, corny as it sounded. Good over evil, this was the issue. This was the cause, and Executioner Bolan knew that he would never find a better one to live for. To *live* for – not to *die* for. There was no victory in dying … ; the victory lay only in the death of evil, and Mack Bolan found himself irreversibly committed to that undertaking.[10]

According to Toronto psychoanalyst and sociologist Don Carveth, the enemy assumes many different forms from book to book because the kind of anxiety these fantasies assuage in various ways is a diffuse feeling of helplessness in the face of large and anonymous social forces. As Carveth explains,

> As early as the 1950s, sociologists like David Riesman in *The Lonely Crowd* talked about the shift from the inner-directed individual to the other-directed organization man, and the strains that this was creating in American society. In this genre you have the rugged individualist being celebrated versus the huge organization. Rambo, for instance, is fighting the CIA; he asks his colonel, "Do we get to win this time?"

Carveth describes another of the genre's central themes as "the simplified moral universe" common to much fantasy literature. The black-and-white world view of the novels reflects what is known in psychoanalytic terms as

> the preambivalent world of the pre-oedipal child, character-ized by a defensive splitting of the whole object, the whole image of another person who is both good and bad, into two objects, one of which is all good and can be idealized and loved and protected, and another which is all bad and is to be hated and vilified and destroyed. And one doesn't have to cope with moral confusion in a world like this.

The genre's extreme transparency in plots and power relations is nowhere more evident than in its sexual politics. In heroic literature, women are traditionally secondary characters: the mythical hero must not stray from his quest, and no one really expects the Lone Ranger to settle down with the local schoolteacher. Often the hero is spurred into action by some threatened or actual violation of a woman close to him – a mother, a sister, a lover. But lately the influence of feminism appears to have crept into the books, with the emergence of the woman warrior, neither siren nor victim:

> The concerned look in April's eyes was that of a lover who cares about her man....
> April wore a .44 Magnum with a six-inch barrel in a fast-draw holster on her shapely right hip. She was also carrying a spare gun-holster rig.
> The lady handled weapons like a carpenter handled a saw.
> But still beautiful, yeah.[11]

Appealing to a growing female readership and changing values, women in the stories now figure not merely as the familiar support-ing love interest but as partners and competitors at war. The action / adventure heroine might be a tribal chief's daughter, leader of a mer-cenary team, a spunky secret agent or a major in the Soviet army. But whether dedicated accomplice or fierce opponent, she is always lim-ited in her power. Varda Burstyn comments:

> The woman is there to show that the hero's heterosexual cre-dentials are intact, but the moment she comes into his pres-ence, her attitude is one of deference and acquiescence, and it's described in terms of her body language, in terms of the dia-logue, and particularly in terms of the fact that he orders and she obeys. That establishes the hero's superiority all the more,

because he is able to have the deference of women who are supposed to be independent in their own right.

> A sharp, single gun report punctuated the sounds of the rain. April emitted a piercing scream and became a deadweight back in Bolan's left arm. He wrapped his arm tighter around her to keep her from falling, knowing already what had happened.
> *Oh, God, no,* he thought. *No!*[12]

In the end, even the new woman warrior seems to fare little better than the traditional damsel in distress. Mack Bolan's beloved girlfriend, the multitalented April Rose – ex-model, solid state physicist, expert markswoman, mission controller – was killed by a KGB bullet aimed at her man; but in reality this fictional superwoman was sacrificed by the publisher as a marketing strategy to "re-energize" the Mack Bolan character. Despite the new veneer of sexual equality, then, action / adventure fiction preserves the status quo. Gender is actually a secondary issue: the anxiety addressed in the books has less to do with feminism than with men's feelings about their relationship to one another within corporate society. Varda Burstyn relates the attitude of nihilism and desperation reflected in this genre to the film noir of the postwar period.

> What we see in film noir is a kind of anger against women, but what is really happening is that there's a displacement onto women of blame for problems occurring in society as a whole, which are rooted in the hands of powerful men in social institutions. Those problems have really been exacerbated today, so that gender anxiety, which seems fairly easy to spot in these novels, is actually hiding a deeper anxiety. And that's one of the reasons why the action takes place between men, and between men and a kind of evil, amorphous society; and that's why women are in second place. It's not only a sexist plot – it also says something about where the real difficulties are.

> Blood Alley could only be marched by a loner. War Everlasting was this nightfighter's mistress, and Bolan would never be free of her....
> For a man who lives large, the good fight would always be worth it.[13]

The solitary man of purpose has always held a romantic allure, and action / adventure's largely male, white-collar readership – particularly its adolescent component – can freely identify with a "man's man." With the loss of faith in social and political institutions that has characterized the past three decades, the ideal of absolute individual power becomes all the more compelling. And from this fantasy of brute masculine force emerges a fierce devotion to the buddy system:

> Every combat soldier knew that feeling. Knew that you'd take on crazy risks because the other guy was your buddy. Do things for him you'd never do for yourself.
> Like die for him.
> And Mack Bolan was his buddy. Friend. Leader.[14]

Women can play only a marginal role in a world where men make love to their guns and grenades; where violence brings the ultimate emotional and psychological high. The admiration of women is easily won; the respect and support of one's fellows are harder earned, and have a correspondingly higher value.

From Riesman's *The Lonely Crowd* in the 1950s to Christopher Lasch's *The Minimal Self* in the 1980s, critics have pointed to a crisis in North American society: a conflict between our basic individualism and our need for community and commitment. In the 1980s, the quest for "personal empowerment" has created what Lasch describes as a "siege mentality" – a preoccupation with psychic survival that finds its fantasy ideal in the cult of the warrior. Some critics see the themes of action / adventure as typical, in psychoanalytic terms, of the syndrome of "phallic narcissism" – a stage that children of both sexes go through from ages 3 to 5, but which is also characteristic of some adults and probably all men in Western culture. In its exaggerated form, it can be seen as a defence against certain infantile anxieties, especially castration anxiety and earlier fears of separation and helplessness. As Don Carveth explains,

> In our culture – a patriarchial culture – the image of the castrated, passive, dependent, helpless object is associated, of course, with the female. And so in this literature, instead of being castrated, feminine and soft, the hero is phallic, virile and hard; instead of fearing separation, his isolation and independence are celebrated as virtues; instead of being helpless, he possesses an omnipotent self-sufficiency; instead of being con-

fused and therefore incapacitated, he has a clear vision and purpose, and doesn't have to cope with ambivalence or ambiguity.

> Somewhere, somehow, the whole savage and bloody thing mattered. It was not a senseless game, from which a guy could just disengage any time the going became a little rough. It was life, and Mack Bolan meant to live his to the bloody, bitter end.[15]

Despite his high-tech gear, the warrior has returned on a wave of nostalgia. Literary critic Leslie Fiedler, longtime defender of popular literature, speaks of the secret desire to restore the ideal of the macho hero:

> Every movement creates its backlash: you have enough anti-machismo, then you get pro-machismo. And it's not merely men who would like to restore the notion of the supermale; in fantasy at least, if not in fact, it's women too.

But in today's terms, the macho can return only as a clumsy cardboard figure. The nihilism that pervades action / adventure fiction simply adds poignancy to the image of the new warrior. The social and political causes for the hero's unrest – the U.S. defeat in Vietnam, the unfinished business of American prisoners of war, the rise of international terrorism, the changing position of women in society, the economic recession, disillusionment with government and frustration with bureaucracy in general – have combined to create a burden so great that the warrior can never lay down his arms. And so the lonely heroes stand at arms on the bookracks, prepared to do battle in endless versions of the same story. The vision of action / adventure fiction is finally a bleak one: in an arbitrary, hostile world, there can be no ultimate triumph over evil.

NOTES

1 "Shootout on the New Frontier" is based on research and interviews for the two-part radio documentary "The New Warriors," prepared and presented by Sandra Rabinovitch and originally broadcast on CBC Radio's "Ideas" series on November 7 and 14, 1986.

2 Don Pendleton, *The Executioner: War Against the Mafia* (#1) (New York: Pinnacle Books, 1969), pp. 166-67.

3 Don Pendleton, *Mack Bolan: Paramilitary Plot* (The Executioner #45) (Don Mills, Ont.: Worldwide Library, 1982), pp. 17-18.

4 *Ibid.*, p. 145

5 Don Pendleton, *The Executioner: Nightmare in New York* (#7) (New York: Pinnacle Books, 1971), p. 9.

6 Don Pendleton, *Mack Bolan: Teheran Wipeout* (The Executioner #76) (Don Mills, Ont.: Worldwide Library, 1985), pp. 47-48.

7 Don Pendleton, *The Executioner: California Hit* (#11) (New York: Pinnacle Books, 1972), p. 111.

8 All comments by Varda Burstyn, Don Carveth and Leslie Fiedler quoted in this article are taken from interviews taped for the radio documentary.

9 Don Pendleton, *Mack Bolan: The New War* (Executioner #39) (Don Mills, Ont.: Worldwide Library, 1981), pp. 105-6.

10 *The Executioner: War Against the Mafia*, p. 77

11 (Don Pendleton's Executioner), *Mack Bolan: Day of Mourning* (The Executioner #62) (Don Mills, Ont.: Worldwide Library, 1984), p. 49.

12 *Ibid.*, pp. 183-84.

13 *Mack Bolan: Teheran Wipeout*, pp. 184-85.

14 *Mack Bolan: The New War*, p. 148.

15 Don Pendleton, *The Executioner #8: Chicago Wipe-out* (New York: Pinnacle Books, 1971), p. 187.

PART THREE
ACTING FOR PEACE

THE CONTRIBUTORS TO this section are all women who have been activists in the Canadian peace movement after World War II. Their articles reflect both unity and diversity. The unity is derived from a shared recognition that the end of the war brought with it a new and terrifying set of circumstances. As the late Margaret Laurence put it: "My generation was the first in human history to come into young adulthood knowing that the human race now had the dreadful ability to destroy all life on Earth and possibly the Earth itself."

The recognition that modern warfare carries with it the risk of total annihilation has transformed peace activism in the last half-century, not only in Canada, but all over the world. It has fired peace activists with a sense of urgency, because war has become not only immoral, but also profoundly irrational.

In addition to this shared sense of urgency, women peace activists of our period have shared a belief that there are connections between war and other issues, most notably between war and the destruction of the environment, war and racism, and war and sexism. Such links are, for example, self-evident to Adele Ratt of Prince Albert, Saskatchewan, who has been involved in opposing uranium mining in northern Saskatchewan. Ratt points out that "the mining kills people before the uranium ever becomes a bomb." Adele Ratt is not a conventional member of the mainstream peace movement: her primary involvement is with the advancement of the rights of native people. Yet it is clear that she sees the despoiling of the environment and the health hazards involved in uranium mining as essentially connected to the threat of annihilation through nuclear war.

Like Adele Ratt, Joy Kogawa has had direct contact with racism. For Kogawa, the varieties of hate that human beings have spawned can only be combatted by their obverse: the human capacity to understand, and even to love, "the enemy." Joy Kogawa believes that the injustices suffered by Canadians of Japanese heritage at the hands of their fellow citizens and their government are rooted in a racism that war encourages and inflames. But, at the same time that she protests the injustice, she calls out "for reconciliation, for forgiveness and for mutuality" as our only means of defence, against both racial injustice and war, which "threatens to destroy us all."

For Elizabeth Richards and Shelly Romalis, feminism and peace activism are closely connected. Their contributions to this section offer reflections about the meaning of that connection. Romalis's discussion of the women's peace camp at Greenham Common in Eng-

s questions about the features of the Greenham movement
al critics have perceived as antithetical to feminism (its
g...............on of motherhood," its support for "traditional role expectations") but concludes that, in spite of the validity of these criticisms,
"Greenham has been a powerful force in undermining traditionalism
in Britain."

The tension between the values of femininity and those of feminism, between women's peace activism that accepts traditional
notions of femininity and feminist peace activism that names and
rejects the oppression of women, exists in Canada as well as in Britain. That tension forms part of the history of the most important Canadian women's peace organization of our period, the Voice of
Women. In her account of VOW's history, Kay Macpherson, one of
the organization's outstanding leaders, gives us her own personal
reflections on this tension. It seems clear that when VOW began in
1960, it drew its strength from the traditional justification of women's
activism which rests on women's special role as mothers. But VOW
transformed the thinking of many women on the issue of feminism.
Macpherson says, "VOW got me into the women's movement, feminism and politics." As she worked for VOW, the connections among
peace activism, concern for the environment, defending the rights of
minority groups and women's issues became self-evident.

I have said that the pieces in this section reflect unity. But they
also reflect diversity and disagreement. Two major issues about
which there is disagreement are the use of nonviolent civil disobedience and – much more contentious – the use of potentially or actually harmful weapons (such as firebombs) in the course of civil disobedience. Civil disobedience has a long history in the contexts of
both feminism and peace activism. For women in Britain, for
example, this history extends from the militant suffragists to the
women of Greenham Common. Several of our authors discuss the
question of nonviolent civil disobedience, but Janice Williamson
deals with it centrally in her account of the protest against Litton Systems in Toronto organized by Women's Action for Peace in
November 1983, and the subsequent trial of twenty-nine women
charged under the Ontario Provincial Trespass Act.

Williamson recognizes the "controversial status of civil disobedience as a political strategy for change." Although the action she participated in did involve breaking the law, it was nonviolent in intent
and in actuality; moreover, the twenty-nine defendants used the
courtroom deliberately and collectively as a way of making a politi-

cal statement, not simply to the public, but also to the presiding judge. The fact that the defendants were allowed to make political statements in the courtroom, and that their expert witnesses were allowed to be heard, is seen by Williamson as representing a partial victory, because the justice system did acknowledge the group's political motivation. For these twenty-nine women, then, it was important not only to protest against militarism as big business, but also to force the courts to recognize their right to do so. Such a strategy, while profoundly critical of society's structures, at the same time reflects a commitment to them, and a faith that they can change.

Ann Hansen presents a different point of view. The piece included in this section is her statement to the British Columbia court which, in February 1983, sentenced her to life imprisonment. Ann Hansen, a member of the group Direct Action, was tried for her involvement in the firebombing of Red Hot Video outlets (video stores renting pornographic materials) in Vancouver, the bombing of the Litton Systems plant in Toronto, the bombing of the Cheekeye-Dunsmuir hydro substation, and conspiracy to rob a Brink's truck. At the Litton bombing, people were injured. She was tried along with one other woman and three men; collectively the group became known as the Vancouver (or Squamish) Five. Clearly, for Ann Hansen, the conflict is between those who share her beliefs on the one hand and the institutions of the state on the other: "The politics of Direct Action saw the interconnectedness of militarism, sexism, environmental destruction and imperialism. We saw that all these problems are rooted in the value system and way of thinking called capitalism and patriarchy" and in the institutions that maintain society, which are there "to protect big business, wealthy individuals and the status quo." She explains, "It was because there was no legal way to stop these crimes against humanity and the earth that I felt I had to use illegal actions to do so."

As readers of this section will discover, all the contributors agree on certain issues, most notably on the terrible threat to humanity and to the earth itself that is posed by nuclear warfare, but they would disagree on others. Some Canadian women peace activists ground their activism in liberal pacifism. Others have a commitment to radical politics which leads them to oppose imperialism, the nuclear arms race and superpower politics, but to support the use of armed struggle in conflicts they define as wars of liberation. Some women believe that a nonviolent policy must always be adhered to in working for peace and social justice. Others reject this view.

And what of women and peace? All the contributors speak as women, but speaking as a woman means different things to different women. For some, women's commitment to peace is rooted in biology: they believe that women, as actual or potential mothers, have a special responsibility to speak out for the preservation of life. Others believe that there are compelling reasons why women must act for peace but ground that activism in a feminist analysis – an analysis that posits no biological connection between women and nonviolence, but asserts that militarism and the oppression of women are inextricably linked.

Finally, it includes activists of many varieties. Some, like Kay Macpherson, have devoted their energies to overt and direct political activism over many years. Others, like Margaret Laurence, have contributed primarily through writing and speaking out. We would suggest that writing, speaking out and teaching are also ways of acting for peace. And the message that is conveyed by all the voices that speak in this section is that we must all act, even though acting in any way is difficult in the face of the combined power and irrationality of late twentieth-century militarism.

–D.G.

My Final Hour[1]

Margaret Laurence

I AM BEING GIVEN a unique opportunity. I will not have to postpone until my last gasp the imparting of the wisdom of my accumulated years to a breathlessly awaiting world. Just as well, as I have never been much of a believer in "famous last words." I suppose this is why King Lear's words "Prithee, undo this button" seem infinitely more moving to me than any high-flown rhetoric purportedly uttered by some well-known person when on the point of departing this vale of tears. Anyway, here I am, faced with the prospect of delivering the message of My Final Hour. I do not promise that it will be My Finest Hour, but I will do my best.

First, I would like to pass on one piece of advice. If, as you grow older, you feel you are also growing stupider, do not worry. This is normal, and usually occurs around the time when your children, now grown, are discovering the opposite – they now see that you aren't nearly as stupid as they had believed when they were young teenagers. Take heart from that. True, your new-found sense of stupidity will no doubt be partly due to the fact that the technology of the age has far outstripped any feeble knowledge of it that you may once have felt you had.

It may, however, also be due to the fact that at last you may be learning a little healthy humility – humility in its true and indeed religious sense, which of course has nothing at all to do with self-effacement but with a recognition of your human limitations. I would not claim that I have learned that kind of humility – that struggle to learn will never cease. But at least I now can accept with some sort of equanimity that many things are beyond my power. I can try to help friends or family or strangers, but I can never "save" another in the profoundest sense. I can do what is within my human power, that is all. Anything else is delusion or spiritual pride, or so I believe. My limitations extend to many fields. I know now that I will never know an enormous amount about music or painting. My knowledge of science is likely to remain minuscule. I will never know as much as I would like to about the planets and their patterned courses. Even in my own area of so-called expertise, I will never read all the novels I would like to read, even though I read great numbers of them yearly. I will also never write a novel with which I am really satisfied.

There is so much to do, so much to learn and experience, and one lifetime, however long it may be, is too short. I think of the verse from Psalms 39: "Hear O Lord, and give ear unto my cry; hold not thy peace at my tears; for I am a stranger with thee and a sojourner, as all my fathers were." Mothers, too, I feel compelled to add. Sojourner, yes, but this need not mean "tourist." My lifetime here is a short span, but I am not here as a visitor. Earth is my home. I have tried to read as widely as I can; I have always believed I had to live as well as write, to be a citizen and a person and a mother and a friend as well as a writer. But basically, I have spent a great part of my adult life in learning a profession – or, as I prefer to call it, a trade – that can never be mastered in its complexity and richness. I am fond of the story about the brain surgeon, who, meeting a novelist at a party, says, "Oh ... you're a novelist, eh? When I retire, I plan to take up novel writing." "How interesting," the novelist replies. "When I retire, I plan to take up brain surgery."

Well, an acceptance of limitations does not mean that one is not constantly trying to extend the boundaries of knowledge and accomplishment. And it certainly does not mean an acceptance of defeat, in whatever fields our endeavours take place. It is my feeling that as we grow older we should become not less radical but more so. I do not, of course, mean this in any political-party sense, but in a willingness to struggle for those things in which we passionately believe. Social activism and the struggle for social justice are often thought of as natural activities of the young, but not of the middle-aged or elderly. In fact, I don't think this was ever true, and certainly in our own era we are seeing an enormous upsurge of people of all ages who are deeply and committedly concerned about the state of our hurting and endangered world. There is a line from the old Anglo-Saxon poem, "The Battle of Maldon," that I think of frequently. It is this: "Mind must be the firmer, heart the more fierce, courage the greater, as our strength diminishes."

So the basic message of My Final Hour would have to be – do not despair. Act. Speak out. In the words of one of my heroines, Catharine Parr Traill, "In cases of emergency, it is folly to fold one's hand and sit down to bewail in abject terror. It is better to be up and doing."

We are faced now with an emergency that concerns not only our own personal lives, but the lives of all people and creatures on earth.

Ours is a terrifying world. Injustice, suffering and fear are everywhere to be found. It is difficult to maintain hope in such a world, and yet I believe there must be hope. I want to proclaim my belief in the social gospel, as a Christian, a woman, a writer, a mother and a member of humanity, a sharer in a life that I believe in some way to be informed by the holy spirit. I do not think it is enough to hope and pray that our lives and souls will know grace, even though my entire life as a writer has been concerned with my belief that all individual human beings matter, that no one is ordinary. The new commandment of the man of Nazareth speaks very clearly. "Thou shalt love thy neighbor as thyself."

The social gospel is no easier now than it ever was. My generation was the first in human history to come into young adulthood knowing that the human race now had the dreadful ability to destroy all life on Earth and possibly the Earth itself. Only later did we realize the full extent of the destruction of life, a continuing destruction passed on to the then-unborn children of survivors, but we *did* know that after Hiroshima, August 6, 1945, the world would never be the same again. The annihilation caused by the first atomic bombs was unthinkable, but it had happened. Also, we had taken it for granted that through wars, through disasters, yet would the Earth endure forever. It was clear to many of us in 1945 that this was no longer to be taken for granted. We have lived with that thought ever since, and have yet borne our children, lived our lives, done our work. The will to survive and to pass on caring to future generations is very strong. But today we have to realize that the bombs used at Hiroshima and Nagasaki were *small* bombs, compared to today's nuclear weapons.

Think of the Holocaust in Europe, when the Nazis murdered a very great part of all the Jewish communities. That horror, surely, must *never* be forgotten. No amount of mourning will ever be enough for those millions of children, women and men whose lives were torn from them by the group of de-humanized humans who had taken power in Hitler's Germany. Are we to remember the Holocaust and the horrors of Hiroshima and Nagasaki and yet remain silent when we hear today about a "winnable" nuclear war or a "limited" nuclear war? I think not.

Our lives and the lives of all generations as yet unborn are being threatened, as never before, by the increasing possibility of a nuclear war. I believe that the question of disarmament is the most pressing practical, moral and spiritual issue of our times. I'm not talking about abstractions. I'm talking about my life and your life and my kids' lives and the lives of people everywhere. If we value our own lives, and the lives of our children and all children everywhere, if we honour both the past and the future, then we must do everything in our power to work nonviolently for peace. These beliefs are not only an integral part of my social and moral stance but of my religious faith as well. Human society now possesses the terrible ability to destroy all life on Earth and our planet itself. Can anyone who has ever marvelled at the miracle of creation – who has even looked closely at a tree or a plant or a river – fail to feel concerned and indeed anguished, every single day, at this thought?

A central disagreement, of course, exists between those who think that more and yet more nuclear arms will ensure that nuclear arms will never be used, and those of us who believe that the proliferation of nuclear weapons brings us closer all the time to the actuality of nuclear war – a war that no side could possibly win; a war that would be so devasting that we cannot begin to imagine that horror. Whatever we are being told about a "limited" or a "winnable" nuclear war, the fact remains that such a war could destroy all that we, as humankind, have aspired to, have achieved. It could destroy the future, not only of the world's peoples but of all creatures that share our planet with us.

As America and Russia develop more and more nuclear arms, so the other will inevitably respond in kind. Nuclear arms have long since ceased to be a "deterrent" if indeed they were ever so, and have become by their very existence a monstrous threat. Daily, the chances are increasing for a nuclear war to break out by accident, by a failure of the intricate and not totally reliable control and warning systems on either side, or simply by human panic and a mutual mistrust between the superpowers.

Dr. Helen Caldicott, that courageous woman who has done so much in the struggle against nuclear arms, has said that both America and Russia have now enough nuclear weapons to "over kill every person on earth sixteen times." Think of that. Do the world's leaders really suppose that it is all just an act on TV and that the dead would get up again and take on a different role in another TV series so they might be killed again and again? I fear greatly that many of the world's leaders have so little imagination and so little caring that they cannot visualize at all what a nuclear holocaust would mean. Do they really think that they and their families and executive staffs would survive in deep-buried bunkers? And if, by any unlikely chance, they did, what kind of a world do they think they would emerge back into? It would be a dead and a putrefying world. Dr. Helen Caldicott says, "If we look behind the headlines and understand the historical perspective we realize that America is preparing to fight a nuclear war. Now, that should make us all distinctly uncomfortable. In fact, we should be screaming in the streets, if we really care about ourselves, our children, and if we really love this planet." With well-researched figures, Dr. Caldicott also says, "In the event of a nuclear war, we predict that within thirty days after an exchange, 90 percent of Americans will be dead. So will Canadians, probably Mexicans, certainly Russians, certainly Europeans, the British and probably the Chinese."

Roger Molander, a former White House nuclear strategist for the National Security Council, in an article in *The Guardian* in April of 1982, tells of one of the many things that made him decide to give up that job. He is now executive director of Ground Zero, an anti-nuclear weapons project. He says, "The final chance event that confirmed my determination to help correct our flaws involved another military officer. It happened at a meeting in the Pentagon when a navy captain offered the view that in America and Europe people were getting too excited over nuclear war. He argued that people were talking as if nuclear war would be the end of the world, when in fact only 500 million would be killed. Only 500 million. I remember repeating it to myself ... only 500 million...." Exactly. These are cold figures, statistics. It takes no time at all to say 500 million. But it all looks different, as it did to Roger Molander, if we think of each one of these people as our own children, ourselves, our parents, our friends.

It is precisely this failure of the imagination on the part of militarists and leaders that is so dangerous today, the failure to visualize what a nuclear holocaust would mean, the apparent inability to imagine the scorched and charred bodies of children ... our children or children of Russian parents or parents anywhere, and to know, by an extension of imagination, that all children are our children. The jargon of the militarists is a distortion and a twisting of language, of our human ability to communicate. Language itself becomes the vehicle of concealment and deception. Such words as "overkill" and "megadeath" do not convey in any sense at all what would really happen – the dead, mutilated and dying people clogging the ruined cities and towns like so much unvalued discarded rubbish, the suffering humans screaming for help with no medical help available, no water, no relief of death for all. Any shelters that the few might reach would in time turn into tombs. Civil defence plans are a sham. In a nuclear war there would be nowhere to hide, and nowhere except a dead and contaminated world to emerge back into.

I profoundly believe that we must proclaim that *this must not happen*. Yes, but what about the Russians? If we try to persuade our government to refuse Cruise missile testing, aren't we playing into the hands of the bad guys? Won't the Soviet Union, as soon as they have clear superiority in nuclear arms, blow us all to hell without a second's thought? I do not think so. Isn't it necessary to have more and ever more nuclear weapons in the hands of the Americans so that we can feel safe? I do not think so. Let me make it clear that I hold no brief for the present Russian system of government. I hold no brief for *any* system of government that is repressive and cruel, and this includes those far-right regimes in countries such as El Salvador, to whom the U.S.A. is determinedly giving so much military aid. The U.S.A. and Russia, the two superpowers, must, I believe, coexist in this world, even if there are some terrible things wrong in both systems, and there are. Russia suffered horribly in World War II, whereas war has not been fought on American soil since the Civil War. I cannot believe that the Soviet leaders are all that anxious to begin nuclear war in which the Soviet Union would be, if not totally annihilated, then certainly devasted beyond any hope of recovery. George Kennan, formerly U.S. ambassador to the Soviet Union, who has been awarded both the Pulitzer Prize and the Albert Einstein Peace Prize, and who is a distinguished diplomat, academic and writer, says in his book *The Nuclear Delusion*:

> Aren't we then ... being unrealistic in the amount of attention we devote to protecting ourselves from the Russians who, God knows, are not 10 feet tall, who have all sorts of troubles of their own, who can't run an agricultural system that really works, who can't adequately house their population, who are rapidly losing their prestige and leadership in the world Communist movement, and have to reckon with China on their long frontier in the East? Isn't it grotesque to spend so much of our energy on opposing such a Russia in order to save a West which is honeycombed with bewilderment and a profound sense of internal decay?

Quite frankly, I can't believe that Russia any longer has hopes of a world revolution. I can believe, though, that the Russian people, the ordinary people who love their children just as much as I love mine, are frightened, just as I am frightened, just as a very large proportion of the American people are frightened and are expressing that fear and outrage. The American people are indeed our cousins, and a very great many of them, young and old, are saying virtually the same things as I am saying here.

No American president has as yet declared himself willing to embrace a policy of "no first strike" in terms of nuclear weapons. President Ronald Reagan recently made the statement that America must reduce Marxism-Leninism "to the ash heap of history." If he proposed to do this by making his country such a true and fine example of social justice, of caring for the poor, of equal rights for women, of peace-making on the international scene, and of a refusal to support corrupt and violent regimes in, say, Central and South America, so that people the world over would look to America, as indeed once they did, as the home of the free, then I would say – Great. But I do not think that is what he had in mind. The president also, not long ago, addressed a group of fundamentalist Christians and told them that good and evil exist in the world and that the good must utterly destroy evil. By evil, he was not referring to organized crime in his own land, or unemployment or poverty in the richest nation in the world. He was talking about America as wearing the white cowboy hat (to use a metaphor from his Hollywood days) and Russia wearing the black one. Good guys and bad guys. George Kennan says:

> I do not have, and have never had any sympathy for the ideology of the Soviet leadership. I know that this is a regime with which it is not possible for us to have a fully satisfactory relationship. I know that there are many important matters on which no collaboration between us is possible, just as there are other matters on which we can collaborate. There are a number of Soviet habits and practises that I deeply deplore ...
>   All this being said, I must ... say that I find the view of the Soviet Union that prevails today in large portions of our governmental and journalistic establishments so extreme, so subjective, so far removed from what any sober scrutiny of external reality would reveal, that it is not only ineffective but dangerous as a guide to political action ... And we shall not be able to turn these things around as they should be turned, in the plane of military and nuclear rivalry, until we learn to correct these childish distortions ... until we correct our tendency to

see in the Soviet Union only a mirror in which we look for the reflection of our own virtue – until we consent to see there another great people, one of the world's greatest, in all its complexity and variety, embracing the good with the bad, a people whose life, whose views, whose habits, whose fears and aspirations, whose successes and failures, are the products, just as ours are the products, not of any inherent iniquity but of the relentless discipline of history, tradition and national experience. Above all, we must learn to see the behavior of the leadership of that country as partly a reflection of our own treatment of it. If we insist on demonizing these Soviet leaders ... on viewing them as total and incorrigible enemies, consumed only with their fear or hatred of us and dedicated to nothing other than our destruction – that, in the end, is the way we shall assuredly have them, if for no other reason than that our view of them allows for nothing else, either for them or for us.

In a moving essay written in 1982 titled *A Christian's View of the Arms Race*, Kennan also says, "utterly unacceptable, from the Christian viewpoint as I see it, is the holding of innocent people hostage to the policies of their government and the readiness or the threat to punish them as a means of punishing their government."

Our Prime Minister recently asked the NDP leader, Ed Broadbent, who was seeking to have the whole issue of the Cruise missile testing debated in the Commons, if he, Broadbent, had written to [then] Soviet leader Andropov to tell *him* to stop testing, too. This snide remark was, of course, beside the point. Our federal government, at the present time talking out of both sides of its collective mouth, says that on the one hand the actual testing of the Cruise hasn't yet been agreed upon and on the other hand Canada must honour its commitment to NATO. According to Pauline Jewett, NDP defence critic, who has done much research on this matter, Canada's commitment to NATO does *not* include the necessity of our allowing *America* – America, not NATO – to test nuclear weapons here. My point is that Canada could have – and must have, in my view – considerable impact as a mediator in nuclear arms talks, as a non-nuclear nation, as a country that might conceivably be helpful in lowering the present climate of hysteria between the two superpowers and in bringing about world disarmament.

This is why I think we must keep on trying to make our government hear us. Why would I write to Andropov or Reagan? I don't have a vote or a voice in those countries. I have both a vote and a voice here, though.

I believe that our land should be declared a nuclear-weapons-free zone, with absoutely no testing of nuclear arms by both sides, monitored by neutral countries, and that there should be a freeze on the production and testing of nuclear weapons. Canada could be a strong influence for a "no-first-strike" agreement among nations, for multilateral disarmament and for world peace.

Canada is not powerless nor are we insignificant in a world sense. Yet our present government appears to be quite willing to allow the Cruise missile to be tested over our land, in Alberta. The Cruise missile, an American nuclear weapon – it was designed as a "first-strike weapon." Its presence in the nuclear arsenal will not be verifiable, thus making any kind of nuclear-weapons control virtually impossible. The Litton plant in Ontario is producing, with the aid of millions of *our* tax dollars, guidance systems for the Cruise missile.... These are only a few of the many examples of Canada's complicity in the nuclear arms race.

Do we care so little about our children? Do we honour life so little that we will not speak out? I believe we do care, passionately and profoundly. Indeed, one thing that gives me hope is that so many of our churches and synagogues, so many people of all faiths, of all professions and trades, of all ages are speaking out against the arms race and the descent into total madness. Physicians for Social Responsibility, active in this country as well as in America and elsewhere, are telling us what human damage would be done and how impossible any thought of medical aid would be in a nuclear war. Interchurch groups such as Project Ploughshares are making strong representations to our government, as are labour unions, academics and indeed and perhaps most importantly, women and men everywhere, in every walk of life. This is true in so very many places in the world today. When I speak of lobbying our own government, that is because we must begin where we are. But we join our voices with those everywhere who believe as we do.

The money spent on arms, including nuclear arms, continues to mount. Recently I read that $550 billion dollars are being spent, worldwide, yearly, on arms. An even more recent estimate puts it at $600 billion dollars. That is so great we cannot really comprehend it. But we *can* comprehend that for the cost of *one* Trident nuclear submarine, malaria could be wiped out from the world. Think of that for one minute. I think of the people in the world who are suffering from thirst, from starvation, from preventable diseases, from ceaseless fighting and the brutality of oppressive regimes. I think, too, of the growing number of unemployed people in our land. I think of the Reagan program in America – more and yet more money spent on nuclear arms, less and less spent on social programs and help to the poor and the disabled.

I have to speak about how I feel as a writer. I don't like calling myself "an artist," but I guess I am, and would join with my tribal sisters and brothers in many ways. I believe that as a writer – and artist, if you will – I have responsibility, a moral responsibility, to work against the nuclear arms race, to work for recognition on the part of governments and military leaders that nuclear weapons must never be used and must systematically be reduced. Throughout human history, artists have affirmed and celebrated life. Whether we work in words, in music, in painting, in film, in bronze or stone or whatever our medium may be, the artist affirms the value of life itself and of our only home, the planet Earth. Art mirrors and ponders the pain and joy of our experience as human beings. In many parts of the world and over many centuries artists have risked and even given their own lives to portray the society around them as they perceived it and to speak out against injustices. Since the most ancient times, artists have passed on to succeeding generations the tales, the histories, the songs, the sagas, the skills of their trade. Can we conceive of a world in which there would be no suceeding generations? A world in which all the powerful works of the human imagination would be destroyed, would never again be seen or listened to or experienced? We must conceive that this is now a possibility, and one not too far in our uncertain future, either. We must not, as artists, or so I feel, stand by and passively allow this to happen. The death of the individual is the end which we will all one day meet, but in the knowledge that our children and their children will live, that *someone's* children will go on, that the great works of humankind will endure in art, in recorded history, in medicine, in the sciences and philosophies and technologies that our species had developed with devotion and a sense of vocation throughout the ages. The individual is the leaf on the tree. The leaves fall but the tree endures. New leaves are born. This concept has been the mainstay of our species from time immemorial. Now the tree itself is threatened. All art is a product of the human imagination. It is, deeply, an honouring of the past, a perception of the present in one way or another, and a looking towards the future. Whatever the medium of any particular artist, art is reaching out, an attempt to communicate those things which concern us most seriously in our sojourn here on earth. Artists, the real ones, the committed ones, have always sought, sometimes in ways prophetic and beyond their own times, to clarify and proclaim and enhance life, not to obscure and demean and destroy it. Even the so-called literature of despair is not really that at all. Despair is total silence, total withdrawal. Art, by its very nature of necessary expression is an act of faith, an acknowledgment of the profound mystery at the core of life.

As a writer, therefore, I feel I have a responsibility. Not to write pamphlets, not to write didactic fiction. That would be, in many ways, a betrayal of how I feel about my work. But my responsibility seems to me to be to write as truthfully as I can, about human individuals and their dilemmas, to honour them as living, suffering and sometimes joyful people. My responsibility also must extend into my life as a citizen of my own land and ultimately of the world.

I do not claim to have done this well. There are no personal victories in those areas. The individual, here, becomes part of a community and only as a part of that community can one person ever be effective and true to herself or himself. There has to be the resolve not to give up and to join with all others who believe that life itself is more important than our individual lives, important though these certainly are.

Dr. Helen Caldicott speaks of "psychic numbing," the temptation to shut out from our minds and hearts all the terrifying things in our world. To think that the problems may just possibly go away if we ignore them. To feel that we are totally helpless, and so ... why bother trying to do anything? What Dr. Caldicott calls "psychic numbing" I would call "despair," and although I would take issue with the early Church Fathers on many things, I would agree that despair is rightly placed as one of the deadly sins. The problems of our world will not go away if we ignore them. It is not all happening on TV. It is happening on our Earth, and we, humankind, are the custodians of that Earth. We cannot afford passivity. We must take on responsibility for our lives and our world and we must be prepared to make our government listen to and hear us. Our aim must be no less than human and caring justice and peace ... *for all people that on earth do dwell.*

So, if this were indeed my Final Hour, these would be my words to you. I would not claim to pass on any secret of life, for there is none, or any wisdom except the passionate plea of caring. In your dedication to your own life's work, whatever it may be, live as though you had forever, for no amount of careful and devoted doing is too great in carrying out that work to which you have set your hands. Cultivate in your work and your life the art of patience and come to terms with your inevitable human limitations, while striving also to extend the boundaries of your understanding, your knowledge and your compassion. These words are easily said; they are not easily lived. Learn from those who are older than you are; learn from your contemporaries; and never cease to learn from children. Try to feel, in your heart's core, the reality of others. This is the most painful thing in the world, probably, and the most necessary. In times of personal adversity, know that you are not alone. Know that although in the eternal scheme of things you are small, you are also unique and irreplaceable, as are all your fellow humans everywhere in the world. Know that your commitment is above all to life itself. Your own life and work and friendships and loves will come to an end, because one day you will die and whatever happens after that, or if anything happens at all, it will not be on this earth. But life and work and friendship and love will go on, in others, your inheritors. The struggle for peace and for social justice will go on – provided that our Earth survives and that caring humans still live. It is up to you, now, to do all that you can, and that means a commitment, at this perilous moment in our human history, to ensure that life itself *will* go on.

In closing, I want to quote one verse from that mighty book – more like a vast library – that Dr. Northrop Frye calls *The Great Code*, and which has so shaped, sometimes so ambiguously, the imagination, the art, and the many facets of faith in our world. This verse is from Deuteronomy, Chapter 30:

> I have set before you life and death, blessing and cursing; therefore choose life, that both thou and thy seed may live.

NOTE

1 This is a reprint of a speech given by Margaret Laurence at Trent University in 1983.

Is There a Just Cause?[1]

Joy Kogawa

IS THERE A JUST cause? In any age or place a particular cause may be deemed to be just, but in the next generation or among other people, that same cause could be judged a crime. Perhaps we will never be fully adequate to see the whole picture of which the causes we uphold are a part. But inadequacy is not an excuse for inaction. The private and the public, the personal and the political, the internal and the external are all co-extensive. Inadequacy is a universal experience, and we are all broken and incomplete like jigsaw-puzzle pieces. Our wholeness comes from joining and from sharing our brokenness.

Many feminists would say that the images of inadequacy and brokenness are inappropriate ones for women and for minority groups and do not assist us to the kind of transforming strength which is now needed. It is true that doubt and ambivalence can sometimes so immobilize us that in the end we serve to maintain oppressors in their positions of power. But healthy doubt also prevents us from succumbing to the demonic forces of an unthinking trust.

Rather than abandoning the way of brokenness, I believe we need to remember the paradoxical power in mutual vulnerability. Where there is doubt, the authority of certainty is put aside, but the capacity to hear is heightened. We broken ones, then, are not people who shout and stride, confident that our cause is just. But we listen, and we limp. In our limping we may discover that we walk with others who also limp and that even our enemies know pain. That sudden "eureka" when we recognize a fellow human being where once we'd seen only the delusions of our monstrous imaginings is a miraculous moment. As Jacob said on returning to Esau, that moment is like looking on the face of God. If we cannot have such moments, if we cannot risk ever being weak, if we are unable to seek to understand an opposing position, we must admit our blindness to that other's reality. And a cause born in such blindness cannot presume to be just.

The injunction to love and to attend the enemy has puzzled us for generations. With the holocausts in Europe and in Japan and with

2,000 years of Christanity behind us, many of us have gone through the collapse of our faith. We suspect that the commandment to love the enemy, to hear the enemy, to care for the enemy, was an impossible command, and has never matched the power of the will to win and to conquer. In the light of our awareness of the human capacity for evil we are bewildered and confounded. Some of us, at some primitive level, experience that bewilderment as a sense of divine abandonment, and, though we might not admit it out loud, we still secretly wonder whether there might not be some higher power to which we can address our longing and our despair.

Feminist theologian Rosemary Reuther tells us that each of us must discover for ourselves the secret key to divine abandonment – that God has abandoned divine power completely and utterly into the human condition that we may not abandon each other.

In other words, the secret is that within the reality of our universal inadequacy, uncertainty and blindness lies a limitless capacity to reach out to one another, to hold one another, a limitless energy, a limitless empowerment which is available and accessible directly in our finite limited condition.

I dare to believe that this is true.

In that midnight moment when the compass of our hearts points to vengeance and the will to ill, we have available to us the fiery weaponry of prayer. Whether we err or fail in our causes, we can abandon ourselves to the transforming and miraculous power of an utterly unlimited and terrifying love. We can limp triumphantly in the certitude that as we entrust ourselves to that love, we will be transformed, enemies will become friends and the just cause of love will yet be won.

The trouble with that statement is that although I believe in it fervently, it is an abstraction. And what draws us together is not sermon, but story. Who are you? Who am I? What is your cause? What is mine?

It was suggested that I tell you about my identity as a Japanese Canadian. The burden of that particular identity is a heavy one for me these days. My experience of the Japanese Canadians, especially in the last several months, is of a vastly and profoundly disparate and broken people. David Suzuki tells me flatly that there is no Japanese-Canadian community.

Many Nisei, like myself, who suffered the drawn-out trauma of racial prejudice during our formative and young adult years have a deep timidity burned into our psyches with the injunction that we must never again congregate, never again risk the visibility of community. Perhaps as a result, no "Japan-town" exists anywhere in Canada today.

The Sansei, the children of the Nisei, are the most vocal and fearless in their belief that Canada is best served by a full exposure of Japanese-Canadian history. They have a tenacious faith that democratic and open dialogue is possible among Japanese Canadians.

Apart from the Nisei and the Sansei, there are a dwindling number of aged and dying Issei, the ones who suffered the most measurable trauma and who today are, of all Japanese Canadians, the ones most abused, forgotten and politically powerless. These are the pioneers who with their lives and limbs cleared Canadian forests and created farms, established mines, businesses and fishing industries, built churches and community halls and infused this land with their gentle dignity and their endurance. They still endure – without the comfort and care that other aging Canadians take for granted.

One by one, I have heard graphic and horrible stories of Issei in white nursing homes who, unable to adjust to the radically different diets, die within days or an average of a month or two. Facilities and assistance are desperately needed, but not one Japanese-Canadian nursing home or hospital any longer exists across this entire country. What does this speak of? It speaks of a people who are weak, separated and broken and have not been able to unite on this most crucial need. It speaks of a governmental bureaucracy that has been unable to enter into substantial dialogue with that brokenness and to assist it. No single group in Canada has been so plundered and abused by officialdom as the Issei. That same officialdom today is implicated in this ongoing victimization.

To speak of one endeavour alone, a group of professional people in Toronto concerned for the Issei there approached the government's Central Mortage and Housing Corporation in 1976 for assistance in developing a nursing home and were rejected outright. They then applied to the provincial government for nursing home licences as an alternative. From 1976 to 1982 they were shunted from department to department until in desperation they abandoned their approach and decided to seek assistance for a geriatric complex instead. This application is on file at CMHC and is yet waiting to be reviewed.

As a Canadian I am embarrassed by my country's bureaucratic racism at home and its condemnation of racism in other countries, by its failure to name its many crimes against Japanese Canadians in the past or to face its wrong in the present. As a Canadian I am identified

with this country's act of destroying the Japanese-Canadian community and demanding that they never again speak as a people or with a
united voice. I'm also identified with this government's current
demand that this people which is scattered now miraculously speak
with one united voice. Whether this demand will work for good or
for ill among us is yet to be known.

If I were a white Canadian I might fear the resurrection of a
Japanese-Canadian voice. I might fear that it would besmirch our
Canadian image or cast aspersions on the good names of our political
leaders in the past. And if I were a white British Columbian I might
find lurking in my heart the fierce thought that the boats, homes, lush
farms, businesses, factories, industries, mines and artifacts which
once belonged to Japanese Canadians must be forever secured for
my white children and my white grandchildren – not theirs.

As a Japanese Canadian, I am caught in the pain and the furor of a
divided people struggling to be heard, struggling with the urgency of
attending the needs of the Issei, struggling with a bureaucracy whose
concern for efficiency exceeds the concern for a people's suffering –
a bureaucracy that seems at times to support rapacious policies
aimed at dividing, conquering and silencing minority groups.

Japanese Canadians are a minority among minorities, minute in
numbers but of a great symbolic significance at home and interna-
tionally. There was a time when I believed that a people who had
suffered in a particular or unique way faced a particular responsibility. But I no longer think that that form of uniqueness and special-
ness applies to any one group. Rather, I now feel that the calling to
liberation is universal and individual. Each person and each group,
no matter what their identity or what their cause, has a special and
particular responsibility to follow the direction of that uncompromis-
ing compass within that points to health. It ignores what is popular,
or what will simply win, or what will give us short-term ease and fill
our bellies. Beyond our doubt and confusion lies our capacity to
recognize what suffering is and where health lies and to identify with
both. I believe that it is the identification of, and with, suffering at
every level, in every condition and in every person that magnetizes
the compass of justice and points us to home.

As a Japanese Canadian I would plead that the suffering of the
Issei be immediately attended to by swift and practical acts of compassion. Let it not be said of our country that we preached democracy and practised racism until the very last Issei died. Not only Vancouver and Toronto and Southern Alberta, but wherever they were

forcibly flung into isolation across Canada, there is need of appropriate health care, extended home care services, nursing homes and financial assistance to local groups that are working to help the Issei. I would plead that the very best Canada has to offer be granted to the Issei, in their homes, wherever they are or wherever they wish to be, that the few who are left may find some comfort and joy in their last days. In our deeply troubled times, their peace would be small beacons of hope that the conscience of Canada towards the Issei was not completely extinguished.

As for the rest of us, the Nisei, the Sansei, and others – the sheep, the wolves and the shepherds – we are in a time of ferment as the world of conscience and consensus pertaining to questions of redress struggles to be spoken. We are weak, we are easily tyrannized, we are factionalized and fractured in our hearts. But I believe that if we keep our eyes on the reality of those who suffer most among us, we can cut through the corruption that rages in times like these – when power struggles with power. Instead of using the Issei and their compliance as pawns for quick and easy political ends, instead of declaring their urgency as an excuse to eliminate and forestall the wholesome process of dialogue, we should maintain the clarity of our distinct and separate needs so that neither the Issei nor the rest should be deprived of healing.

It should not be required of Japanese Canadians to bear any further burdens of suffering arising from crimes committed against us. But my experience is that we are suffering now, and we are surrounded by a sense of the enemy.

In naming our enemies, I believe we should begin from that which is most knowable – the enemy in our own hearts. When we can see clearly the face of the enemy within, I believe we can more accurately identify the enemy on the outside – in the community, the country and the planet.

I am aware of three enemies, three fears that I have been facing recently. First I have been tyrannized by the simple need to be liked. It has been one of the most painful experiences of my life to have been publicly vilified, lied about and identified by some Japanese Canadians as an enemy of Japanese Canadians because of my belief in the need for a democratic and open dialogue among us. My fear of being further vilified drove me into silence and withdrawal.

My second fear arose from an awareness of blindness – from my fear of being unable to see or recognize the friend within the ones who name me as an enemy. This sense of the Japanese-Canadian enemy of Japanese Canadians fosters a course that is factionalizing and self-devouring, and we are in danger of doing irreparable harm to that unseen Japanese-Canadian friend that hides within the perceived Japanese-Canadian enemy. This second fear also drove me to public silence.

But my third fear was that by silence I would be bowing down to the tyranny of fear itself. By silence, I could be a collaborator in chaos, guilty of inaction where action was required. So I am speaking publicly now about these matters for the first time and with no small terror, for I still fear the vilification and I still fear my own incomplete knowing.

During this time I have discovered the sickly taste of that seductive and corrupting drug that oozes through the heart, the will to win. Where, I am wondering, is the antidote to that drug that threatens to destroy us all.

I know that before our collective story is ended, we will all be requiring of ourselves and of each other forgivenesses of many kinds. It behooves us then to wield the weaponry of our truths with great caution.

In this our not-yet-completed storytelling time, I believe the strong from within us should be silent that the weakness from within might speak. As we move towards the naming of our public friends and our public enemies, I trust and believe that the energy for healing, for reconciliation, for forgiveness and for mutuality are endlessly, endlessly accessible to us. In our own Canadian and Japanese-Canadian backyards we can build countless missiles of hope. The tinier and more invisible those missiles, the greater their impact. With all my heart I believe in that explosive, atomic power for good that rockets through us as we pray.

Is there a just cause? We cannot all hear all the crying in the world. But I believe that when we listen, we can recognize specific voices calling us out of specific sufferings, and the voices that call our names are the ones to which we are each accountable.

NOTE

1 This article was presented originally to the Canadian Caucus on Human Rights, December 1983.

Moving Heaven and Earth

Elizabeth Richards

FEMINISM IS OFTEN described as a process, whereas peace is more often than not described as the end of a process. We hold it up as the goal that we are working towards, the result of a long struggle. After seven years of involvement in that struggle, I am convinced that this interpretation of peace is too limiting. Certainly, peace is an ideal. But it is equally a process. It is the means we employ to realize an ideal. As the Quakers say: "There is no way to peace. Peace is the way." If we attempt to impose universal parameters, we run the risk of arguing over semantics. Academics in the field of peace research have debated definitions of peace for decades, resulting on occasion in major splits in the community. When peace researcher Johan Galtung popularized the notion that the word "violence" implies more than simply the kind of violence imposed by weapons, he broadened the debate considerably. If violence includes social injustices such as poverty and racism, then its antithesis, peace, is also broad and inclusive. Some academics questioned whether the word "peace" should be used to define the field anymore. Peace studies, they argued, should be confined to the study of war and alternatives to war.

Although disagreements are often constructive and can motivate people to think more critically about an issue, the problem with disagreements about peace is that they are accompanied by self-righteousness. Will the person who knows what *real* peace is please stand up? I have resisted the temptation to ask that question at conferences, and what prevented me was the fear that nearly everyone in the room would stand up. In retrospect, an even greater apprehension was that everyone would stand up while I remained sitting. The more I worked for peace and read about it, the less I knew and the more ignorant I felt.

Fortunately, I have friends who admit to being just as ignorant as me, and we got together to discuss why it is that we still didn't understand peace after all those years. One of the first things we discussed was the role that fear played in motivating our initial involvement in the peace movement. Looking back over my first years of peace work, I can see that they were motivated almost entirely by fear: fear of nuclear war, fear of the future, fear of being alone, fear of failure. Added to that was a hefty dose of anger and frustration over wars and poverty and myriad other injustices in the world. In short, the fire of my inspiration was negative emotion. And it took me a long time to admit it.

I can thank my involvement in the peace movement for forcing me to confront that negative emotion, and to learn how to transform it into constructive action. I have learned to appreciate "peace," and to appreciate my own ignorance because it is a stimulant to personal development. If one approaches peace as a process that entails personal as well as social change, then it is interactive and dynamic and alive. But along the way to that realization one has to leave behind the corpses of a number of fears. Perhaps some people accomplish that task gracefully, but in my case the process was as graceful as falling down an abandoned mine shaft.

The experience of discovering my own "peace," of discovering the pool of diamonds at the bottom of that mine shaft, was even more traumatic than the experience of becoming a woman. I still don't know why exactly, but I'm working at it. In the meantime, the only peace offering I can make is to share my personal story, with the understanding that there are probably others who have had similar experiences. I hope that we can learn from each other.

Although I had been working full-time on peace issues for a few years, the real work began as the result of a dream I had in 1984. In the dream, I was floating above the earth's surface and observing the aftermath of a nuclear explosion that had occurred on the west coast of the United States. What I can describe only as "spirits of life" – hazy forms of people, animals, trees, and even lakes and land masses – formed undulating clouds which swirled above the surface of the earth and emitted a haunting, mournful sound.

The feeling was so real, I awoke with the sensation that I had heard, tasted, and smelled a nuclear explosion. As I dressed and rushed around my apartment in search of papers and documents to take to work, I couldn't stop crying. My inclination was to accept the dream at face value and then forget about it as soon as possible. On a conscious level I did forget it, almost immediately. But something else was operating on an unconscious level.

I was building up a potentially explosive internal arsenal. For some time my life had revolved around nuclear war. Obsessed with it, I spent all my time thinking it, reading it, writing it, and supposedly working to prevent it. Rarely did I stop to question what might happen if we actually achieved this thing we chanted in slogans and demanded of governments, this thing called "peace."

I understood that weapons of mass destruction had rendered war obsolete because "victory" is meaningless. But what can realistically replace war? Nations were built with it and protected by it, and war predated nation-states by a long shot. I asked Gwynne Dyer, who had completed an excellent TV series about war, whether he would make a documentary about peace someday. "How can I document something which doesn't exist?" he asked. When I stopped to think about it, peace was a concept even more frightening than war. At least I understood war. Peace was the unknown, and the possibility of attaining it was becoming more and more remote.

I was working on a peace campaign for the Labour Council of Metropolitan Toronto at the time. The knowledge that I was advocating the abolition of nuclear weapons and war but had no idea what to replace them with made me feel that I was deceiving myself and others. I realized that even the films I used to "educate" people about disarmament contained little more than weapon counts and scenarios of nuclear war – describing in detail what we would like to avoid, not what we would like to create.

Five months into the campaign I took a vacation to try to sort things out. I travelled to Manitoulin Island in Lake Huron, where I have stayed every summer since I was a child. When I was about 10 I decided that Manitoulin Island was the place I'd run away to when a nuclear war occurred. That was during the Cuban Missile Crisis, when we kept transistor radios in our school desks to listen to news, and naively organized emergency escape plans during recess. Years later, when the arsenal inside was ready to explode, it was indeed Manitoulin that I escaped to.

The morning after I arrived I was swept up in a state of emotional trauma that would be pointless to describe. Suffice it to say that I let go of a lot of pent-up grief and anger, so much that I felt numb for several days. But, most important, I experienced a heightened sense of awareness of everything around me, as if a filter that had separated my perception from reality had lifted. I began to see things and people differently. Above all, I was able to see how I had deceived myself, and especially how I had used the peace movement as a vehicle to avoid making peace with myself. I began to write poetry to help clarify a jumble of new ideas and feelings.

The first poem was inspired by a meeting with a leading European peace activist who for years had been a role model for many of us. When I met her in person, I was able to see that Petra Kelly was using her activities in the peace movement partly to avoid resolving some internal wars. The only reason I was able to perceive her dilemma was because Petra unintentionally held up a mirror in which I saw a reflection of myself. After meeting her I wrote a poem that expressed my disappointment. The poem was not written about Petra, however. I had sought out a personal hero who made no attempt to hide her vulnerability. In all fairness, Petra was merely an innocent victim of my circuitous path to Self.

SEX IS JUST POLEMIC SLEEPING WITH APOLOGY
I found you in the dark with your back to the door;
This is the price of fame, you said,
hiding in obscurity

And looking in your eyes, I see
the Revolution lives in fear of itself,
paying dues for being born middle class
and starving for affection

You file yourself at night in a suitcase
packed with folded fantasy and flesh,
No Time, you said
No Time, you repeated

Burn-out is holy absolution for the true believer
It's politically correct to hold your breath
until your face turns blue

I knelt down on my knees in that Bonn café
while we planned another war on war,
and prayed they keep the future burning
while we prey upon the ashes of our past.

Gradually the poetry became less vitriolic, and when the initial mass of emotion was explored, digested, and swept away, I felt prepared to rejoin the peace movement with a new perspective. From then on, my direction was to be towards peace, not war. If I was going to be obsessed with anything, it was the desire to search for alternatives to war and to push my intellect "beyond the bomb." One of the first steps in this new journey was to explore feminism.

My understanding of feminism was entirely subjective. I was unfamilar with its history, literature or philosophy. I sought out a knowledgeable friend who could provide some insight, and together we decided to research a proposal for a radio documentary, tentatively called "Feminism and Peace." Our immediate objective was to agree on a definition of feminism, hoping this would provide a perspective to bring "peace" down to earth. With this goal in mind, I travelled to a conference on feminism and peace in Rome. Contrary to my expectations, I did not discover a definition of feminism there. What I did discover was no less illuminating.

In attendance were women from developing nations, wealthy women who owned law firms and ran for political office, women who spent their time knitting flowers to decorate fences around military bases, rich feminists, poor feminists, socialist feminists and radical feminists. Within a few hours, it became obvious that aside from being women, we did not have much in common. Some of us tried to conform to whichever ideology was apparently leading the day. Others rebelled.

When several women swayed in a circle in a symbolic gesture to "matriarchal goddesses," a trade unionist from West Germany expressed bemused discomfort.

Another woman said women who are "tough" and resist such displays of sentimentality are "really men." She backed that up by stating that Margaret Thatcher and the late Indira Gandhi are also men, but "even worse because they're against disarmament." "What could possibly be worse than men?" I asked. She thought I was serious. I thought I was making a joke. If one takes this theory to its ultimate conclusion, I thought, the solution to inequality as well as war would be to ensure that everyone conforms to standard genitalia, preferably female. But what about the women who are "really men?" If on-site verification in the arms race is controversial, it would be devastating in a sex race.

A number of women considered the matter of gender biological. Women can bear children and are the "mothers of society," which makes them "closer to the earth" than men. I wonder if that makes those women who are more interested in mothering a book than a child sexual deviants. I do not have children – not because I don't want children, but simply because I don't *have* children. Does that make me less "nurturing" than a mother? A number of sons have mothers who "nurture" them into joining the army, precisely because they feel the military protects their near and dear. Oddly enough, the conference provoked a sense of relief that feminism and peace cannot be precisely defined. What disturbed me was the realization that those who preach tolerance and flexibility often practise the opposite, making war with peace.

Peace activists, for the most part, point out that relations between peoples should not be "them versus us" and that we must cease to blame or stereotype. Feminists, for the most part, demand equality and point out that hierarchical structures are inherently unproductive and unfair. I therefore found it difficult to swallow the idea that men are the enemy. It goes without saying that men dominate the military and that women are generally underprivileged. But women in industrialized nations are generally less underprivileged than many men in developing nations, and women in those nations are possibly most underprivileged. Within the spectrum of feminist analysis one naturally would expect a parallel range of views regarding the focus and emphasis of feminist action.

Similarly, "peace" has a variety of meanings depending on historical, linguistic or cultural contexts. In Latin the word "peace" implies the notion of order; in Sanskrit it means mental tranquillity; and according to Webster's it means simply the absence of war. Even if we confined the definition of peace to the notion of warlessness, there is no one accepted means to achieve that end. Although comparing definitions of peace can be an exercise in superficiality, it is nonetheless important to guard against imposing Western values on the rest of the world. However, if we accept the notion that peace and feminism are concerned with process and understanding more than with absolute truths, then I am confident that intolerance can be avoided or overcome.

The conference in Rome provided me with yet another inspiration, and an apprehension. Pacifist and feminist movements are largely transnational. To a limited extent, they illustrate the "global society" many of us would like to realize. Nation-states are today's primary war-waging sociopolitical organizations. It is possible that transnational movements are a stepping-stone towards ending nation-state wars. It would be a mistake, however, to assume that ending nation-state wars would solve our problems. Nation-states could be replaced by other boundaries based on adversarial relations, be they racial, sexual, or twenty-second-century tribal. It was Einstein who predicted that World War IV would be fought with sticks and stones.

The Chinese have a saying: "A journey of a thousand miles begins with one step." And Japanese Buddhists say "If you want to see the moon over Kamakura, do not stop on the last mile." But no one has made up lovely sayings about the middle parts of journeys. Beginnings and ends are interesting; middles are boring. We focus a great deal on envisioning the end, on the extremes of nuclear holocaust versus a world that lives in peace and security. In Christian mythology the Earth lies somewhere between heaven and hell. People lie somewhere between peace and war. It is time to focus our attention on the middle and examine the *means* we are employing to achieve the ends we desire.

I returned home from Italy without any answers. Although this prevented me from writing a documentary on feminism and peace, I was far from disappointed. I gained instead a host of new questions which have since led to still more. Perhaps there are no "answers," but merely new and more challenging questions. British historian E.P. Thompson ended a talk on peace by suggesting that "it may be poetry that we will need most of all." I tend to agree.

REFERENCES

Dyer, G. *War.* New York: Crown, 1985.

Galtung, J. *The True Worlds: A Transnational Perspective.* New York: Free Press, 1980.

Galtung, J. "Twenty-Five Years of Peace Research: Ten Challenges and Some Responses." *Journal of Peace Research* 22, no. 2 (1985), pp. 141-58.

From Kitchen to Global Politics:
The Women of Greenham Common

Shelly Romalis

WOMEN IN CLASS societies have traditionally been on the margins of political action, and the form their protest takes is often unconventional and imaginative, incorporating the emotional and the personal. The Greenham Common peace camp in Berkshire, England, crystallizes many of the contradictions about women and peace. Greenham has become an international symbol and a focus for the women's peace movement. I joined a Greenham support group and became involved as a peace activist while on sabbbatical in England during 1983 / 84. In May 1984, I returned to England to study the network more closely. Although I had known about the camp, media coverage in Canada was scarce, and I had no idea if it still existed. And I had no knowledge of the extent of the women's network which supported Greenham.

The Greenham Common Peace Camp began in December 1981, when forty women and a few men and children walked to Greenham from Cardiff, Wales, and chained themselves to the high wire fence encircling the military base. Their purpose was to protest the lack of media interest in antinuclear issues. Although the base is officially labelled RAF Greenham Common, everyone knows it is a U.S. air base. Its nine-mile fence encloses self-sufficient living quarters for large numbers of British and American soldiers and their families, as well as housing nuclear missiles and other military hardware. Women in the peace camp named the nine access gates for the colours of the rainbow, then set up camps outside the gates.

Greenham was to be the site of ninety-six of the more than four hundred Cruise missiles NATO planned to deploy in Europe. A number of missiles arrived in November 1983, despite serious attempts by the Greenham women to sabotage their delivery.

Although the women suffered a terrible loss of morale, the camp continues. There may be as few as ten women, three on a cold wet winter weekday; numbers increase on weekends. In summer, visitors flock there from all over Europe and North America. Babies have been born at the camp; children play; flowers and vegetables are grown. Life on the perimeter is active, a vivid contrast to the deadly weapons and stark landscape on the inside. The women weave spider-web symbols and paint flowers on the fence. They cut holes in the wire and "trespass," stage theatrical actions (a Hallowe'en party) inside the fence, dance on the silos on New Year's Eve, and organize large-scale actions in which thousands of women hold hands around the perimeter of the base and sing.

Everyday life at the camp is extremely difficult. The women suffer daily evictions by bailiffs sent from the nearest town of Newbury. They are no longer allowed to construct dwellings on the land. Tents and lean-tos have replaced the once-common polyethylene "benders." There is no running water except for one standpipe at the main (yellow) gate. The women rotate on night-watch in order to scrutinize the Cruise deployment exercises and inform their networks.

Those who camp permanently at Greenham are only a fraction of those who call themselves "Greenham Women." Throughout Britain, women belong to groups that visit their favourite gate on weekends, deliver food and firewood, organize local demonstrations (singing at a local supermarket, leafleting, staging mock funerals), raise money for the camp and their own activities, and participate in actions at the camp itself. They come from different age groups (teenagers to grandmothers), social classes and political backgrounds, and vary in marital status and sexual preference. The media have sensationalized the lesbians, the punks and the freaks, but Greenham defies stereotyping. As a place and as a symbol, it has been tremendously effective in organizing women across classes and political lines and focusing their concerns for peace.

The women feel that Greenham, as a women-only camp, provides them with a place to be themselves and build confidence. They claim that in mixed camps, men are more vocal and dominating, and women assume more traditional helpmate roles. The women want to make decisions by consensus rather than by majority. They feel less likely to be victims of police harassment or violence in all-women than in mixed groups. (In fact, they have been subjected to harassment of all kind – from local intruders, residents of the town, and the police.) Men have functioned as babysitters during actions at Greenham and during local group meetings. They are quietly tolerated as day visitors, but are never welcome to stay overnight at the camp or accompany the women on peace actions.

Greenham's detractors feel that this exclusivity further divides an

already factionalized peace movement and ignores the deep involvement of many men in peace issues. They feel men could contribute
to Greenham in a more active way. Some feminists have denounced
Greenham's single-minded antinuclear focus, convinced that it
diverts the attention of large numbers of women from more immediate issues of sexism, poverty and racism. Others feel that the
glorification of motherhood, combined with a commitment to nonviolence and personal sacrifice, ultimately serves the military effort by
encouraging passivity in women. Still others are concerned that the
ideology and methods of nonviolence and the use of dramatic techniques trivialize the issues. They see the women's behaviour as con-
forming to traditional role expectations and thus perpetuating institutions and values that underlie gender inequality and women's subordination.

I would argue, however, that Greenham has been a powerful
force in undermining traditionalism in Britain. Women who have
never before thought in political terms, who have been isolated from
others, are now beginning to understand the relationship between
the economy, militarism and sexism. A woman coming to Greenham
to make a simple statement about the importance of home and family soon finds herself part of an engulfing process, discussing media
coverage, governments' military strategies, plans of Greenham
actions, and peace activities in other parts of the world. She would
hear about arrests, police harrassment, court procedures and prison
sentences, all of which she might eventually experience. She might
travel to other peace camps, or to conferences, and be exposed to literature produced by the European peace network. A woman's initially superficial involvement with Greenham can thus be the beginning of an educational process involving a new consciousness of
national and international politics.

The apparently nonproblematic focus on "peace" provides
women with an opportunity to consolidate ideas and branch out to
other issues. One Greenham support group has adopted a women's
school in Ethiopia and sends the school money, work tools, clothng
and household items. This movement from kitchen to global politics
is a common one for women. Resistance to or struggles against injustice are likely to begin at home (e.g., food strikes) and become
related to larger issues.

My own association with Greenham has had a profound influence
on my life. It has made me intensely aware of how resourceful the
powerless can be. I have learned how consensus decision making

works – how disagreements are chewed over towards a common understanding of the larger issues. Greenham has forced me to confront my own fears and feelings of impotence, and to come to terms with feelings of guilt that I wasn't "doing enough." Struggling with the splits between my academic and activist, rational and emotional selves, I have learned what I have in common with a whole spectrum of women whom I would otherwise never have met. Many have become very dear friends. Perhaps most important, Greenham has contributed to a sense of optimism regarding the value and role of women's collective action and solidarity.

Greenham Common as a source of peace education emerges uniquely out of British society. In Europe, war isn't an abstraction – everyone has experienced a personal loss. Moreover, Britain is a highly politicized country whose people are acutely aware of discrepancies in class and power. It has a history of pacifist movements which contrasts with its military tradition. In Canada, as in the rest of North America, we have not experienced a modern war on our soil. Our cities have never been bombed. Our huge size gives us a false sense of security. Although we have many kinds of peace organizations and even peace camps (on Parliament Hill in Ottawa; at Nanoose on Vancouver Island), they attract little public attention and minimal media coverage. Peace activists are seen as an alarmist fringe whose efforts are both irrelevant and unnecessary. The reality is that nuclear war (whether by deliberate decision or accident) and the potential of nuclear accidents are ever-present dangers. Sophisticated technology (Star Wars) is being madly developed by military contractors who have a vested interest in the execution of new projects. This, we know, rather than protecting us, increases the chances of world destruction.

Greenham Common cannot be re-created in Canada, nor can the peace network here remotely resemble the British one. It is extremely difficult, given the size of this country and the distances between population centres, to keep track of peace activities in one's own city, let alone other provinces. Greenham can be a symbol and a source of inspiration to the Canadian peace movement. The message from its existence, and from the relentless efforts of the women connected to it, is that small-scale resistance is vital. Keeping track of Cruise exercises or demonstrating that an air base is vulnerable to terrorists makes it that much more difficult for the process to run smoothly, for militarism to accomplish its tasks.

Greenham's other message to Canadian women is that we must

be engaged in continuous consciousness-raising regarding the social structures that promote oppression and how we can resist them. We should move towards exposing militarism's link to oppression and inequality by designing new programs in peace studies, by incorporating peace issues in our courses and in our scholarly efforts and by bringing together our political and academic concerns.

This article was based on a talk given in 1986. By the terms of the Intermediate Nuclear Force Agreement, signed in the spring of 1988, Cruise missiles are being removed from Greenham. The women have vowed to remain at the base until the last missile is gone and are urging a return of the common land to the public. The women are aware, however, that the treaty covers only a minute percentage of the strike force and that militarization is still a major problem. At this time some women are still camping at Greenham while some are moving to other bases in Britain. The support groups continue to plan and carry out demonstrations remaining active in their struggle against militarism and its consequences.

A Power We Have Been Taught to Bury[1]

Janice Williamson

THE ACTION

November 14, 1983, was a day of resistance for women nuclear protesters in Toronto. It was a day of reclamation of our power as women – a power we have been taught to bury. Our reclamation enabled us to demonstrate our resistance to Litton Systems' participation in the largest build-up of nuclear weapons in history; a build-up which is making companies like Litton Systems rich.

On that day, two hundred women sang, danced and read poetry outside the gates of Litton's management building. Yellow police barricades and lines of officers protected Litton from us. Twenty-nine women attempted to make a citizens' arrest of the president (Ronald Keating) and the corporate management for violating the Criminal Code of Canada.

– Sara Adams,
a defendant in the trial
and an active member
of Women's Action for Peace,
Our Times, March 1984.

THE LITTON ACTION of November 14, 1983, was my first political act of nonviolent civil disobedience. Two days before, my commitment as a feminist and anguish over the proposed testing of the Cruise missile had led me to participate in a day-long nonviolence training session organized by Women's Action for Peace. Originally I had planned to provide support during the action for those women committed to making their citizens' arrest, but, as Pamela Millar was to say during our trial, "For many of us, the revolution begins at the fence." As the women began their difficult progress towards the Litton management building, I took a few deep breaths, abandoned my pack, asked for a lift up and was catapulted over the fence.

On the other side, a chorus of twenty-nine female voices

addressed the assembled fifty or so police officers, two on horse-back, many of them policewomen. We requested that the police assist us in our arrest of the Litton executives for their participation in a variety of "crimes against humanity" including conspiracy to commit mass murder, fraud, possession of a dangerous weapon, making and storing an explosive substance and advocating genocide. The police did not offer assistance but instead charged us with petty trespass, and we were unceremoniously dragged to waiting police vans.

This was the first of three days of civil disobedience during the November week of resistance. In all, 127 women and men were arrested protesting Litton's production of the guidance system for the Cruise missile. After two court hearings several weeks later, the second judge would grant us the right to group trials and set three trial dates according to our day of arrest. The largest trial of women would begin February 20, 1984.

THE TRIAL

Outside Etobicoke Courtroom 208 on Monday, February 20, 1984, a list of defendants was tacked to the wall: Sara Adams, Kari Brown, Sharon Chimming, Helen Durie, Susan Dyment, Deborah Ellis, Kathie Froelick, Margaret Hancock, Teresa Hibbert, Colleen Howe, Leeann Irwin, Lorree Lawrence, Rosalee Martin, Pamela Millar, Vicki Miller, Carol Milligan, Susan Milwid, Mary Moon, Wendy Moore, Ruth McMurchy, Nancy Prescott, Emily Smith, Marlene Tadman, Pamela Tadman, Nancy Watts, Janice Williamson, Sarah Winterton, Martha Waldon, Maria Louladakis. Twenty-nine defendants were charged under the Ontario Provincial Trespass to Property Act and faced a maximum penalty of a $1,000 fine and two years' probation. The defendants came from Montreal, London, Ottawa, Kingston and upper New York state, so it was left to the Toronto members to act as agents and represent those from out of town. For two months a small group had met to organize our defence. Lawyer Marion Cohen participated as legal counsel and resource person. One of the defendants, Pamela Millar, in the midst of her bar exams, was to provide her research skills. The rest of the group had little or no experience with the court system.

We agreed to have a collective counsel which would rotate according to trial day and purpose. Thus, several defendants were assigned to work with our expert witnesses in developing their testimony. Martha Waldon consulted with engineer and peace activist Dr. Ursula Franklin of the University of Toronto; Wendy Moore developed testimony with Sister Rosalie Bertell, an international expert on the effects of radiation; and I questioned sociologist Dr. Dorothy Smith of OISE. Teresa Hibbert, Pamela Millar, Marion Cohen and I remained as counsel throughout the week, while several of the defendants, including mother and daughter Marlene and Pamela Tadman, represented themselves and cross-examined each other. Midway through the first day of the trial, before Justice of the Peace Bernard Gottleib, the Crown finished presenting its case. Prosecutor Diane McAleer called three policemen, one policewoman and Litton security services manager Ronald Peterson to the stand. Elaborate descriptions of the fencing around the Litton management building and sometimes contradictory testimony as to the events of November 14 followed. In our cross-examination of Peterson we established that Litton was in production that day, that the Litton management offices were indeed located at 1 Cityview Drive in Rexdale, where we were arrested, and that Litton had been contracted to produce the guidance system for the Cruise.

Testimony from seventeen defendants and our three expert witnesses followed. Kari Brown told the court that "to speak of going over the fence belittled the purpose of why we were there." And, when the Crown questioned me on the stand about whether I knew I was on private property, I appealed to Gottleib, noting that these technical issues had nothing to do with my presence at Litton. "Feminism taught us the difference between the language of science and technology versus the language of politics and ethics [I silently thanked feminist theorist Sandra Harding for this formulation]. If we had intended to debate technicalities we would have come to court with surveyors, cartographers, fence builders and pole vaulters as expert witnesses." Gottleib allowed me to continue.

Each of the defendants described how she attempted to enter the management building by a variety of daring means – "jumping," "leaping," "flying over the fence." As the trial progressed, the defence counsel agreed with the Crown that to expedite the proceedings our defendants needn't describe the details of their arrest, but should restrict their testimony to the motivation and beliefs which led them to participate in the action at Litton. This agreement signified a radical reversal of any previous trial proceedings concerned with civil disobedience at Litton, where defendants were either refused or badgered by the prosecutor when their testimony strayed from evidence directly related to the charge of trespass. In addition, none of the other trials were to allow all of the defence counsel's expert witnesses to speak. The previous week's group trial had been marked by a particularly unthinking and callous incident. Hiroshima survivor and peace activist Setsuko Thurlow was refused permission to speak on the effects of nuclear war because, while she might have "some interesting stories to tell," her first-hand experience was not "expert" knowledge.

Was it the novelty of our feminist defence, the collective defence counsel, the benevolent curiosity of Gottleib, or a combination of the above which enabled us to proceed with a thoroughly political trial? Defendants throughout the week explained the philosophy of nonviolent disobedience and analyzed patriarchy. "Mad old men run government: cruise protester" headlined the Thursday, February 23 *Toronto Star* article detailing Vicki Miller's testimony that "a group of mad old men are conspiring against the planet and our species." When Gottleib became defensive about men who, like himself, opposed nuclear arms, it was carefully explained to him the difference between "masculist" and masculine. We were not suggesting that *all* men supported war preparations and *all* women opposed them.

However, Dr. Dorothy Smith pointed to the minimal role women play in political decision making and the qualitative difference this exclusion makes in our culture. While military strategists speak statistically of the projected number of dead in a nuclear war, women have been socialized to relate to the individual body as sister, as brother, as mother, friend, lover, father, child – not as an empty cipher in an endless column of numbers. Defendants also pointed out that women make up the majority of the poor in Canada and are less capable in economic terms of effecting social change. The economic picture expanded when we pointed out that one-half of the world's population, 2 billion people, live on a total income equivalent to world military expenditures. The international perspective was developed by Marlene Tadman, who discussed how women and men in Central American liberation struggles were battling mercenaries trained in camps constructed by a subsidiary of Litton's American parent company.

In order to prove our defence of necessity we had to point to the "imminent peril" which we face. Dr. Ursula Franklin described the Cruise as "different in kind, unmanned, undetectable since it travels at a low altitude." Its delivery system can be as commonplace as an ordinary truck. Martha Waldon reported on figures provided by the Cambridge Study Group on Nuclear Disarmament, which showed that 3,707 false alarms of a nuclear attack were recorded in an eighteen-month period from January 1979 to June 1980. Sister Rosalie Bertell pointed out Litton's participation in a history of nuclear production which has resulted in the damaging of 16 million people since nuclear production began in 1945. "The casualties have already begun in World War III and continue at the rate of two hundred per day."

When asked to describe her motivation for her civil disobedience, 17-year-old Nancy Jane Prescott testified that after pamphleting and demonstrating against Cruise testing, she had "not only a right, but a duty to go to Litton." Defendant Vicki Miller affirmed the same commitment. "Silence is complicity. I cannot be a part of those who commit the sins of omission. I felt I had to be there. I didn't have a choice."

By the end of the fourth day of testimony, a central question remained. Would Gottleib accept our challenge as outlined by defendant Hibbert: "We women refuse to maintain the cultural silence of the dispossessed. The challenge to the law is clear: Is it on the side of private corporations who make weapons for profit, or on the side of these defendants who pose their dissent and rationality against Litton's irrationality?"

THE FINAL ARGUMENTS

On the morning of Friday, February 24, the final stage of the trial began. The week had been long and demanding. Justice of the Peace Gottleib was sniffling with a cold, and several of us were struggling through various stages of flu. A few of us acting as agent and counsel worked most of Thursday night preparing our final arguments to the court. By now we had developed a complex series of six defences.

Our submissions began with Pamela Millar's presentation of detailed legal cases and precedents supporting our defences. She cited Canadian and U.S. law which justified our presence on Litton property to make our citizens' arrest of Keating. Documenting our second defence, she justified our interference in what we saw as Litton's "breach of the peace" in its production of the Cruise guidance system. Millar referred to our "common law defence of necessity" which justified our actions on the grounds that Litton's activities threatened us with serious harm and represented a far more serious criminal act than our simple petty trespass. My final argument developed this "defence of necessity," which is often presented in civil disobedience trials.

Earlier testimony by Sister Rosalie Bertell and Wendy Moore had introduced international law into the proceedings, and Hibbert developed this line of defence: "There are thirty-four traditional wars now being waged on this planet. The Nuremberg Principles established in 1946 by the British Parliament and adopted by the UN General Assembly, of which Canada is a member, prohibit the threat of or preparation for war. These principles of international law are binding on all citizens. Canada is breaking this law by funding the production of the guidance system and testing the Cruise." Hibbert then referred to our fifth defence, Section 7 of the Canadian Charter of Rights, which guarantees us "the right to life, liberty and security of the person," a right which is denied by the production of the Cruise and the threat of nuclear war.

Our sixth defence was detailed by Marion Cohen, who tackled the charges of trespass. According to Cohen, the Crown had failed to prove two crucial sections of the trespass act. First, the defendants were not, as required, "directed to leave its premises by an occupier of the premises or a person authorized by the occupier." In fact, defendant Brown had testified that she was "requested," not directed, to leave. The officer had asked, "Would you like to leave?" Brown replied, "No." And second, Cohen continued, the police were not properly authorized by Litton to direct us to leave in any event.

On hearing our final arguments, prosecutor McAleer asserted that she had proven that we had trespassed, and criticized our feminist defence. Ignoring much of the testimony, McAleer was puzzled that the issue of women's exclusion had been underplayed in our final submissions. And, misinterpreting our position, she complained that we didn't recognize the concern some men had shown about the threat of nuclear war. McAleer saw a contradiction between our reference to women's poverty and exclusion, and the presence of the more than one hundred women at Litton on November 14. "Weren't they free to act?" she asked. She wrapped up her argument with a plea to Gottlieb that an acquittal would give us "a ticket to do what we wished to do" and allow us to disregard "the force of law and how it must guide our everyday lives." However, her final comments indicated the growing ambivalence of her position. "There is no evidentiary basis to prove that Litton has produced a perilous situation. In five or ten years the situation may be different. As of today's date, no crime is being committed at Litton."

On this day of final submissions, the Metropolitan Toronto Police Department had provided the courtroom with a generous half-dozen police, compared with the one or two officers who had attended earlier in the week. All were armed, and carried protruding billy clubs. Was this their not-very-subliminal cue to the justice of the peace: "Make no mistake in your verdict. These are dangerous women"? When Gottleib thanked us all for our submissions and left the court until March 7 to consider his judgment, we wondered how he would process our defence. As we were to discover later, our consciousness-raising hadn't really proceeded beyond mezzanine level.

THE VERDICT
Our judgment day fell between two polarized events. On Tuesday, March 6, a Canadian Federal Court judge rejected Operation Dismantle's injunction against the testing of the Cruise, saying that there was no persuasive evidence that testing the guidance system would "jeopardize humanity or bring on nuclear holocaust." On March 8, we would celebrate International Women's Day.

On Wednesday, March 7, however, we all returned to Courtroom 208, where once again six armed police dotted the walls. Three more stood outside in the hall, deliberately lying and obstructing the entry of five of the defendants into the court until after the judgment had been read.

In his judgment, Gottleib praised the defendants for their "courtesy and cooperation," and thanked the three expert witnesses, who were "a delight to have in the court." He referred to the variety of our defences from "the Criminal Code, the Charter of Rights, the status of women, the effects of radiation, international law, and the defence of necessity,"presented "with sincerity and zeal by the defendants and agents." He didn't want "to divide issues on a gender basis," because statements like "the mad old men of government" were counterproductive. He noted the previous day's Canadian Federal Court decision supporting the Cruise test and quoted extensively from U.S. Supreme Court Justice Abe Fortes's pamphlet "Concerning Dissent and Civil Disobedience." According to Fortes, the American civil rights and antiwar movements were supported solely by legal protest and devoid of civil disobedience actions by hundreds of people. Gottleib assured the court that "most of us share the desire for peaceful existence and a nuclear-free world. But," he said, and here was the catch, "the charge concerns trespass at Litton." Thus, he found us guilty.

McAleer requested that we each be sentenced to a $250 fine and a year's probation. However, the defendants and agents responded with a number of counterproposals. Since women earn 62 percent of the male wage in Canada, Pam Millar suggested that we be fined 62 percent of the recent $50 fine given to the mixed-gender trial the week before. She continued, "The law required that we be found guilty, but justice doesn't require that we be punished." I pleaded for a symbolic $1 American (or 80 cents Canadian) fine to symbolize Canada's moral and economic servility to the U.S. and our participation in war preparations. The day before, Prime Minister Trudeau had announced with cynical duplicity that the testing of the Cruise missile did not make Canada a nuclear power. Marion Cohen pleaded that any probation would "chill the freedom of expression of the defendants about a very important issue." One cent was the fine suggested by Ruth McMurchy, who hoped the justice of the peace had "listened with his heart" to the testimony of the defendants. In his sentencing, Gottleib said that he did not doubt the sincerity of our beliefs or that we had acted out of conscience. He did not want to punish us, but to deter us from breaking the law. Therefore, he gave us all suspended sentences, except the three women arrested twice during the week of resistance, who were given fines of $50 each. However, we were all placed on six months' probation and assured that this would not restrict us from all legal expressions of political dissent.

Was this a victory? Although we weren't acquitted, Gottleib did listen to all of our testimony, and unlike the judges at the other trials, he accepted the submissions of our expert witnesses. Several weeks earlier, in the first group trial, another judge had fined each of the sixty-three defendants $75. And, in the same court, only hours after we were sentenced, Justice of the Peace Kashuba would refuse the defence testimony of four young members of the Peace Camp charged, like us, with petty trespass at Litton, and sentenced to two years' probation and fines of $300 to $500 each. Are we to believe that justice is not arbitrary?

For many of our defendants, a real victory would have been acquittal. Defendant Hibbert addressed Gottleib after the sentencing, interpreting the probation as "an admonishment, a punishment," not a deterrent. Central to Gottleib's guilty verdict was his refusal to "internalize" our defence and hear our plea that the manufacture of nuclear weapons poses an imminent danger to the world. Susan Milwid commented later that "our concerns were invalidated. We don't want to be in a situation of 'I told you so.' That's my greatest fear."

What was my response to the trial? Sarah Winterton described the justice of the peace as "a big father" who had listened to the "ladies," as he called us. For me, the trial *was* like a return to the patriarchal nuclear family. Black-robed, perched on his throne above the throng, Gottleib reigned over the courtroom. We were the dutiful daughters gone wrong. The Crown prosecutor (the queen?), like the nuclear family mother, expressed her divided affections, supporting from time to time the pleas of her daughters, but in the end upholding the law of the father.

These curious feelings were compounded by a sense of isolation. Once the trial begins, one struggles against alienation, even when working as a collective. Defendants are forced to respond to a specialized legal language in a public space which makes them the interloper watched over by billy-club- and pistol-wielding police. And, throughout the week of our trial, aside from a handful of close friends and family, few women from the feminist community appeared in the courtroom to show support. Perhaps this was a result of the out-of-the-way location of the courtroom, but more to the point it may be symptomatic of the controversial status of civil disobedience as a political strategy for change. Forgotten are history's women and men who risked more serious terms of imprisonment and physical harm in struggling for women's vote, improved working conditions and a nonracist life.

How would I evaluate my participation in the November action and our trial? Martin Luther King Jr. described how "nonviolent direct action seeks to create a crisis and foster such a tension that a community which has constantly refused to negotiate is forced to confront the issue." But this doesn't explain the revolution that occurred inside of me: what I learned about myself, group process, the legal system and the politics of this nuclear era. I echo Ruth McMurchy's response to our verdict: "The value of the action stands alone no matter what the judgment. It's always an educational experience for the person who goes through it, for the people around them, for the reporters and the people in the courtroom who are exposed to what we are doing and why we are doing it. But even if all that didn't happen, it would be important for me personally to keep doing it."

As we left the courtroom that day, a Canadian Defence Department spokesman announced that the Cruise testing is just the beginning, for "the United States has asked Canada to approve a new list of

military weapon tests which could include artillery equipment, helicopters, surveillance and identification systems, advanced non-
nuclear munitions, aircraft navigation systems and the guidance system for more advanced unarmed nuclear missiles." We are supposed
to feel consoled that the list does not include "tests for chemical and
biological weapons or armed nuclear weapons."

I return to my home south of Toronto's Junction Triangle, where
local residents have just learned that the Canadian General Electric
factory down the street is processing 550,000 tons of uranium a year
for Ontario Hydro in an area with more than 3,000 immediate residents. Our work – our revolution at the fence – has just begun.

AFTERWORD

During our trial we had been reminded by Gottleib that two legal
strategies, through the police and the courts, were available for us to
challenge Litton's production of the guidance system. While these
legal routes had been followed earlier and unsuccessfully by peace
activists, we decided to try again.

On May 5, 1984, fifty people travelled to 23 Division of the Metropolitan Toronto Police to collectively inform the police of Litton's
criminal activities and request an investigation. Two representatives
from our group were allowed to enter the station. The police were
shown a copy of the section in Litton's product manual which outlines the Cruise guidance system's capabilities as both a navigational
and a triggering device. While a photocopy is sufficient evidence for
police to act on, they insisted we bring them the original to prove
that Litton manufactured the guidance systems, a fact that not even
the courts had disputed the month before.

Our parallel strategy involved a meeting between Teresa Hibbert,
Martha Waldon and Justice of the Peace Gottleib to "lay an information" and initiate hearing procedures against Litton. Our concerns
focused on Section 79 of the Criminal Code, which makes it illegal to
make explosive substances with the intent "to endanger life or to
enable another person to endanger life." Under Section 2, the guidance system could be classified as an explosive substance if defined
as "anything or any part thereof, used or intended to be used, or
adapted to cause, or to aid in causing an explosion in or with an
explosive substance." After lengthy discussion and consideration
Gottleib set a hearing date for August. However, on April 26, a hearing was quickly held without notifying the informant. Deputy Crown

attorney Norman Matusiak erroneously concluded that " the only device manufactured at Litton Systems Canada is an inertial guidance system of the same type used in 747s, DC-10s, L1011s and A300s and many other general aircraft." Claiming that there had been "an extensive investigation into the allegation," he asked that the charges against Keating, who had appeared in court, be withdrawn. Our next attempt to lay an information will be in August; this time we plan to bring along experts to support our claims.

AN UPDATE

According to an internal Litton document leaked to *The Toronto Star,* Litton Systems lost the contract for the Cruise missile guidance system as a result of the bad publicity generated by the ongoing civil disobedience at Litton Systems, and their increased security costs (Litton's security budget jumped to $2 million a year after the bombing and nonviolent protests). Dave Collins, a member of the Cruise Missile Conversion Project, notes that another factor in the contract loss must have been an embarrassingly "bad product." In fact, Litton Systems manufactured a guidance system which apparently did not guide the Cruise missile in the right direction. Most often the missiles dove off their mark into the Albertan tundra. Thus it was no surprise that when Litton finished its ten-year Cruise missile system contract ahead of schedule it was not asked to make a bid on the next-generation Stealth Cruise missile. But in spite of the company's poor military production history, Litton has stepped up its work in the area. In fact, the company has expanded military production of components for nuclear and conventional arms in both dollar terms and overall production. According to Collins, Litton got a large part of the $1-billion-plus contract for work on the Tribal Class Destroyer and "a fair chunk in the military upgrading" set out in the Mulroney Conservative government's White Paper on Defence.

The Cruise Missile Conversion Project, active between 1979 and 1987, was a core of about a dozen women and men who were committed to collective process, nonviolence and conversion as strategies for nonmilitarist social change. With additional supporters across the country, CMCP was active in leafleting workers at Litton Systems about the advantages of converting their plant's production to peaceful industries. A new conversion group, "River," continues this work. Interested activists can contact River c/o Glen Rhodes United Church, 1470 Gerrard Street East, Toronto, Ontario, M4L 2A3.

NOTE: My thanks to Marion Cohen and members of Women's Action for Peace for their assistance in producing this article. I am grateful to Judy Oleniuk, Ollie Shakotko, Vivien Smith, Jane Springer and Miriam Nichols for their support during these events. The opinions expressed and any errors or omissions are my own.

NOTE

1 Variations of this article first appeared in *Broadside* and *Canadian Forum*.

Direct Action: Ann Hansen's Statement to the Court[1]

Ann Hansen

INTRODUCTION

One option to strike back against institutionalized violence that many women fantasize about and a few participate in is direct action. In 1982, two women took direct action to its logical conclusion and firebombed Red Hot Video outlets in Vancouver.

In January 1983, Julie Belmas and Ann Hansen were arrested for these actions. Along with Brent Taylor, Doug Stewart and Gerry Hannah, they were also charged with the Litton bombing, bombing the Cheekeye-Dunsmuir hydro substation, and conspiracy to rob a Brink's truck. Together they became known as the Vancouver (or Squamish) Five.

I was in Vancouver last February and decided to go to the trial. I was only there for a few minutes, and I didn't realize how much the experience affected me until a few days after I came home when I began to cry in telling some other women about it. The five people in the dock looked like any five people I might know. I knew they were operating from an idealistic and analytic base, just as I do. Seeing them up there scared me to death.

Julie Belmas got twenty years, even though she plea bargained. Ann Hansen got life. When they asked Ann Hansen if it was worth it, she hesitated and said yes. But I don't believe it. How could anything be worth life in prison? But can you let the fear stop you from what you believe needs to be done?

Undoubtedly some people will turn to direct action. The Vancouver Five will not be the only ones to present us with this moral dilemma.

It was clear to me who needed protection from whom in that courtroom. The criminality of the defendants was nothing compared to the criminality of what they were fighting against.

By Moe Lyons

WHEN I LOOK BACK on the past year and a half, I realize that I have learned a lesson. Not the kind of lesson that some people would hope I had learned, but rather through direct life experience I have re-learned what I once only understood theoretically – that the courts have nothing to do with justice and prison is where they punish the victims of this society. For many years now I have understood that the justice system was actually a system of injustice when seen in the broader social context. I was aware that parliament is where men make laws to protect big business, wealthy individuals and the status quo. Police were employed to enforce the laws, courts were created to prosecute those who broke the law, and prisons were built to punish the guilty.

My faith in the justice system began to erode as I grew up and saw the big businesses ripping off people by selling poorly produced products at high prices, resource companies gouging and raping the earth, governments producing nuclear arsenals capable of destroying life on earth many times over, pornographic magazines that normalized and glamourized rape, incest and sexual assault, and Indians being herded onto reservations to die. All these crimes against humanity and the earth are legal. They are protected and sanctioned by Parliament, the courts, the law and the police. This was all very wrong.

In Oakalla, where I have spent the past sixteen months, I have found that 70 percent of the prison population are Indian womyn, even though Indian people make up only 1 percent of the total outside population. This disproportionate number of Indian people in prison is reflected in prison populations across the country and reflects the racism of our society.

Everyone I have met in prison is poor. No one owns cars, homes, land or anything. They are there because they were forced to commit crimes to survive in a society that has no place for them. They have never owned forest companies that rape whole mountains of their forests, or handled nuclear murder weapons or stolen oil from Arab lands to be sold at scalper's prices in North America.

In the beginning when I was first arrested, I was intimidated and surrounded by the courts and prison. This fear provided the basis for the belief that if I played the legal game, I would get acquitted or perhaps less time. This fear obscured my vision and fooled me into thinking that I could get a break from the justice system. But this past eight months in court has sharpened my perceptions and strengthened my political convictions to see that the legal game is rigged and political prisoners are dealt a marked deck.

From the beginning in January 1983, the police illegally orchestrated press conferences and furnished the mass media with evidence, photos and information that became the basis for nationwide news stories convicting us as terrorists. We were portrayed as dangerous, psychotic criminals without politics.

Then our charges were separated into four separate indictments, of which the first was the Brink's conspiracy, so that we would be criminalized. This would make it harder for people to understand us as political people for our future trials.

During the voir dire, it became obvious through police testimony that the different police departments had committed illegal acts during their investigation. The Security Service in all probability watched the WFB (Wimmin's Fire Brigade) do the firebombings since Julie and I had been under intensive twenty-four-hour surveillance by the ss for days prior to and during the day of the firebombing.

CLEU (Co-ordinated Law Enforcement Unit) had committed illegal break-ins to plant the bugs in our house and in Doug's apartment among other illegal activities. But despite this, the judge permitted the wire-tap evidence. This taught me that there is one law for the people and none for the police.

But the event during the court proceedings that has had the most politicizing effect on me was Julie's sentencing. The judge ignored the fact that she had plea bargained and slapped her with the maximum prison sentence suggested by the Crown – twenty years. During the sentencing, the judge said that this case is criminal not political, yet the twenty-year sentence contradicts this view and instead reflects the real political nature of these proceedings. The twenty-year sentence was justified by the judge as a necessary social deterrent, which indicates that the court is so threatened by the potential of social upheaval that it takes a twenty-year sentence to deter others. That is political. It seems that the severity of the prison sentence is in direct proportion to the perceived level of discontent in society.

I understand why I have participated in the legal system up to now, but, in retrospect, in order to be honest to my political principles, I should have refused to collaborate in this legal sham and instead simply stated my political reasons for doing what I did.

Since I didn't then, I have the opportunity to do so now. Over the last couple of days we have heard witnesses who are activists around the different issues. They have spoken at great length about their efforts and the efforts of other groups to prevent the testing of the Cruise and the construction of the Cheekeye-Dunsmuir line and to stop Red Hot Video. I think it has become fairly obvious through their testimony that in each case they had exhausted all the legitimate channels of social protest in order to stop these projects and businesses. It was because there was no legal way to stop these crimes against humanity and the earth that I felt I had to use illegal actions to do so.

I didn't just feel that I should; I felt I had a duty and responsibility to do everything in my power to stop these crimes. At this dangerous point in human history, we have a moral responsibility to stop the arms race, violent pornography and the destruction of the earth. This moral responsibility far overrides any obligation to adhere to man-made laws.

I would prefer to live in peace but, when I looked around me, I couldn't find it anywhere. Everywhere I looked, the land was being destroyed, the Indians were victims of genocide, Third World peoples were oppressed and massacred, people lived in industrial wastelands and womyn were being raped and children molested. I could never live in peace, only quiet – the kind you find in cemeteries.

Even though I knew that a few militant direct actions would not make the revolution or stop these projects, I believed that it was necessary to begin the development of an underground resistance movement that was capable of sabotage and expropriations and could work free from police surveillance. The development of an effective resistance movement is not an overnight affair – it takes decades of evolution. It has to start somewhere in small numbers, and whether or not it grows, becomes effective and successful, will depend upon whether we make it happen.

I believe these direct actions of sabotage complement the legal radical movement and serve a purpose that it can't fulfil. Not that the legal movement is ineffective: although its efforts often fail to stop a project, its work will increase people's consciousness. The important thing is that the above-ground and underground support one another because our strength lies in unity and diversity.

Although I did do these three political actions, they were the result of the culmination of a legal struggle around the respective issues. In fact, the point of an underground resistance movement is to develop a strategic political analysis and actions that are based on an understanding of the economics and politics of the corporate state. Instead of reacting to every issue that pops up, we carried out actions that were based upon an analysis. This way, if an effective resistance movement does develop, we can be subjects who determine history instead of reacting to every singularly obvious symptom of the system's disease.

The politics of Direct Action saw the interconnectness of militarism, sexism, environmental destruction and imperialism. We saw that all these problems are rooted in the value system and way of thinking called capitalism and patriarchy. These values are passed on from one generation to the next through the institutions of this society – the multinational corporations, schools, mass media, church and commercial culture.

The main value of this society can be boiled down simply into one word – money. All life on this earth is reduced to its profit value by the capitalist economic system. Women, animals, Third World people, and the environment are reduced to a product and thus are objectified. Workers are valued for their productivity, women as sex objects, animals for food or furs, the environment for its potential as a natural resource base. If some living being is of no economic value in relation to the capitalist system then it is valueless. Consequently, traditional Indian people become victims of genocide and huge areas of the earth are designated as "Natural Sacrifice Areas." So the Litton action, Cheekeye-Dunsmuir action and WFB action, at least for me, were not issue-oriented actions but were our resistance politics transformed into action.

Contrary to the Crown's and police's theories, Direct Action and the WFB were two different groups. Of the five of us charged with the Red Hot Video fire-bombings, only Julie and I did the firebombings. There were no men involved with doing the firebombings. Doug, Brent and Gerry just happened to either live with Julie and me or visit us. The WFB was not an ongoing underground group, it was simply a group of womyn who came together for the purpose of firebombing Red Hot Video because we felt there was no other way for us to stop the proliferation of violent pornography.

Direct Action carried out the Litton and Cheekeye-Dunsmuir actions. I do sincerely regret that people were injured in the Litton bombing. All precautions were taken to prevent these injuries and an explanation as to why it happened was released almost immediately after the bombing. But I must also add that I criticize the Litton action itself because it was wrong for Direct Action to place a bomb near a building that people were working in, regardless of the number of precautions taken to ensure that nobody got hurt. In carrying out actions, revolutionaries should never rely on the police or security guards to clear out buildings and save people's lives.

There is no excuse for these mistakes, and I will always live with the pain that I am responsible for, but these mistakes should never overshadow the incredible amount of pain and suffering that Litton contributes to every day and the potential for planetary extinction that the Cruise missile embodies. Every day millions of people are slowly starving to death because so much money and human effort is diverted into the international war industry instead of being used to feed the people of the world. In Canada, essential social services are cut so that the government can pour more money into the war industry and megaprojects. For example, the federal government has given Litton $26.4 million in subsidies to build the guidance system of the Cruise.

The use of 1984 double-think has become an important part of today's psychological warfare against people developing radical consciousness. We experience it every day, even in this courtroom. I am called a terrorist – one who tries to impose their will through force and intimidation – by the court and press. But I am not a terrorist. I am a person who feels a moral obligation to do all that is humanly possible to prevent the destruction of the earth. Businesses such as Litton, B.C. Hydro and Red Hot Video are the real terrorists. They are guilty of crimes against humanity and the earth, yet they are free to carry on their illegal activities while those who resist and those who are their victims remain in prison. How do we, who have no armies, weapons, power or money, stop these criminals before they destroy the earth?

I believe if there is any hope for the future, it lies in our struggle.

NOTE

1 Ann Hansen's "Statement to the Court" and the "Introduction" by Moe Lyons were originally published in *Hysteria*, vol. 3, no. 2.

An Interview with Adele Ratt[1]

Shari Dunnet, Interviewer

I was born and raised in La Ronge, in northern Saskatchewan, but I live all over Saskatchewan. I travel around, so I don't really have a home yet. I'm 29, with two kids and another one coming. I'm from the Cree Nation. Most of the people around La Ronge and that area are Crees. The first six years of my life were spent out in the bush, living with the land and learning that way, until the school laws came up and we were sent away to schools. So I spent most of my growing-up years, from 6 to 18, away from home, in the city – Prince Albert. That's where most of the kids were sent that couldn't go to school in La Ronge because their parents – trappers, fishermen – lived out of the community.

Prince Albert Boarding School – it was one of those assimilation schools where they wanted us to be nice little brown / white people. I found it really hard. Really lonesome. A lot of people who went through that system didn't survive. They're alive, but either they've been assimilated completely into the white society so that they've lost their language and rejected their Indianness, or they've turned to alcohol or committed suicide. Very few of us really survived to be active in trying to change the way things are. It's only been in the last ten years that I've relearned my own culture and my own language.

Reclaiming our culture feels good. It gives you a sense of direction where before you were completely lost. You didn't know where you belonged or what to do. And trying to work within the system, which I did for about three years after I left high school, was hard because you know it's not you. It's not a part of you. It just furthers the destruction that's happening to the people and removes you further from the land and any kind of understanding of what the land means. So it feels better now. It's hard because of the poverty we have to live with, but it's better in the sense that you know who you are. So you have some kind of sense about what's right and wrong now and you can do something about it.

In 1977 I became involved in the Native Women's Association of Saskatchewan. And I started learning why the conditions in the communities are the way they are – the high rates of alcoholism, suicides and the way the schools turn people's minds away from who they are.

I guess that's when I first found out about uranium mining. It had already been going on for quite a few years, but the dangers and the environmental problems had been kept covered up. Several people I got involved with were working to stop uranium mining, and that's how I learned about it. People like Lloyd Madsen, who was with the Communist Party. He took me under his wing for a while. He's lived with the Indian people for a long time so he knew what I was going through. I learned a lot from him. I'm not a communist. I don't believe in communism or capitalism. To me, they're the same thing. But he taught me a lot about where I come from because he worked with my dad and he'd worked with people like Jim Brady, who was really the leader in Saskatchewan for the Métis Association. He revived the whole Métis Association after the rebellion was squashed.

I also learned a lot on my own, studying. I took a personal interest in it because it affected me so deeply, because of my parents and my brother being trappers. The people were being moved off the land into little communities – the whole relocation that happened in northern Saskatchewan. It's really the same thing that's happening at Big Mountain right now, for the same reasons. It was done more insidiously here, more covertly. Over there everybody knows who's on what side. But here, they tricked the people – sort of like the whole treaty-making process. They tricked the people into believing that moving away from the land into these smaller centres would be better for them, that they would receive a lot of benefits. Nobody was aware of the problems that would come from that.

In the beginning I was mostly going to meetings and talking to people about what's happening, what the uranium is doing and how the government operates. And now people are aware. It's just that the feelings of powerlessness to do anything about it keep people where they are, keep them from being active and from trying to confront the government on it because they're so busy trying to survive.

It's so hard to survive now, away from the land, when you don't know the system. You don't know how it works and it just sucks you in. It sucks the whole life out of you and it's a struggle just to survive on the streets or in these smaller communities. You don't have much time to think about social change or the future.

So that's what we're trying to work on most right now, the smaller centres in the north, trying to make the people aware of these things.

And they know it's not good for them, but because of life, the way it is, they're forced into accepting the jobs that it offers and the little bits of money that trickle through. There's billions of dollars in uranium and resources coming out of the north that passes through La Ronge every day, because La Ronge is the centre of the north. That's where they do everything, all the leg work to go out and do the exploration and the mining. And all the money changes hands in La Ronge, yet the people there are the poorest in all of Canada, with the highest unemployment.

The greatest concentration of uranium mining is happening here in the north right now. The only reason the mining companies are there is to maximize their profits, and any kind of benefits the people are going to receive are going to be minimal and will last only a short time. Only a few individuals will benefit – individuals who are aware of the system, who have assimilated into and who have accepted that way of life. That will benefit people like Sol Sanderson, the head of the FSIN [Federation of Saskatchewan Indian Nations], running the SINCO [Saskatchewan Indian Nation Company], people like that. But even they can't be unaffected by it, because they're handling this stuff. And they know they're being lied to, so in some way they'll pay for it, sometime down the line.

The Wollaston Blockade was one of the most powerful actions I've been involved in. Survival gatherings are very powerful – although it's not really an action – because you are actively informing people and exchanging views and ideas on how to stop this thing. But as far as an action, a confrontation type of thing, Wollaston would be it. It's the first time that a native community has requested outside help on its own, without us having to come in and do anything to try to change things there. It's come from the people. After ten years of trying to get the government to listen to them, the frustration led them to do something, and they were just so together and so strong in the community about that. In any other community that is fighting against uranium mining, there are always so many problems that come up for people trying to work together – the differences override the issue, cover it up, and it gets lost somewhere in all that jumble and confusion. But in Wollaston, it was so together. Everybody was focused on the issue and why we were there; that was the number one motivating thing and nobody strayed from it.

The blockade happened in June 1985. The Wollaston Lake Lac La Hache band sent out a letter calling for help. We got it in Saskatoon. We were still working as the Group for Survival then, before we became the Big Mountain Support Group. One of our members went up to talk to the people in the band to see what we could do to help, and that's where the whole blockade thing came from – that meeting with the chief and the council. We just did all the leg work of putting out the word that the blockade was going to happen.

That appeal for help went out all over the world. We couldn't organize as we should have because of the lack of money, resources, no cars to go places to tell people about it, and things like that. We had to rely on the media, and the corporations own the media; they pay them to do their job, so they're not going to put out the total story, the whole truth. A lot of things got distorted. The forces that are out there were putting out word that AIM [the American Indian Movement] was going to come up and bring guns and bombs. That scared a lot of people out of coming. Plus the timing of it too – June. Kids are still in school and a lot of people aren't on their holidays yet. I think there'd have been a lot more people if we'd held it in July or August; I think it would have been a lot more powerful.

There were about 50 people from across Canada and about 250 local people and people from surrounding communities like Lac Brochet, Black Lake, Fond du Lac. Places like that all came, all native people. The actual blockade went for four days. We had a survival gathering for five days before the blockade, so it went for about ten days altogether.

It was really pleasant. There were no squabbles. Everybody was really solid and together, worked together to keep the camp going. The people would bring in food, and we set up an arbour, and there were tents alongside of the road. We had a fire going twenty-four hours and a little bit of security set up after the police were kicked out of the camp – they confiscated a spray-paint can and everybody got really upset. Before, the police were walking around freely, talking to people, trying to create divisions. And we could see what they were doing, so the elders asked them to leave, and to leave their guns if they had to walk through. They were walking through the camp going to the Eldorado security people on the other side of the gate, talking to them, telling them what we were doing. We had meetings constantly. Whenever an issue came up, there was a meeting pulled together right away to make the decision. There was no one leader; everyone was leading, and that was what was really great about it. Kids were there, little kids.

When we went back to the community after the blockade was pulled down, everybody was feeling kind of defeated, that they hadn't really done anything. We'd stopped the trucks for five days, sure. And it was really amazing. They were waiting.... It must have cost them a lot to not have those trucks running through, because they had to fly the necessary things in and that cost a lot more than trucking them in. There were twenty-two trucks within a half-hour after the blockade was pulled down. They were waiting just down the road for the word to go ahead. So they must have known; they knew somehow when it would happen. They were ready for it and they pushed a confrontation. And the chief had no choice because he was worried about his people; protecting them. The people wanted to stay, but in the best interests of everybody he decided that it was time to pull it down and that we could continue it later if these meetings that Eldorado had agreed to didn't work out.

Later, when we went back into the community, people were feeling defeated but they asked us to come back. They wanted two of us, myself and a man, to stay and help them for the winter to keep doing that work, but we just couldn't do it then. It wasn't time – the climate just wasn't right and we thought something really bad would happen if we stayed, because that's usually what happens. When you do an action in a community, it's very important that you keep the support strong there, because of the backlash that happens. We learned this from Wounded Knee. There were 385 native people or something like that killed – AIM supporters killed by the federal people; agents and the people that they called the "goons" on the reservation, the BIA (Bureau of Indian Affairs) police.

We more or less just went our separate ways, and it was really hard to maintain the contacts. I think the book we're doing, *Voices from Wollaston Lake*, is going to be important in keeping that network alive and letting the people in Wollaston know that we're still doing something, that we haven't forgotten about them. I think that's a general feeling in the community right now, that the world has forgotten their protest. Women are the backbone of the resistance. We keep it alive and convince them that any kind of change is going to come from the women, because we're the strongest. And I don't say that to belittle men, because I think we all need each other in this struggle. It affects our whole communities; it affects our families. Uranium destroys our families. So, in order to be strong, we have to keep our families together, no matter what the cost.

Men are attacked in this society and they are victims of the society – they've been weakened, too. And their roles have been destroyed, their traditional roles. I'm thinking of Indian men now, but generally speaking, the man in this society was the provider and now he's not. Now the women are. You can see that in a lot of homes in the community: men can't find jobs, Indian men especially. It's really hard if you're not assimilated and you have a doctorate or something like that. And if you don't have the education or the training for any other kind of work, most of the time you're unemployed. Indian men in the movement are especially in jeopardy. Unemployment does a lot to destroy self-respect, and that's where you get a lot of wife-beatings and things like that from. We have all these things to deal with, and women have survived it, and they've become stronger because of it. So they're really the leaders in the communities for any kind of change that's happening.

In AIM, men initiate a lot of things, and they get a lot of community support, but the women do all the work. It takes all of us to keep it alive, to keep it going, but I think it's the women that are the true leaders in the community. And you see that any time anything happens, even in these little communities. If there's a wake, it's the women who put it on, who make sure everybody's fed and has coffee or is comfortable. They're the ones who go and help the people, the family.

In the Indian movement elders play an important role. In Saskatchewan, there are a lot of elder women involved, farm women. To me, farm women and Indian women are the same, because of their connection to the land. We need the land to survive; that's what feeds us. In the Indian community, the elder women are probably the strongest. They're the ones who tell us, "OK, go now," or "Come back." We take our direction from them.

That's very visible in Big Mountain. In Big Mountain, it's the elder women that are leading that resistance. They're the ones who say, "OK, tear that fence down," or, "All right, we're going to have a sundance this year," and things like that. Any kind of major decisions that have to be made come from them. And it's really good because our societies were matrilineal, matriarchal. And it's coming back even stronger.

The elder women have the wisdom and the vision to see that what we do today affects our kids in the future. Even the men will listen to them because the elder women know, they've been there; they've faced soldiers before. They were there during the rebellions and the Indian Wars.

In the north, in Saskatchewan, the women were the ones who carried the medicine bundles when the church came in. The church had a big part to play in destroying the traditional, cultural ways of the people in the north, more so than the fur-trade people. And you can see it really strong still in the communities. A lot of our elder women who are involved in the resistance are Christian. But they remember. I think they hid in Christianity to protect the ways for later, when they knew it would be safe to bring it out again.

This happened on the West Coast too. If you've ever read *Daughters of Copper Woman*, you can see it very clearly there. But here it's still slow. It's coming out more and more. They saw; they had to watch their medicine being burned in mass piles, and they buried the people that died from smallpox. They've lived such a long time that they just know what is going to happen. So they're always there, waiting for the young people to come to them and say, "Look, we need help to do this." And I think more of us are starting to do that, which is good.

So, even if there is nothing happening, they're there and they're talking; they're teaching the little ones. They tell them legends. They tell them the stories of what happened when we had to bury all these people. Kids retain that, and sometime later, in their consciousness it's there and it comes out: "Oh yeah, I remember my grandma saying that. It's true." And that's where more people come into the resistance, through the elders.

And then us, the younger ones who are really aware of what's happening – we're active. But I think our greatest role will be when we are elders. Right now we're just running around talking to whoever will listen to us about this stuff and hoping that some way we can keep the struggle alive.

I think right now there is a regrouping happening. We were brought down by different things that happened. I can see it clearly in the Group for Survival, how they destroyed us. They separated the men we looked to as our leaders. They separated them and caused divisions between them. That's when the women came in. Now we're coming back, and we're saying the same things. But it's really hard because you're working from a limited resource base. A lot of us, like myself, don't have a home, and that's necessary – even if you have kids, you have to travel. If you stay in one place, they're going to neutralize you. And that's a fear that's always there, but it's not like I'm running from it because no matter where I go, it's there. It makes me feel good to know that sometimes they don't know where I am. So I keep moving; I think that's why we're called the movement!

The poverty. Most of us are welfare moms and you can't make

ends meet. There's no way. It's just barely subsistence. A lot of times the fridge is empty, and you spend a lot of time trying to keep the kids fed. So whenever we do organize something, it usually is really good, because you put everything into it. You sacrifice a lot.

My feeling has been more and more to pull away from the mainstream peace movement, though I can't help but be a part of it because of the uranium issue. We see uranium mining as just another attack against us on the land. It's probably the most dangerous thing we've ever come up against – it's the new killer, and it's affecting all races and all people all over the world. In that sense, we see the peace movement as supporting us, but it's a very limited view. It's too narrow a view, and there's too many factions. There are just too many groups who don't see eye to eye, and I think they let their personal differences get in the way of any real change that could happen. A lot of people are doing good work – I don't want to say that they're all screwed up, because a lot of us are, too, but at least we know where we stand most of the time.

I went to the fortieth anniversary of Hiroshima in Japan last summer as a representative of the Canadian Uranium Resistance Network. I found the biggest problem with anybody getting any work done was that they couldn't decide if they wanted to support nuclear energy for the power and oppose nuclear weapons. But you can't, because one goes with the other. And they think the ultimate thing is the bomb, killing people, but they don't see that uranium mining, from the beginning exploration process, kills people. And so they're divided on that. And that's what I mean; it's too narrow a view. You have to look at the entire thing because you can't build a bomb without mining that shit out of the ground. And the mining kills people before the uranium ever becomes a bomb. So, that's what I'd like to say to them – which I did say to them when I was over there.

I don't want you to be an Indian, because you can't be. I think we just have to accept our differences and try to live with each other, like the bears and the elks live in the same forest. The bear doesn't try to make the elk into a bear, because it's impossible. It's the same with people. We're here for a reason. We're taught in our ways, in our spiritual ways, to always look at the other person as your brother or your sister. You always have to remember that in any kind of dealings you have with each other in this movement, you have to respect the people's ways when you're in that community. I think western society and industrial nations can learn a lot about respect and ecology from indigenous people.

That's been our biggest problem with the peace movement, working with peace people – like Greenpeace, for example, or people who come from overseas who don't really understand us. They try so hard; they try too hard sometimes, and they just end up stepping on people in the process, and that's what we're trying to avoid. We want people to listen to us, for a change, and to really hear what we're saying. It's caused problems for us in the past in trying to work with peace people because of the cultural differences. There's just no understanding, and nobody's really willing to listen because they all think they have the answer. There's got to be better communication, for sure, somehow.

Peace is being able to sit down, wherever you want to sit, and to have nobody bother you. Peace is that feeling of security inside that you know that you're OK, that you're going to be OK, and your kids are going to be OK, that nobody has to go hungry – no war. It's hard to describe what it is because we've never known it. I don't know if we ever will. Well, I shouldn't say, "If we ever will"; we will; when we die, we know peace. But do we have to die to know peace? I think it can happen before, but maybe at one time ...

When I think about our history, our tribes weren't always at war with each other. There were certain territorial things but they were respected. I think something happened, even to the Indian people, to change a peaceful coexistence with each other into war. Even before the white man came, we were at war with different tribes, over territory. It wasn't like the Indian Wars with the whites, or the world wars – then it was all just killing, nothing but killing and killing for killing's sake. The wars between tribes were a little different. You tried *not* to kill the enemy. You were considered a better warrior if you could get close enough to the enemy to touch him without killing him.

I would do the same today. We have to look at this word "nonviolence" very closely. To me violence is: You're participating in a violent act if you just watch it happen and not try to stop it, or if someone is beating you up to try to defend yourself. And that's why I respect the women in the "Take Back the Night" movement a lot, because they are doing something, they're not saying, "Well, I'm nonviolent so I'm not going to strike back." But I don't know what happened to destroy peace. At one time the earth was at peace; the people were at peace; and something happened to destroy that.

I think until more people ask that question – "What do you think peace is?" – and really think it out, nothing's ever going to change.

But I don't know if I can answer it myself. I think it's your own individual thing inside that maybe nobody can explain.

But world peace – we know what that is. It means no more war. It means people pulling together to help one another and not fighting any more. We were a flight animal before we were a fight animal. We would run from danger before we would confront it. And we've got to bring that back, because these people have done something to change that. They've forced us to think fight before flight. Our instincts are to run – so I guess people have to listen more to their instincts. And we know these people that we're up against, the corporations, the heads of the corporations, the ones who make the decisions to do these things to the people – it's all a deliberate act. Even bringing alcohol into the communities was a deliberate act of war.

There was one other thing I wanted to add about peace. You know how everybody looks at Canada – you hear it all the time in the news, how Canada is one of the leaders in world peace. And that's a real ego thing for the politicians. But when you look seriously at what's happening to the Indian people in this country, you come to realize the parallels between apartheid in South Africa and apartheid in Canada. The way we are treated is no different. They're not shooting us down in the streets with bullets, but the bullets they use are just as deadly – bullets of racism, sexism, classism let you know you don't have the same chance as your next-door neighbour. Our people are dying just as fast as the South Africans from hunger, from poverty, from suicides, from alcoholism – those are the bullets that kill us. There is no protection whatsover against uranium mining. That was one of the things that was promised. In all the inquiries they did to open the uranium mines in the north, they said the people would be protected; the people will benefit in all these ways; there'll be lots of money; there'll be lots of employment. And that's not true. There's less employment. They told us native people would be getting the jobs in the mines. The only jobs we got were the pick and shovel, the dirty jobs where you're breathing in that dust.

It's the same as what's happening to the Navajo uranium miners in Arizona – Windowrock, Redrock, and all those places. They threw them down in the pits after they blasted, and they're the ones that are dying left and right now from that.

It's really hard to get statistics up here on who's died from uranium mining because they always have another reason why that person died – "It wasn't directly because of working in the mine." But I've heard stories from guys that I know that their hair started falling out. My brothers work for the uranium companies, drilling, and they say none of their bosses who have worked in the field for a long time now have any hair. A lot of them can't have kids. And they don't tell them those problems. They say that uranium is clean, it's safe, and it's gonna make you rich, but what we're seeing is the complete opposite.

Most of the uranium in North America, particularly in Canada, is on native lands; it's native people that are living with the consequences of uranium mining. They have sacrificed the native people of this country, of North America, for what they consider progress. In South Africa, they are relocating the South Africans off their lands, their traditional lands, to what they call Bantustans, and it's an exact replica of the reservation system in North America. It's for uranium, for the exploitation of the minerals on the land, that they're doing it. And that's just part of the ongoing war – a five-hundred-year war against Indian people. It hasn't stopped. Only the faces and the names of the attackers have changed.

NOTE

1 Excerpts of this interview are included in the series, which was originally produced for Vancouver Co-operative Radio (102.7 FM in Vancouver, B.C.).

Adele Ratt was interviewed in Prince Albert, Saskatchewan, on September 28, 1986.

The Voice of Women[1]

Kay Macpherson

SINCE ITS FOUNDING in 1960, Voice of Women (VOW) has attracted many women: saints, eccentrics, individualists, "groupies," prima donnas, "retiring violets," old revolutionaries and young idealists (and young revolutionaries and *old* idealists). I wish all their names and achievements could be included here, because every one is a part of the patchwork of VOW.

During the fall of 1960 our family returned from a sabbatical year in England. We had heard Bertrand Russell speaking in Trafalgar Square, and seen antinuclear buttons for the first time. "Ban the Bomb" was the slogan, and the Aldermaston peace march was an annual event. Soon after we were home, one of my friends called.

"There's a new women's peace group which might interest you. It's called the Voice of Women." The name conjures up a vision of ladies in hats holding teacups and calling for peace around the world. I forgot about it. After all, by going to England for a year, I had managed to get *out* of two organizations. Why join another?

Later on in the winter, another friend phoned me.

"I've been asked to get a few women together who might help organize a conference," she said. "It's for the Voice of Women, and they said they knew that Women Electors are good organizers." (We both belonged to that association, which monitored the goings-on at City Hall and the Board of Education). So down we went to meet the national president of Voice of Women, Helen Tucker. A small group of us squeezed into the tiny office, and I learned about the plans for international meetings and conferences and worldwide contacts with people whose names we only knew from headlines: Thérèse Casgrain, Margaret Mead, Jawaharlal Nehru, Philip Noel-Baker, Mrs. Sirimavo Ratwatte Dias Bandaranaike (Prime Minister of Ceylon) and others. Helen had a genius for contacting headline makers, and we set about doing that and much more in the cause of peace.

That was the beginning for me. Thousands of women had already responded to Lotta Dempsey's May 21, 1960, *Toronto Star* column which had sparked the formation of Voice of Women. The world that spring seemed on the brink of nuclear war. The U.S.-U.S.S.R. summit conference had failed. An American U2 spy plane had been shot down over the Soviet Union. A 1964 *Toronto Star Magazine* article continues the story:

> In the course of her column, Miss Dempsey dropped the casual comment that men were too concerned with political systems and economic considerations, while women were more concerned with people, and she added, "It seems to me that if we had a summit conference of women dedicated to the welfare of children all over the world, we might reach an understanding."
>
> The seed fell on fertile ground. A number of Toronto women got busy on their telephones and at a peace meeting already planned in Toronto's Massey Hall Helen Tucker presented their plans for women's peace action. A month later an organization was born, called simply the Voice of Women, with Helen Tucker as President and Jo Davis as Vice-President.

The founders, among whom were media women, senators and Mrs. Lester B. Pearson, declared that humankind "must find another way than war to settle international differences." Their slogan was "construction not destruction."

Members, support and letters poured in; provincial and local groups were formed. A newsletter provided ideas for action. Campaigns were launched. Contributions ranged from one woman's "money I was saving for a washing machine but.... peace is more important," to Old Age Pension cheques from a Saskatchewan couple who wrote, "We are fed up with this war talk. It won't matter to us if this world is destroyed, as it may well be, but it matters to our grandchildren."

During the summer of 1961 vow branches were also formed in Japan, Australia, New Zealand, Nigeria and Jamaica, and contact was established with women's peace movements in other countries.

In the early 1960s, following the postwar baby boom, thousands of women were raising children, not yet thinking of returning to the work force and not yet confronted by Betty Friedan's *The Feminine Mystique*. One of vow's strong points was the means it provided for women who were often tied to their homes and children with time but little money to take responsibility for action, to do something constructive and effective. This lessened the feeling of isolation. By joining together, they could make the weight of women's concerns felt in the places where decisions were being made. "What Can One Person Do?" was a favourite flyer, giving ideas and information about how to write letters or interview officials.

As far as I know, no one ever did a survey on the effects of all this activity on the husbands and menfolk of these busy VOW members. It was more than some men could cope with, to find, coming home to "supper and slippers by the fire," that children had been parked with neighbours and the "little woman" was off interviewing the local Member of Parliament. Often there was a cryptic note: "Hot dogs in fridge. Please bathe Johnny. There'll be 20 women in basement stuffing envelopes at 8. Love, B." There were several casualties: some men couldn't take this unconventional, independent type of wife, and separations and divorces resulted. However, while unacknowledged by these women and men, they were in fact part of the beginning of the contemporary Canadian women's movement. Many husbands were towers of strength and totally supportive, glad to see their wives involved, effective and happy. We called them the men's auxiliary. They did the dishes, babysat, edited briefs, answered the phone, drove cars and ran messages. Two husbands acted as baggage masters for delegations of women visiting Canada and overseas. Others were experts at fund raising and producing potluck supper dishes.

CAMPAIGNS

Voice of Women has mounted a number of significant campaigns. As well as addressing specific recommendations to the relevant authorities, campaigns have encouraged maximum involvement and action on the part of VOW members and other sympathetic individuals and groups. This technique of top-level political action and grass-roots involvement has been followed effectively in non-VOW campaigns, including Media Watch, action on pornography, and television surveys preliminary to submitting briefs to the CRTC.

VOW's first campaign raised funds for the Canadian Peace Research Institute. Its most successful campaigns have been the Anti War Toys campaign, the Baby Tooth collection, and the Knitting Project for Vietnam children.

War Toys

The Anti War Toys Campaign has ebbed and flowed over the years. It has involved thousands of women and their children. At one time,

Eaton's had fourteen pages of war toy ads in its Christmas catalogue. Women all over the continent tore out the pages and mailed them, with a few well-chosen words and "no-purchase orders," back to the store. Women wrote articles, leafleted street corners, picketed the stores, and attended spring buyers' exhibitions. Child psychologists were interviewed, and busy mothers dreamed up constructive alternatives. The Lionel Christmas ad in the *New Yorker* demonstrated that the peaceful point had been made by showing a toy train with the caption "This train does not shoot, kill, stab, etc., etc., it just goes round and round on its track."

Radiation and Baby Teeth

When Ursula Franklin told me she thought her most important job as vow's chair of research was to prepare a brief on fallout monitoring, I didn't know what she was talking about. She had to explain that radioactive strontium 90 and other lethal materials from nuclear tests in the Pacific were carried in the stratosphere and deposited all over North America. They got into the vegetation and, through the food chain, eventually into our milk and other foods. The Canadian government was not doing much to monitor the fallout and so knew little about what these dangerous substances were doing to Canadians' health.

It is typical of vow to link health concerns with scientific and political actions. Thus, a concurrent campaign was launched to collect baby teeth from children all over the country, in order to assess amounts of dangerous minerals by region. Thousands of teeth (easily available bone which absorbs strontium) were required by Dr. A.M. Hunt of the Department of Dentistry at the University of Toronto. vow members took up the challenge, organizing collections at boards of education, dentists' offices, libraries, the CNE and other public events. Hundreds of women collected, sorted and documented the specimens (breast or bottle-fed, age, where conceived and born, statistics about mother and child, etc.). At the vow twenty-fifth anniversary party on Hornby Island, B.C., in 1985, fifty women recalled the rows of documented teeth on their living-room floors. I was lucky enough to accompany Ursula Franklin to lobby Ottawa officials with the radiation brief. Later that fall, she eventually obtained an interview with Judy La Marsh, then Minister of Health and Welfare. Eventually, the government improved its monitoring and the Test Ban Treaty was signed.

Vietnam Knitting Project

Without detailing the letters, leaflets, meetings and knitting instructions, the sorting, folding and ironing of garments and blankets, the speeches, interviews, press releases, posters and fund raising, Lil Green describes the Knitting Project:

> This Voice of Women activity was one of the most consistent projects for aid to the Vietnamese people. For roughly ten years – 1966-1975 – it involved hundreds of concerned men and women, not only in eastern Canada but in the United States, where it was against the law "to aid and abet the enemy."
>
> The Project was a full time after-hours voluntary job.... Every single item of the final total of 30,000 knitted garments and cot blankets for the children of Vietnam and Laos eventually came through the dining room headquarters in my home. Every participant was thanked either personally or by letter. Many joined Voice of Women and were active. Every item was received, re-packed and expressed to the Canadian Aid for Vietnam Civilians in Vancouver, B.C., from where shipments were made free of charge with other medical aid, etc., to Vietnam by Soviet ships.

Some of us doubted at first the validity of what was essentially an "aid" project. But time and time again women would give variations of "I took my knitting to school / church / meeting / laundromat," etc., and when I was asked why I was knitting baby clothes in dark green or brown or blue, I would explain that in Vietnam babies have to live mainly underground – sometimes floating in baskets and bowls in flooded trenches – and light-coloured clothing meant they could be seen and bombed by American planes. Women were horrified.

Thus many new VOW members began their work for peace. Local and regional groups devised campaigns or joined local actions. Nuclear activities of the U.S. and Canadian armed forces at Comox and Nanoose Bay off Vancouver Island provoked vigils, demonstrations, visits to bases and leaflet distribution, often backed up by questions in the House of Commons from local Members of Parliament.

Halifax has had visits from nuclear submarines; Labrador has to contend with low-flying jets that devastate human and animal populations. In Saskatchewan and Alberta, VOW has demonstrated against chemical and nerve warfare research at Suffield, and against Cruise missile tests. Manitoba has faced the training of NATO troops and Emergency Measures practices. There have been countless vigils and watches – at Litton Systems outside Toronto, on Parliament Hill, at Bomarc missile sites, at the U.S. border, at embassies and consulates of many countries, and at the United Nations for many reasons. VOW has confronted visiting politicians on various issues: for example, British Prime Minister Harold Macmillan on nuclear tests and Henry Kissinger on the U.S. role in Greece. For nearly ten years the Vietnam war was a focus of dozens of political actions, such as the knitting project and the Draft Resister program. VOW was active in Quebec's Quiet Revolution and opposed use of the War Measures Act in 1970. VOW members have acted on human rights issues at home and in other countries, on threats to the environment (pollution, toxic waste, acid rain, chemical spraying) and on nuclear power in all its dangerous aspects.

The National Action Committee on the Status of Women (NAC), of which VOW was a founding member group, held its first workshop on survival at its 1981 annual meeting. About seventy delegates saw the film *If You Love This Planet* and responded enthusiastically to Sister Rosalie Bertell's call "to be passionate about survival."

That passion inspired my statement to the June 12, 1982, disarmament rally in New York:

> Today we have started to turn the tide of the arms build-up. We the people must make our governments turn to disarmament. We women and men have the power to give the world a future. Thousands of Canadians say, in the words of our Women's Petition for Peace: "We say no to war. Non à la guerre! We say yes to life. Oui à la vie!"

The enthusiasm and euphoria of the New York rally – a million people coming together for disarmament and peace – led subsequently to renewed interest and action within Voice of Women.

Here is another Voice, that of Dorothy Inglis:

> As a VOW member who started in B.C., transplanted to Newfoundland and spent a half dozen years in between in Central Canada, I have a personal overview of VOW in various regions and a reflection of an organization that lit candles of hope across the country and kept them burning.
>
> The contribution that VOW made with all the briefs, the conferences, the analysis, the monitoring of events provided a

platform for the women's movement.... The National Action Committee on the Status of Women has embraced the concept that peace is a women's issue and every annual general meeting reinforces the support delegates give to this topic as high priority....

In every province VOW left its mark....

VOW's work goes on. We have to replace the use of the threat system with a new agenda and a new, nonviolent, cooperative process of negotiation. Women have developed some of these processes around their kitchen tables, dealing with their children, in their communities and workplaces. It's time for them to be used in public and international life.

As Terry Padgham says, "The unifying theme of VOW's story is the tenacious instinct for survival that women possess, and Voice of Women members channel this instinct into a life-long commitment to peace."

NOTE

1 Edited sections of this article have appeared in *Atlantis: A Woman Studies Journal* 12:1 (Autumn 1986).

PART FOUR

IMAGINING PEACE

FEAR, RAGE AND CONFUSION emerge when we contemplate the fragility of life in the nuclear age. Women writers transform these and other responses in narratives informed by the knife-edged precision of parody, the playful rich ambiguity of sound poems, and the haunting insight of the lyric. Louky Bersianik poses the feminist dilemma: "on what should peace be constructed? ... on the murderous and ferocious rivalries that the co-existence of people depends on, between individuals, between sexes, between skin colours, on the scorn ingrained in politics so as to instill the fascist values of the patriarchy?" The terms of this rhetorical question are staged and reimagined by the women's writing collected here.

Contributions by Bersianik, Kate Lushington, Leslie Hamson, Faye Scott Rieger, Greta Hofmann Nemiroff, Erin Mouré and Betsy Warland were originally published as part of "Women's Peace Write / Rite des Femmes pour la Paix," a campaign which sent women's "prose, poetry, dialogue and song lyrics" about peace to all Canadian Members of Parliament from June 1985 to May 1986. The immediate issues addressed by this campaign were the threat of Canadian participation in Star Wars and "the federal government's recent encouragement of the private sector to actively seek defense contracts." Organized by a feminist collective of writers, the West Coast Women and Words Society, the project followed the initiative established during the 1983 national conference Women and Words when Dorothy Livesay proposed a resolution "That Women and Words support the use of the spoken and written word to endorse disarmament and promote peace on this planet."

The different but familiar faces of war and peace are sighted in Maxine Gadd's "from the Women's Conference / on how to end the war in viet nam." The disastrous impact of "small" wars waged in the name of American democracy is explored by Himani Bannerji in the context of the U.S. invasion of Grenada. The everyday state of siege that exists in totalitarian regimes is recalled in Rosemary Sullivan's "An Argentinian Script." Claire Harris's double-voiced poem, " Where the Sky is a Pitiful Tent," sounds the difference between two accounts of war and revolution. One woman's lyrical voice juxtaposed with the oral testimony of Rigoberto Manchu provokes us to ask ourselves the price of peace in the violent context of Guatemalan totalitarianism.

Kate Lushington's "Griefkit" treats feelings of powerlessness, "the psychiatric effects of nuclear war," with the inflating tactics of satire. What appears to be satirical fantasy in Betsy Warland's etymological excerpt from *serpent (w)rite* is revealed to be the pathetically inadequate "post-nuclear war" theorizing of military strategists. In "Machine. Gun. Nest." Margaret Atwood envisions the other side of war: a hand poised at the end of a gun ready to explore "Some glint of reflected light." The poem asks about a state of mind whch suspends ethical questions in the taut pragmatism of a killing "machine": "Justice and mercy are words that happen in cool rooms, elsewhere. / Are you your brother's keeper? Yes or no, depending what clothes he has on, what hair. There is more than one brother." Phyllis Webb's poem sounds the instructive linguistic echoes of "war crimes" in "war cries." Chanting a long history of atrocities, the poem shifts our attention from a remote "cool room" contemplation of war strategies to the sensate wounded weeping bodies "still warm" then "still still still." Penn Kemp's poem sounds an associative catalogue of terms which play between war's myth and "his tory."

The contradiction between creation and destruction is embodied in the hand that rocks the cradle of Lola Lemire Tostevin's "Einstein." Here, a poet's physics lesson points to what is lost in the abstract rationalizations of scientific theorizing. A concern with children surfaces in a number of the poems. The process of reconstructing our own histories where consciousness is marked by war memories is written into Sharon Stevenson's "The Holocaust" and Marilyn Bowering's "Learning the Bomb." An elemental connection between a mother's birthing and the human planet is posed as an imaginative transformative strategy in poems by Nadine McInnis and Roberta Buchanan.

In some of these poems, nuclear-era anxiety appears as backdrop, symptom or coda. A poem by Daphne Marlatt encourages us to seek beneath the picturesque domesticity of an English landscape framed by "delphiniums blue & geraniums red" to uncover the opportunistic double-talk of a militarized, Thatcherized language. In the calm contemplation of Leslie Hamson's healing meditation, and the grotesque vividness of Faye Scott Rieger's "After the Big Bang is Over," the woman writer works to move, provoke and engage the reader. Central to women writers' engagement with a politics of peace is the twinned knowledge of despair and hope: the painful assessment of a world in crisis and the mobilizing utopian energy necessary to imagine "something better." Sharon Thesen's "Praxis" poses the dilemma: how to move from a state of paralytic contemplation "weeping in *the abattoir*" to engaged action, to "Get up. Get out. Leap / the mossy garden wall."

According to critic Barbara Johnson, "the *literary* ramifications of [... feminism] involve the discovery of the rhetorical survival skills of the unvoiced."[1] For Louky Bersianik, the writer's "white page [is] the hinge between the visible and the invisible. between what is true and what is likely. between reality and fiction. between intimidation and its implications." These texts, while they acknowledge the incursion of a militarized language and consciousness into our everyday lives, challenge us to act beyond suffering and mere survival, towards social transformation.

– J.W.

NOTE

1 Barbara Johnson, *A World of Difference* (Baltimore: Johns Hopkins Press, 1987), p. 31.

from the Women's Conference
on how to end the war in viet nam

Maxine Gadd

it shld be some other language 'speak in Swahili' said the
black women in the elegant turbans and the english words in a swinging
syntax turned
into some village i didn't belong in pretty though, wanting to stop
and sing with the orange bird with the emerald eyes
except knowing the whole schizophrenia
was brought on to drive me away, their huge eyes in a beautiful terror, not
to fascinate, but because they thought i was about to play
Great American Male, but i wouldn't have known it then, thinkin to be
in a blue and green bandana and listening
to the human river

Spain

Dorothy Livesay

When the bare branch responds to leaf and light
Remember them: it is for this they fight.
It is for haze-swept hills and the green thrust
Of pine, that they lie choked with battle dust.

You who hold beauty at your finger-tips
Hold it because the splintering gunshot rips
Between your comrades' eyes; hold it across
Their bodies' barricade of blood and loss.

You who live quietly in sunlit space
Reading The Herald after morning grace
Can count peace dear, when it has driven
Your sons to struggle for this grim, new heaven.

40 days

Nadine McInnis

tomorrow is Ash Wednesday

one day early   we drive north
through blowing snow

dunes   white hands
palms down across the highway
make our journey perilous

on our right
Cold Lake billows into infinity

a satellite tracks the test flight

it registers the lake
as a white puff ball
almost hidden
in lush undergrowth

satellite dishes
planted in barren gardens
speak the language of dead stars

the missile scuds above snow clouds
its engines hiss
ashes to ashes

our signs are frozen
obsolete as prayers
tugged by the wind

a child runs
in the wrong direction
after her sign   a tumbleweed
in slow motion

– March 6, 1984, Cold Lake, Alberta

Learning the Bomb

Marilyn Bowering

In the school-hall
rows of children crouch,
arms clutched over their heads,
learning the Bomb.

Will there be time to cross the field
(fire grappling at clothing,
stumbled by wind),
will there be time to get home,
and what if there are only children
to huddle each other
in the unprepared cellar?

Open the window
and see;
there are fires,
predictable as genii,
all over the city.

Open the window,
and a siren rivers down the street.

We watch with eyes
burrowed by a thousand species.

We still have something:
an occasional fire of the skin,
an amnesia of gentle hands
in a dark with no surname;

but what now,
when we find ourselves
children,
unnamed,
unforgiving?

Grenada 1983

Himani Bannerji

It is dark here
somewhere a sun in a depthless blue
is eclipsed by the wings
everywhere the eagle screams

huge talons flash from the sky
tearing roots shoots branches
tearing the earth from itself
by its hair

the earth, its soul of dove
caught in the steel grips
cradled in the dark wings
in a nest of feathers & blood

the eagle is screaming
its eyes are lightning
flares discovering us
in our hollows, searching the jungles

the sky rains helicopters bombers
paratroopers on us
the streets swallow our marching feet
shrapnel separating the fists from the bodies

dark times are here
mushroom flowers bloom in the sky
a darkness brighter than a thousand suns
the blood of the dove is covering the earth
a dark tide is rising
everywhere the eagle screams

Praxis

Sharon Thesen

Unable to imagine a future,
imagine a future better
than now, us creatures
weeping *in the abattoir*
only make noise & do
not transform a single fact.
So stop crying. Get up. Go out. Leap
the mossy garden wall
the steel fence or whatever
the case may be & crash
through painted arcadias,
fragments of bliss & roses
decorating your fists.

delphiniums blue
& geraniums red

Daphne Marlatt

rose light in the blue, at eye level (where is the dormouse curled?) their kitchen looks out on where it suffuses hayfield, appletree, vegetable-garden hedge – day's amber, stilled & stilling. watch fresh lettuce leaves, curled, disappear in the spinner. watch a child, curled up in himself for comfort, dreaming of blue. roselight makes of their kitchen unearthly hue, seraphic even, in our vision blue, is a healing colour even a bird will spring toward.

but i was blue with cold on the Didcot Platform in a wind the intercity diesels roar on through. torn holes in attention. out of nowhere we are near the source. a shallow brook ripples by a few crosses at fords, a few stone walls for leaning up against – the Thames, really? not that one. wellspring. dayspring. home – when the walls come down, what kind of source?

that was Old Bernie, she said, on his last legs waiting outside surgery with his stick, "they're all full up in there" – refused the chair she offered to fetch from the grocer's. no relief from the blinking exit sign: alone & knowing it.

despite all this pulling together. Taunton, Weirfield. running out on the hockey team blue with cold, "you can't be cold." grown older, painting the open wound with iodine, "it doesn't hurt, it's for your own good really." slogans on the road to selfless, sightless in the guise of ought-to-be – chrysanthemums, say, on the unclipped village graves. when *five-year-olds* (are) *looting burned-out shops* "these days of career marchers & young punks tearing up the streets. it's all me-me, no sense of the common good, now have they?"

& if The Common Good, pointing its nineteenth century hand, has tyrannized all sense of me, small voice essential to life? so that we falls apart, gone mad at the mask of Reason which is still quoting Good in the face of annihilation: tactical advantage, counterforce capability, stockpiling. *the first few weapons arriving do almost all the damage conceivable to the fabric of the country.* have done so, without ever arriving, the nest we live in full of holes these days.

& still: *i suppose all these people know better than i* – doubtful, paws to eyes, small creature at the heart of dreaming some blue otherwhere. *& that is the reason,* the story continues, circling back to its source, the dormouse curls, imagining delphiniums blue, o blue / black hole at centre, folding in on itself.

Machine. Gun. Nest.

Margaret Atwood

The blood goes through your neck veins with a noise they call
  singing.
Time shatters like bad glass; you are this pinpoint of it.

Your feet rotting inside your boots, the skin of your chest
festering under the zippers, the waterproof armour,

you sit here, on the hill, a vantage point, at this X or scuffling
in the earth, which they call a nest. Who chose that word?

Whatever you are you are not an egg, or a bird either.
Vipers perhaps is what was meant. Who cares now?

That is the main question: who cares? Not these pieces of paper
from somewhere known as *home* you fold, unread, in your
  pocket.

Each landscape is a state of mind, he once told me:
mountains for awe and remoteness, meadows for calm and the
  steam

of the lulled senses. But some views are slippery.
This place is both beautiful as the sun and full of menace:

dark green, with now and then a red splotch, like a punctured
  vein, white like a flare; stench of the half-eaten.
Look at it carefully, see what it hides, or it will burst in your
  head.

If you lose your nerve you may die, if you don't lose it
you may die anyway, the joke goes. What is your nerve?

It is turning the world flat, the moon to a disc you could aim at,
popping the birds off the fence wire. Delight in accuracy,

no attention paid to results, dead singing, the smear of feathers.
You know you were more than that, but best to forget it.

There's no slack time for memory here; when you can, you
     plunge
into some inert woman as into a warm bath; for a moment
comforting, and of no consequence, like sucking your thumb.

No woman can imagine this. What you do to them
is therefore incidental, and also your just reward,

though sometimes, in a gap in the action, there's a space
for the concepts of *sister, mother.* Like folded laundry. They
     come and go.

But stick your hand up a woman, alive or freshly –
dead, it is much like a gutted chicken:
giblets, a body cavity. Killing can be

merely a kind of impatience, at the refusal
of this to mean anything to you. He told me that.

You wanted to go in sharp and clean like a sword,
do what they once called battle. Now you just want your life.

There's not much limit to what you would do to get it.
Justice and mercy are words that happen in cool rooms,
     elsewhere.

Are you your brother's keeper? Yes or no, depending
what clothes he has on, what hair. There is more than one
     brother.

What you need to contend with now is the hard Easter-
eggshell blue of the sky, that shows you too clearly

the mass of deep green trees leaning slowly towards you
as if on the verge of speech, or annunciation.

More likely some break in the fabric of sight, or a sad mistake
you will hear about in the moment you make it. Some glint of
    reflected light.

That whir in the space where your left hand was is not singing.
Death is the bird that hatches, is fed, comes flying.

Einstein

Lola Lemire Tostevin

1.

It wasn't unusual in the early days
to rock the cradle of his son
with his left hand
while working on the electrodynamics
of moving bodies
with his right

in a cradle
the relative place of a body
is that part of the cradle
which the body fills and moves together
with the cradle

and relative rest
is the body in space
in which the cradle and all it contains
is moved
is rocked

one force in its ellipse
about the heart
about the earth
around the sun

        light years bent by the rim
        caught by the cradle
        or the high sandstone ridge by the River
           Aare
        before their endless journey
        into time and space

        to the source
        nature's course
        light into body
        body into light

2.

Einstein
in his own time
in his own space falls free
from all magnetic fields
family friends houses

converts the universe
into perfect equations
of rhyme and reason

fourth dimension
of where and when
one man's now
another man's then

3.

and there was his music
and there was his sailing
on the Zuricksee
or on Lake of Thun

the small red pennant on the mast
vertical for the sailor on deck
while it moved forward
for the bathers on shore
and for the gulls flying above
it fell back and disappeared

on the calm constant motion
of water
there is no absolute

relativity is the only rule

4.

formulas melted in his mouth
'give muscle to flesh' he said
'but to make them into bombs
would be like shooting at one bird
in the dark ... '
and scribbled more riddles on the back
of old brown envelopes
where there is no bird

split the message
from the code

                    alpha / beta

the flesh to bear the mark
of an equation
the burn cold metal gives
as it unlocks what's latent
at the core

atomic

common denominator that spins
its own intrinsic chain
of love or hate
in quantities relative only
to the one who measures

5.

On August 11, 1945
after Hiroshima and Nagasaki
Einstein is quoted in the Union-Times
' ... we did not draw upon supernatural strength
we merely imitated the sun's rays ...
atomic power is no more unnatural
than when I shall sail my boat on Saranac Lake ...'

Y 2-Q 2-B 2-CL

Louky Bersianik,
Translated by *R. McGee*

EH.
The Atomic bomb as fine-art. The tHermonuclear super-bomb a
supra fine art. BOMB EH. JESUS H. BOMB!
**If children yet to be born could read today's papers, they
would arrange their own abortions. As would the children of
Hiroshima had they known what their human brothers had in
store for them.*** Written in 1961 and still applicable today.
No more bomb, eh no more H. bomb now we have MINI-MISSILES!
Superfine art – arts: limited assassinations! radioactive survivors.
post-war "action painting". facial features melted like a lost-wax
mold. to remodel. to remake the mold. pouring in the liquid flesh. an
artist working in perspective. Pollock-style "drippings".
**We are preparing a generation of twisted bodies of repug-
nant monsters a generation of effigies of intolerable suffering
a crazed generation of disfigured mental amputees.**
a monday morning in the month of august. a vacationing school-
girl feels a familiar caress on her black hair. she smiles as the sun's
long fingers clearly signal rise and shine bathing her in warmth. the
sun that day was perfectly normal until exactly 8:15. a second later it
falls into the city and its populace is in ashes. it but brushes by the
house and the house turns to dust. friday the little girl is bald and
thinks the sun has gone crazy. the following month she is back at
school in the open air in the charred black woods.
If the earth is "a field of multiple slaughter" as Georges
Bataille has said, and if despite this we continue to pull beings
out of the void and install them on this same earth, we cannot
continue to take this risk.**
gigantic arsenals. "Department Store Catalogue." to celebrate the
end of a century we dream of apocalyptic deployments. we stock the
atom silos. live missiles lie buried. waiting their chance to spring
from their coverts and send a charge through the more-than-dead.
the artificers are preparing a massive launch of invulnerable Polaris
from diving submarines to crown the millenium. nostalgia for the big
bang theory. oceanic and planetary sentimentality. men are in love
with, yes in love with Death, thought Sylvanie at the convent at

Erémo. from her energy. from her ecstasy. from the overwhelming light of Death. "You Can't Hug Kids With Nuclear Arms."**

While through silk curtains the newborn perceive their first amazing days, the wise men committed to our security emerge from their laboratories and lift a finger to the air, not to gauge the wind's direction, but rather to calculate the rate of radioactivity and arrive at the degree of contamination.

the planet itself is a bomb quilled with fuses that humanity can't wait to light. humanity itself as explosive as dynamite balancing precariously on the edge of the abyss. humanity burning to try out its new masterpiece "Nuclear Strike Capability."

And we say CHILDREN ARE DISARMING! (...) the allotment of cradles is filling with what we call "le petit de l'homme" – the main component in the Great Massacre's recipe, the necessary ingredient when prescribing the bomb and whose dosage is limitless; this alignment of cradled little people does not deter the Big Guys.

a new cause of death: atomic death as if the planet had cancer of the latitudes. a collective execution: the silent majority with their heads screwed on right and their mute jawbones: a particularly patriarchal image pushing this majority to the wall in total silence.

(...) "si vis pacem para bellum". They are right: Peace will come. (...) The peace so desired by all peoples cannot compete with the great universal peace which will be the result of massive mortality and immediate and hopeless infirmity. Combat will cease. Not only because of the combatants, but because of the battleground itself. For each of the duellists seeks to make the earth shake the other off his feet. They will both succeed.

in this impossible war: neither winner nor loser. in this "programmed hell" nothing new can emerge, there is only total horror. "Nous voulons, tant ce feu nous brûle le cerveau / Plonger au fond du gouffre, Enfer ou Ciel, qu'importe / Au fond de l'inconnu pour trouver du *nouveau*"(Charles Baudelaire).

It would be preferable for humanity to go out with a whimper by not reproducing the species instead of dragging its chancre through creation. The day Total Disarmament is proclaimed, we can reclaim our rights to procreation. Until that day let our nights be sterile (...)

While we hold the power to utterly destroy humanity many times over, we have replaced concrete reality with a demented fiction. in fact, once it is destroyed, can humanity be destroyed a second time, a third and fourth time in the same spasm?

What we call life in biology would have a different name. That word would be stricken from the dictionaries. It would be replaced by another word which would be defined as: "A state of radioactivity in dissembled substance, radioactivity common to plants and animals".

The chunk of barbarism that is in each of us has been looted and examined to its atomic core. Out of it we will make as many firewords as a head count of this planet. we will need an international arbitration of barbarism.

And of this obsolete "reasoning" animal will be given the following description: though we now consider the human being to be among the most inferior of beasts, it once held sway over other organisms.(...) We are contradicting evolution to perform a stupid about-face towards a lower life form.

aerial flora: ivy crawling or atomic mushrooms. human fauna and its sounds: music will cease forever. volutes will not speak of themselves, won't fashion their winding convolutions to the heavens. architextures won't roll out their spiral sculptures. yesterday's asleep with no future, without form without colour. barbarian hordes will have only cinders to conquer. seasons will have reached the point of no return. no longer the era of nuclear freeze, this is the deep freeze. as for mankind ... "it is when he unleashes on cities the ultimate in human excrement that man finally feels he has *transcended nature* for good; the rest is silence ..." (L'Euguélionne).

He will end up vomiting his brains and wearing his bones on the outside as a suit of armour. The disintegrated human will find himself on a par with invertebrates; a shelled mollusk, an abject husk of flesh devoid of any semblance of humanity.

constant menace of "nuclear guerilla war". olympic terror games. inconceivable fiction. weightlifters with bursting arteries and cardiac muscles. hoisting the hemispheres; balancing the terror. we accept living on this powderkeg. nuclear energy should lead to planet-wide political unity. who would effect this unity? the patriarchy? on what should peace be constructed? on patriarchal values? on institutionalized, accredited and subsidized violence? on the murderous and ferocious rivalries that the co-existence of peoples depends on between individuals, between sexes, between skin colours, on the scorn ingrained in politics so as to instill the fascist values of the patriarchy? such a peace could not but be nuclear. could not but be another sadistic competition in the cynical race for Greatness. **For a country is great only if it has the bomb. It is very great if it has several. It is supreme if it breaks all records in the quantity and quality of its sacred product.** how did that human ash stay standing on that August morning in 1945, just before 8:15? just before the wind changed. before the 800 km/h winds, before the apparition of the 10 km high mushroom. before the black rainfall fattened with a ten thousand metre high phalloid Amanita. before the wind of fire breathed on the riverbeds. before immense waves washed everything in their path. before the radical wind uprooted all the trees razing all living matter. a wind which transformed inanimate mineral matter into lethal contagion. **No longer can we ask if these humans who are preparing will have a roof, a burrow, some shelter above or below ground to protect themselves from these destructive forces. The burning question is whether they'll have a planet to take those first few tentative steps on (...) Ah well, let's hurry up and pass on to posterity a life we'd be burying alive in the event of a nuclear war. "Do You Know How To Protect Yourself In A Nuclear War?"****

Y 2-Q 2-B 2-CL is the formula that destroyed Hiroshima. it's in morse code: "Low clouds 1 to 3/10 – Medium clouds, 1 to 3/10 – High clouds, 1 to 3/10. Advice: first objective". 20,000 ton of TNT and phosphorus.

war memorial: "alive or dead we were hard put to identify them as human. their skin was raw and blackened. their hair had disappeared. features had melted from their faces." must archaeologists of the future work amid radioactive ruins? "War Memorial".**

for forty years peace has been as nuclear as the patriarchal family has been for 2,000 years. the core that holds women, men and their children together in an uncertain equilibrium of terror undergoes fission and the family explodes. as the patriarchal world, having only an embryonic respect for life, also explodes. the nuclear era is a symbol of the necessity of this explosion. so that the world be unified. that a female culture can emerge. with its active and its life-nurturing forces (not to be confused with so-called pro-life movements that have respect only for an embryonic life).

Einstein: it is easier to break an atom than prejudice.

Inhabiting a verdant sphere among the mysterious spheres of this star-struck world, being on the verge of hanging our

lanterns on the other globes we trot in the limitless expanse of space, we are conspiring in the conflagration of our own star. Clearly, the mystery lies with man.

in a world where the Value of Life will be first and foremost in the Catalogue of Values, nuclear deterrences as an obligatory modus vivendi would make no sense, would no longer be necessary.

art is conscience of the invisible. politics would be the more or less erroneous application of this conscience.

essential lucidity. weighing the arguments against pacifism: "pacifism against peace" (Boukhovski, a Soviet dissident who discerns in this movement an instrument of U.S.S.R. diplomacy.)

"up to now this movement has mostly weakened the democracies." (Pierre Melandri)

a poll in the U.S. in 1982: yes to "nuclear freeze". no if it is impossible to get the other side to comply.

"the missiles are in the East and pacifists are in the West". (Francois Mitterand)

the artist works on his/her canvas, the writer on his/her white page, the hinge between the visible and the invisible. between what is true and what is likely. between reality and fiction. between intimidation and its implications.

let there be light and may the invisible be. the light of kindness and not that of the planet-wide death sentence.

* Paragraphs set in italic are taken from an article by the writer that appeared in *Cité Libre* in autumn of 1961, under the name Lucile Durand.

** Asterisked phrases are titles of works in the past Powerhouse anti-nuke show.

Untitled

Leslie Hamson

I lay on my back in the soft warm snow
and patched with peace
a great hole rent in the sky
by a long pointed jet

I lay on my back, and with my thumb
erased the long white scar.

Elemental Poem

Roberta Buchanan

EAST WEST NORTH SOUTH
EARTH AIR FIRE WATER

We turn to the East: AIR
Blue space – breathing – the kiss of life
The wind driving sails and waves across the ocean
Impelling clouds across the sky
Blowing away the cobwebs at Cape Spear
We take deep breaths and laugh.
Meditation on the breath
I watch your breathing as you sleep.

Otherwise:

Difficulty in breathing, the poisoned air
Tear gas, poison gas in the trenches
Coughing up one's guts
Emphysema, asthma, bronchitis
Choking, throttled, the breath stopped
The air that kills.

We turn to the South: FIRE
The singing kettle on the hearth
Cooking: the bubbling pot of beans
The barbecue that friends and neighbours share
The camp fire, sitting in a circle
Glowing coals, warmth in winter
Making love by firelight
Candles burning before the shrines
Solar energy
The fiery sunset flowing red
The stars dancing round the sky.

Otherwise:

Smoke from the death camps: Auschwitz
The burning of people
Witches burned alive in the burning-times
The mushroom cloud at Hiroshima
Bombed houses catching fire in Philadelphia
Napalm burns on screaming children
Caught in cross-fire
Fire that destroys.

We turn to the West: WATER
First element, the waters of life
The sea womb of the Mother Goddess, giving birth
To strange creatures, bearing exotic cargoes
Aphrodite rises from the foam
The waterfall tumbling over cliff
The holy well, the sacred spring
That heal our spirits
Swimming in the sunset
Immanence is light on water.

Otherwise:

The flood that destroys, the burst dam
The raging sea, sailors drowning
The Ocean Ranger gone, bodies never found
The water cannon on the protest march
Polluted lakes killing fish; mercury poison
The poisoned water that kills.

We turn to the North: EARTH
Gaea, Mother Earth, the Deep-Breasted One
The nurse of seedlings, infusing the blossoms
Forming the fruit
Digging our gardens
Manuring, tilling, sowing seeds
Until the bean hangs on the vine
Until the lettuces fan out their delicate leaves
Carrots, potatoes plump and swell
The fertile earth, abundantly feeding her children
At the last our final resting-place.

Otherwise:

The parched earth, desert, famine
The rain forests cut down
Defoliation – stripping the earth
Chemical warfare where nothing grows
The earth poisoned with PCBs
Eroded soil, the waste land
The bomb – nuclear winter
The poisoned earth.

EARTH AIR FIRE WATER
Essential elements, natural sources, re-sources:
Extract, extort, exploit, rape, destroy, kill
Or reverence, worship, conserve the sacred grounds of being?

Where the Sky is a Pitiful Tent

Claire Harris

*Once I heard a Ladino say "I am poor but listen I am not an Indian";
but then again I know Ladinos who fight with us and who understand we're human beings just like them.*

Rigoberto Manchu (Guatemala)

All night the hibiscus tapped at our jalousies
dark bluster of its flower trying to ride in
on wind lacinated with the smell of yard fowl
Such sly knocking sprayed the quiet
your name in whispers
dry shuffle of thieving feet on verandah floors
My mouth filled with midnight and fog
like someone in hiding
to someone in hiding
I said *do not go*
you didn't answer
though you became beautiful and ferocious
There leached from you three hundred years of compliance
Now I sleep with my eyes propped open
lids nailed to the brow

---

*After their marriage my parents went into the mountains to establish
a small settlement ... they waited years for the first harvest. Then a
patron arrived and claimed the land. My father devoted himself to
travelling and looking for help in getting the rich landowners to leave
us alone. But his complaints were not heard ... They accused him of
provoking disorder, of going against the sovereign order of
Guatemala ... they arrested him.*

Ladino: descendants of Spanish Jews who came to Guatemala during the
Inquisition

From the testimony of Rigoberto Manchu translated by Patricia Goedicke,
American Poetry Review, January / February 1983.

In the dream I labour toward something
glimpsed through fog   something of us exposed
on rock and mewling   as against the tug of water
I struggle under sharp slant eyes
death snap and rattle of hungry wings
                    Awake I whisper

You have no right to act
you cannot return land from the grave
Braiding my hair the mirror propped on my knees
I gaze at your sleeping vulnerable head
Before the village we nod smile or don't smile
we must be as always
while the whole space of day aches with our nightmares
I trail in your footsteps through cracks you chisel
in this thin uncertain world
where as if it were meant for this mist hides
sad mountain villages   reluctant fields
still your son skips on the path laughing
he is a bird   he is a hare
under the skeletal trees

My mother had to leave us alone while she went to look for a lawyer
who would take my father's case. And because of that she had to work
as a servant. All her salary went to the lawyer. My father was tortured
and condemned to eighteen years in prison. (Later he was released.)
But they threatened to imprison him for life if he made any more
trouble.

Rigoberto Manchu translated by Patricia Goedicke
American Poetry Review, January / February 1983.

I watch in the market square
those who stop and those who do not
while my hands draw the wool over up down
knitting the bright caps on their own
my eyes look only at sandals
at feet chipped like stones at the quarry
There are noons when the square shimmers
we hold our breath while those others
tramp in the market place
Today the square ripples like a pond
three thrown   what is left of them
corded like wood   alive and brought to flame
How long the death smoke signals
on this clear day
We are less than the pebbles under their heels
the boy hides in my shawl

---

*The army circulated an announcement ordering everyone to present
themselves in one of the villages to witness the punishment the
guerillas would receive.... There we could observe the terrible things
our comrades had suffered, and see for ourselves that those they
called guerillas were people from the neighbouring villages ... among
them the Catequistas and my little brother ... who was secretary to
one of the village co-operatives. That was his only crime. He was fourteen years old.... They burnt them.*

Rigoberto Manchu translated by Patricia Goedicke
American Poetry Review, January / February 1983.

As if I have suffered resurrection I see
the way the grass is starred with thick fleshed
flowers at whose core a swirl of fine yellow
lines disappear into hollow stems
so we now into our vanished lives
Dust thickening trees we turn
to the knotted fist of mountains
clenched against mauve distance
Because I must   I look back
heartheld to where the mudbrick huts
their weathered windows daubed with useless crosses
their shattered doors   begin the slow descent
to earth   my earlier self turns in
darkening air   softly goes down with them
The boy only worms alive in his eyes
his face turned to the caves

When we returned to the house we were a little crazy, as if it had been
a nightmare. My father marched ahead swiftly saying that he had
much to do for his people; that he must go from village to village to tell
them what had happened. . . . A little later so did my mother in her
turn. . . . My brother left too . . . and my little sisters.

Rigoberto Manchu translated by Patricia Goedicke
American Poetry Review, January / February 1983.

If in this poem you scream who will hear you
though you say *no one should cry out in vain*
your face dark and thin with rage
Now in this strange mountain place
stripped by knowledge
I wait for you
Someone drunk stumbles the night path
snatching at a song or someone not drunk
I am so porous with fear
even the rustle of ants in the grass flows through me
but you are set apart
The catechists say *in heaven there is no male
no female*   that is far foolishness
why else seeing you smelling of danger
and death do I want you so
your mouth   your clear opening in me

*We began to build camps in the mountains where we would spend the
night to prevent the troops from killing us while we slept. In the day-
time we had taught the children to keep watch over the road.... We
knew that the guerillas were up there in the distant mountains. At
times they would come down in order to look for food, in the beginning we didn't trust them, but then we understood that they, at least,
had weapons to fight the army with.*

Rigoberto Manchu translated by Patricia Goedicke
American Poetry Review, January / February 1983.

You will not stop what you have begun
though I asked in the way a woman can
Since you have broken thus into life
soon someone will make a pattern
of your bones   of your skull
as they have with others
and what will fly out
what will escape from you torn apart
the boy and I must carry
In your sleep I went to the cenote*
in the moonlight I filled my shawl with flowers
threw them to the dark water
the ancient words fluting in my head
your son pinched awake to know what must come

My mother was captured (some) months later ... when all she could wish for was to die ... they revived her, and when she had recovered her strength they began torturing her again ... they placed her in an open field ... filled her body with worms ... she struggled a long time then died under the sun.... The soldiers stayed until the buzzards and dogs had eaten her. Thus they hoped to terrorize us. She doesn't have a grave. We, her children, had to find another way of fighting.

Rigoberto Manchu translated by Patricia Goedicke
American Poetry Review January / February 1983.

* cenote: a well occasionally used in ritual sacrifice (precolumbian)

Oh love this is silence   this is the full
silence of completion   we have swum through
terror that seared us to bone
rage lifted a cold hand to save us
so we became this surreal country
We have been bullet-laden air   fields that sprout
skulls   night that screeches and hammers
we have been hunger   whip   wind that sobs
feast days and drunken laughter
a rare kindness and pleasure
We have come through to the other side
here everything is silence   our quiet breathing
in this empty hut   our clay jugs full of light
and water   we are our corn our salt
this quiet is the strength we didn't know we had
our humanity no longer alarms us
we have found who we are
my husband our silence is the silence of blue steel thrumming
and of love
Our deaths shall be clear

---

*Our only way of commemorating the spilled blood of our parents was
to go on fighting and following the path they had followed. I joined
the organization of the Revolutionary Christians. I know perfectly
well that in this fight one runs the greatest risk.... We have been suffering such a long time and waiting.*

Rigoberto Manchu translated by Patricia Goedicke
American Poetry Review, January / February 1983.

Your death is drenched in such light
that small things   the sky   branches
brushing against the cave mouth   the boy
stirring   make my skin crackle against damp blankets
As one gathers bullets carelessly spilled I gather your screams
all night I remember you utterly lovely
the way you danced the wedding dance
rising dust clouding your sandals
your slow dark smile
You return to the predawn   leaving us
what remains when the flames die out of words
(small hard assertions
our beginnings
shards of the world you shattered
and ourselves)

Their death gave us hope, because it is not just that the blood of all those people be erased forever. It is our duty on this earth to revive it.... I fight so they will recognise me.... If I have taken advantage of this chance to tell the story of my life it is because I know that my people cannot tell their own stories. But they are no different from mine.

Rigoberto Manchu translated by Patricia Goedicke
American Poetry Review, January / February 1983.

This testimony was collected by Elizabeth Burgos. Translated into Spanish by Sylvia Roubaud. This translation was taken from the Mexican publication *Unomasuno*. It was published by *American Poetry Review*, January / February 1983.

Untitled

Penn Kemp

how we age in his story's
stages

his tory rages in our
itinerary

his story call
his stereo
shibboleth

War in all its guises
wears out work clothes
wares out worth close
wreaks out worse weeks

All the guys were wrecked
All disguise is blown
Exit Jesus

Exegesis
come on dear comrads
co-madres

con quest
drag on!

man kills dragon –
woman rides her back

Griefkit

Kate Lushington

Kate Lushington originally wrote and performed Griefkit *for Every
Mushroom Cloud has a Silver Lining, produced by Pelican Players in
December 1982. She has subsequently performed the piece at Theatre
Experimental des Femmes in Montreal, the Women and Words Con-
ference in Vancouver, 1983, and at the Groundswell Festival of
Nightwood Theatre in 1984, among other venues.*

Note: the griefbox is a 12" square blue Birks box, the griefpillow is
covered with red satin, and the safety pin is a diaper pin.

Good evening. My name is Veronica Mandel, and I've come to talk to
you tonight about the psychiatric effects of nuclear war, or what can
be done for mental health after the Bomb has dropped.

American psychiatrist Robert Jay Lifton has identified one of the
major problem areas as "psychic numbing": a profound blandness,
insensitivity and inability to experience grief – or indeed to feel anything at all. This will be detrimental to our continued development as
whole human beings inside the bomb shelter, and may seriously
limit our capacity to form cooperating groups in the new world outside.

The natural mourning process, which could alleviate the severer
symptoms of "psychic numbing," will be inhibited in many cases, or
made very difficult, by the absence of bodies to bury – through
vaporization, incineration, or other forms of corporeal annihilation.
It is hard to bury a shadow on the wall. Another problem with
nuclear devastation is its scale. Try to imagine one hundred million
dead. Try it. And of those of us left, how many will be therapists? On
a more individual level, it is unlikely that we will survive together
with anyone close to us, or even be anywhere near our loved ones at
the moment of impact. In the aftermath, the process of grieving and
saying goodbye to those we have lost may assume supreme importance.

It is vital – and I use the word in its original sense of "essential to life" – that we are all prepared, in the event of nuclear attack, to be our own therapists. There are self-help books now available. For example: *Good Life, Good Death*, by Dr. Christian Barnard; *Positive Thinking at a Time Like This*, by Norman Vincent Peale; Mildred Newman and Bernard Berkowitz's *How To Be Awake and Alive*. These are no longer enough. Researching into more appropriate ways to meet an imminent need, psychologists have devised a "griefkit," to keep always by you in a safe, accessible place. It is very simple, consisting of ordinary household items:
– a box, with a well-fitting lid – clearly marked with your name
– a cushion or pillow
– photographs of the people you love
– a safety pin
– some kitty litter.

In the coming emergency, we believe that grief and mourning must have their place: the dead, as well as the living, need space. To this end there will be racks made available for griefboxes in every government shelter; but it is up to the individual to be responsible for his or her own kit. So, when the warning sounds, be sure to bring yours with you. Your future sanity could depend upon it.

Now, how to use your griefkit:

Place the pillow directly in front of you. Take the photographs one by one and name them, give them a name, their name:

Grandad
Suzy and Michelle
Bill
Jimmy
Anita.

Visualize them. See them smile. Hear them breathe. Now, take a safety pin and pin your loved ones to the griefpillow. Say to yourself: "This is me. I am here and I am alive. These are the people I love. They had their own individual existence, and now they are dead." Take the pillow and hold it to you for a moment. (Pause) Now, bury them: place the pillow in the griefbox, take some kitty litter, a handful should be enough, and sprinkle it over the ones you love, repeating:

"Death is random, death is not fair,
death is random, death is not fair,
death is random.... "

When you are ready to say goodbye, close the lid firmly and put your box away alongside all the others, making sure you can find it again handily should the need arise.

Remember, when the nuclear warning is given, if you bring nothing else, bring this. It may mean the difference to your emotional well-being, after the bomb has dropped. Thank you.

An Argentinian Script

Rosemary Sullivan

for N.F.

You speak of one afternoon –
the sun was doing its yellow dance
across the cafe table.
Above the rim of your cup
a car stopped. Two men
descended a street
as in a film –
where the extras go on with their business
pretending not to notice
and the street is just a pretext
to pull the plot together –
suddenly you knew the script.

All your life
you've dragged these men
behind you.

This is the moment
you dream each night, differently.
But always the same wall,
the same hot hiss of lead,
waking, when the blindfold's off,
among the dead
and the ones whose hair turned white,
five times, five deaths,
undied,
screaming inside your head.

Excerpt from *serpent (w)rite:*
a reader's gloss

Betsy Warland

word play
war *play*
plegan, to pledge for, stake, risk, exercise oneself, plight
                                        flight
                                        race
nuclear arms *race, ers-, err, erratic, erratum, erroneous, error,
aberration* to our
                race, ratio, a reckoning, account

count me in
count me out
can i count on you
are you in the head count

The Count Down
1,2,3,4,5,6,7,8,9,10 – ready or not, here I come

'A few days after the reunion of scientists in 1983, Seth Wyden
Neddermeyer, whose achievement of plutonium implo-
sion at Los Alamos had been pivotal, said: "I get
overwhelmed by a feeling of terrible guilt when I think
about the history of the bomb. This is what bugs me more
than anything else – I don't remember having any strong
feelings about [the bombings] at the time. I guess I just got
caught up in the mindless hysteria."'

comen cumen com cam camen com c(w)omon *come, vulgar,*
to experience orgasm The Big *Bang, vulgar slang,*
to have sexual intercourse with (a woman)

1,2,3,4,5,6,7,8,9,10 – ready or not here I come

Man's Ultimate *fucken, fokken, to strike, copulate (see peig-)*
evil-minded, hostile

1,2,3,4,5,6,7,8,9,10 – pushing The *Button*
bhau-, to strike, in Latine futuere,
to have intercourse with
(a woman)

'War is a brutal, deadly game, but a game, the best   Broyles
there is. And men love games.'

don't get so upset
it's just a game

'Where hysteria is diagnosed, miosogyny is not   Fischer-Homberger
far away.'

here at our skin's horizon
we feel such terrible fears
skin no wall of Paradise
horrors *conspirare, to breathe together*
within our own lungs
our bodies at sea
with pairs of nearly everything
fluid the presence of
The Other
we are 20 square feet of skin
60,000 miles of arteries and veins
and 60 to 70 per cent water
a fluency which....
here at our skin's horizon
we will stop at nothing
to deny our fear's origin
we will kill each other
kill ourselves
kill earth
liquidate it all
obsessed to *control, ret-, round* Paradise Lost
our 20 square feet
our defense against *them, to-, decoy*
Falls for the trap
when The Flood is 60,000 miles within

this is our terrortory

Five Miles from Detonation

Erin Mouré

I am one survivor
who would envy the dead
In the midst of nuclear predicament, not
its aftermath –
Our bright lawns strewn with garbage,
so much rot
I hide away from it, my face in my hands, listen
to the motor of wasps lunging
thru the open window, into old cups of
honeyed tea:
The mire of our being connects for one moment.
I hear them plunge in, & the motor
stops,
& the sun goes on as ever before, making its
tracks on linoleum,
& the schools are out for Easter so
the neighbourhood's quiet
& the white seltzer has settled in my glass, undrinkable
The world ends at last for one wasp
as I sit
citizen, imbecile, reading newspapers
Unable to empty my head of predicament:

Third
degree burns, five miles from
the point of detonation.

Contributors

MARGARET ATWOOD has been active in environmental and free trade activities as well as Amnesty International and P.E.N. International. Her *Selected Poems II* was published in 1986 and a novel, *Cat's Eye*, in 1988.

HIMANI BANNERJI teaches in the Sociology Department of York University, Toronto. *Doing Time* is her second book of poems.

LOUKY BERSIANIK has written for radio, television and cinema. In 1976, she published the first feminist Québécoise novel, *L'Eugelionne*, which was translated into English in 1982. Since then she has published seven volumes of poetry, fiction, essays and plays.

MARILYN BOWERING lives in Victoria. Her selected poems, *The Sunday Before Winter*, were published in 1984. *Grandfather was a soldier* (1987) is her most recent collection.

ROBERTA BUCHANAN, a feminist poet and critic, teaches in the English Department of Memorial University, Newfoundland. At present she is doing research in women's autobiographical writings.

SHARI DUNNET is a writer / broadcaster and graphic artist living and working in the Gulf Islands of British Columbia. She is the producer of "Women Talking Peace," an oral history series on women in the Canadian peace movement.

KIM ECHLIN is an arts producer with the Canadian Broadcasting Corporation. She has travelled in the Marshall Islands, including an extended stay on Ebeye, an island on the same atoll as the U.S. testing facility called Kwajalein.

MAXINE GADD published her selected writings in *Lost Language* in 1982. She lives in Vancouver.

DEBORAH GORHAM is a professor of history at Carleton University. She is the author of *The Victorian Girl and the Feminist Ideal* (1982) and is currently working on a study of Vera Brittain.

LESLIE HAMSON has lived for the past twenty years in the Yukon, where her most recent writing success was a production of her stage play *Last Rites* by the Nakai Players.

ANN HANSEN is serving a sentence at the Kingston Penitentiary for Women in part for her role in the bombing of Litton Systems of Toronto.

CLAIRE HARRIS writes and teaches in Calgary. Her poetry has been anthologized in collections of Canadian and Caribbean writing. In 1985 *Fables From the Women's Quarters* won the Commonwealth Poetry Prize. Her most recent book is *The Conception of Winter,* published in 1988.

PENN(Y) KEMP writes and performs her poetry and plays. *Throo: Wise Cracking C'Odes from the Lunar Plexus* (1988) has many voices from her "old texts and new."

JOY KOGAWA has published four volumes of poetry; a novel, *Obasan*; and a children's book, *Naomi's Road.* She is a member of the Order of Canada and is currently working on a novel, a sequel to *Obasan.*

MARGARET LAURENCE (1926-1987), one of Canada's finest fiction writers, was a tireless activist for world peace and the recipient of many awards for her work.

LOLA LEMIRE TOSTEVIN, a Franco-Ontarian, writes in English and French and teaches creative writing at York University, Toronto. *'sophie,* published in 1988, is her fourth poetry book.

DOROTHY LIVESAY, who lives on the Gulf Islands, has been actively engaged in peace politics for many years and published her first book in 1928. *The Self-Completing Tree* is a recent book of selected poems.

KATE LUSHINGTON, a performer and writer, is the artistic coordinator of Nightwood Theatre, Toronto. She is working on a theatrical adaptation of Josef Skvorecky's *The Bass Saxophone.*

NADINE McINNIS lives in Ottawa. Her first collection of poems, *Shaking the dreamland tree,* was published by Coteau Books in 1986.

KAY MACPHERSON was president of the Voice of Women from 1963 to 1967 and is a founding member of Women for Political Action. From 1977 to 1979 she was president of the National Action Committee on the Status of Women. She is a member of the Order of Canada.

DAPHNE MARLATT, poet and novelist, published her innovative novel *Ana Historic* in 1988, as well as *Double Negative*, a poetry collaboration with Betsy Warland. She was one of the organizers of *Women's Peace Write*.

ERIN MOURE works and writes in Montreal. Her fifth book, *Furious*, won the 1989 Governor General's Award.

SANDRA RABINOVITCH is the Script Editor for CBC Radio Drama and a freelance writer / broadcaster.

ELIZABETH RICHARDS is a journalist and peace activist. She has been a director of the Toronto Disarmament Network.

BARBARA ROBERTS is an associate professor of women's studies at Athabasca University. She is currently writing a book on the history of women's peace activism in Canada.

SHELLY ROMALIS is an associate professor of anthropology at York University, Toronto. She does research and teaching in women's studies.

DOROTHY E. SMITH is the chairperson of the Department of Sociology, Ontario Institute for Studies in Education. In 1987 she published *The Everyday Word as Problematic: A Feminist Sociology*.

DONNA E. SMYTH is a writer and a peace and environmental activist. Her latest novel is *Subversive Elements*.

THOMAS SOCKNAT is assistant professor of history at the University of Toronto. He is the author of *Witness Against War: Pacifism in Canada 1910-1945*.

ROSEMARY SULLIVAN has edited several anthologies of Canadian women's writing and teaches in the English Department at the University of Toronto. *The Space a Name Makes* won the League of Canadian Poets' best first book of poetry award in 1986.

SHARON THESEN is a Vancouver poet. Her fifth book, *The Beginning of the Long Dash*, was nominated for a Governor General's Award in 1988.

BETSY WARLAND, the originator of the 1983 writing conference Women and Words, has published three books of poetry, most recently *serpent (w)rite*, published in 1987, as well as *Double Nega-*

tive, a collaboration with Daphne Marlatt. She was one of the organizers of *Women's Peace Write.*

R.R. (RANDI) WARNE is Program Director for Continuing Education at St. Stephen's College, University of Alberta. Her doctoral dissertation for the University of Toronto was on Nellie McClung.

PHYLLIS WEBB has been active in Amnesty International. Her book of selected poems, *The Vision Tree,* was edited by Sharon Thesen and won the Governor General's Award. Her most recent book is *Water and Light: Ghazals and Anti-Ghazals.*

JANICE WILLIAMSON teaches and writes in the English Department and Women's Studies Program at the University of Alberta. A collection of interviews, *Sounding the Difference: Conversations with Fifteen Canadian Women Writers,* and a collection of fiction, *Tell Tale Signs,* are forthcoming in 1991. She is currently writing a critical work on Daphne Marlatt.